TEIKYO WESTMA W9-BVJ-939

Weakness of Will

WEAKNESS OF WILL

William Charlton

90-312

Basil Blackwell

Copyright © William Charlton 1988

First published 1988

Basil Blackwell Ltd
108 Cowley Road, Oxford, OX4 1JF, UK

Basil Blackwell Inc.
432 Park Avenue South, Suite 1503
New York, NY 10016, USA

All rights reserved. Except for the quotation of short passages for the purposes of criticism and review, no part of this publication may be reproduced, stored in a retrieval system, or transmitted, in any form or by any means, electronic, mechanical, photocopying, recording or otherwise, without the prior permission of the publisher.

Except in the United States of America, this book is sold subject to the condition that it shall not, by way of trade or otherwise, be lent, re-sold, hired out, or otherwise circulated without the publisher's prior consent in any form of binding or cover other than that in which it is published and without a similar condition including this condition being imposed on the subsequent purchaser.

British Library Cataloguing in Publication Data

Charlton, W.
  Weakness of will.
  1. Will
  I. Title
  128'.3   BJ1461

  ISBN 0–631–15758–1
  ISBN 0–631–15759–X Pbk

Library of Congress Cataloging in Publication Data

Charlton, William, 1935–
  Weakness of will / William Charlton.
  p.   cm.
  Bibliography p.
  Includes index.
  ISBN 0–631–15758–1   ISBN 0–631–15759–X (pbk.)
  1. Will.   I. Title.
  BJ1468.5.C43   1988   87–35575
  128'.3—dc19   CIP

Typeset in 10 on 12 pt Garamond Typeface
by Colset Private Limited, Singapore
Printed in Great Britain by Billing & Sons Ltd, Worcester

Contents

Preface

My thanks are due in the first place to Theodore Scaltsas who suggested I should write this book and discussed the contents with me. I am grateful also for advice and help to many friends and colleagues: in particular to J. M. Brearley, P. F. C. Charlton, P. N. Jones, A. A. Long, Paul Smith and David Sachs. David Charles read and commented most generously on a draft of the Aristotle chapter; I am sorry that I was unable to accept all his suggestions, but it is thanks to him if I have been able to clarify the issues between us.

To those who see grammar as the great instrument of masculine domination I should apologize for the frequent use of 'he' as a universal pronoun and 'man' as a word for members of the human species. Perhaps I may receive some credit for referring to female colleagues in the same unceremonious way as to male; or perhaps in forgoing the more chivalrous styles which, all things considered, I think better, I merely betray the weakness of my will.

1
Introduction

Weakness of will is something we all think we know; many of us feel that we constantly experience it in ourselves. 'The good that I would, I do not', says St Paul (Romans 7.15); 'the evil that I would not, that I do'; and this familiar situation is commonly attributed (so Hare, 1963, ch. 5) to weakness of will.

But is weakness of will always to blame? In the course of a walk over difficult country, my companion and I reach a fast-flowing stream some five feet wide and perhaps three feet deep. My companion springs lightly across, I hesitate. The good that I would is to cross, yet I do not do it. Is it because I am physically unable to jump five feet? But I know I can. What is it, then, that holds me back? To say 'weakness of will' does not sound quite right; irrational fear or failure of nerve would be a more plausible diagnosis. Similarly with the evil that I would not. If I betray my friends under torture, or steal from my benefactor to take my mistress on an expensive holiday, I do a bad thing I should prefer not to do; but it is unclear that weakness of will is the culprit rather than lack of fortitude in the one case, or lust or dishonesty in the other.

We speak of weakness of will in two ways, sometimes as a phenomenon to be explained, and sometimes as an explanation of that phenomenon. The phenomenon to be explained is going against one's judgement of how it would be best for one to behave: doing something one thinks bad or failing to do something one thinks good. Sometimes we simply call such behaviour 'weak-willed' to label it. But sometimes we say that people behave in this way *because of* weakness of will, offering weakness of will as a kind of causal explanation of their actions or omissions. The subject of this book is weakness of will in the first sense of the expression; whether this can be explained by weakness of will in the second is one of the questions I shall be considering.

Partly to guard against confusion on this point I shall follow what is
now a fairly common practice among philosophers. Instead of 'weakness of will' I shall use some Greek words taken from Aristotle. The man
who behaves in the ways just indicated I shall call 'the akrates'. His
behaviour I shall call 'akratic'. And unless the context indicates otherwise, I shall use the abstract noun 'akrasia' for this akratic behaviour and
not for whatever it may be in akratic people that is responsible for it.

Translators of Aristotle sometimes render 'akrasia' by 'incontinence'.
I once heard G.E.L. Owen (my first guide in the mazes of Ancient
Philosophy) say that this word has ineliminable connotations of bed-
wetting. Certainly the casual bookshop-browser will not be misled by
the title of the excellent recent work by Paul and Linda Smith
Continence and Incontinence (1987). Another translation is 'lack of
self-control'. Austin's comments on this are well known:

> I am very partial to ice cream, and a bombe is served divided into
> segments corresponding one to one with persons at High Table: I am
> tempted to help myself to two segments, thus succumbing to temptation
> and even conceivably (but why necessarily?) going against my principles.
> But do I lose control of myself? Do I raven, do I snatch the morsels from
> the dish and wolf them down, impervious to the consternation of my
> colleagues? Not a bit of it. We often succumb to temptation with calm
> and even with finesse. (1961, p. 146 n.)

I said just now that akratic behaviour is doing something one thinks
bad or failing to do something one thinks good. That is not a precise
formulation, and when we look at the literature on the topic we find
that different writers have slightly different cases in the front of their
minds. Aristotle says that the akrates does things he knows to be bad
because of passion (1145^{b}12–13); he conceives the misbehaviour as con-
sisting in action rather than omission; the moral judgement against
which the akrates acts must be true (1146^{a}16–21); and the motive is
typically desire for more or less sensual pleasure: not necessarily for pleasant sensations, but at least for activity which involves such sensations.
Aristotle is probably following Plato here, and in recent times he has
been followed by R.M. Hare. What Hare calls 'backsliding' is rather
action than omission, it is motivated by desire for pleasure, and
although Hare's non-cognitivist theory of ethics makes it hard for him
to describe any moral principles as true or false, the backslider goes
against principles which come as near to truth as is possible.

But other writers have different interests. Sidgwick (1893,

pp. 176–7) was interested in 'voluntary action contrary to a man's deliberate judgement as to what is right or best for him to do'. The motive need not be passion or desire for pleasure; it might even be a sense of duty. Writing in the English Whig tradition, he asks us to imagine a Spanish Inquisitor whose better judgement tells him to yield 'to a humane sentiment' but who carries on torturing heretics out of fidelity to his (benighted) moral principles. In recent times Donald Davidson has taken the same line, but with more up-to-date examples. On the other hand writers like Jon Elster and Frank Jackson are interested primarily in rationality and the conflict between reason and emotion. Cases where an agent does something he thinks bad as a matter of principle are not of concern to them unless adherence to the principle is irrational; their attention is centred on cases where the motive is a relatively unintellectual emotion.

Not only does the term 'akrasia' cover a number of different cases related to one another at best by Wittgensteinian family resemblance; akrasia gives rise to a number of different problems. Many writers (for instance David Charles, 1984, p. 109) distinguish two groups of questions. On the one hand there are questions about whether akrasia really occurs. In particular, is it possible for an agent to do something intentionally, thinking at the moment when he does it both that he could refrain and that it would be better all things considered if he did? Philosophers' intuitions vary on this. F. P. Ramsey (1978, pp. 75–6), following Bentham (1827/1962, p. 5) declares that a man 'will always choose the course of action which will lead him in his opinion to the greatest sum of good'. Similarly Richard Robinson: 'It does not happen that a man sets himself to consider, in its totality and all its parts, an argument forbidding him to do a certain act, while at the same time he yields to a strong desire and does as the desire wishes' (1954/1977, p. 85). E. J. Lemmon, on the other hand, says:

> It is so notorious a fact about human agents that they are often subject to akrasia that any ethical position that makes this seem queer or paradoxical or impossible is automatically suspect for just this reason . . . Perhaps akrasia is one of the best examples of a pseudo-problem in philosophical literature: it view of its [sc. akrasia's] existence, if you find it a problem you have already made a philosophical mistake. (1962, pp. 144–5)

John Benson (1968) is probably not alone in wavering: on p. 167 'the situation in which I am quite clear what I really want to do but knowingly give way to temptation to do something inconsistent with it' is 'comparatively uncommon'; by p. 170 it has become 'impossible'.

Related to the question whether clear-eyed akrasia occurs are questions about the interrelations between thinking a course good, wanting to pursue it and pursuing it. Since any course about which there is serious deliberation is good in some respects and bad in others, it may also be asked whether there can be a difference between the course an agent thinks best all things considered and the course he thinks morally best.

The second group of questions concerns the explanation of cases of real or apparent akrasia. Are there such things as wills of varying strengths? Does the agent's grasp of what is best relax at the crucial moment, and if so, how? Is it possible to deceive oneself about whether a course is all right? Is there such a thing as being psychologically unable to resist a motive to go against one's better judgement? Does the psyche have rational and irrational parts, and if so, how do they relate to and influence one another?

Lemmon thought akrasia a pseudo-problem because he thought it obvious that we often do what we know to be evil or disadvantageous. This objection can be countered, as we shall see in chapter 3, by distinctions between different ways in which a person can know something. But there are deeper grounds for scepticism about akrasia as a philosophical (it will always be a practical) problem. It was a problem for the ancient Greeks because, as we shall see in chapters 2 and 3, they closely connected thinking it good to do something with acting intentionally. For them, if I think it best to go to Athens next week I must have some desire to go, and if I am able to go I go. Conversely if I go to Athens intentionally and not by accident or because kidnapped, I must have thought it a good idea to go. David Pears (1984, p. 114) calls the connection running from thought to action the 'forward' connection and the connection running from action to thought the 'backward'. We shall examine the first of these connections in chapter 5 and the second in chapter 6. Clearly the closer we take them to be, the more puzzling akrasia appears.

There exists, however, quite a different view of action from that of the ancient Greeks. In the Old Testament the universe is said to owe its existence to a more or less arbitrary act of will by God. What acts are good and what evil is revealed by God, who commands us to do the former and refrain from the latter. The task of the human agent is to accommodate his will to God's and obey the divine commands.

Whereas Greek philosophers see evil-doing as folly or ignorance, the authors of the Old Testament see it as disobedience. Adam and Eve knew that they ought not to eat the forbidden fruit but ate it all the same. What today we call 'the will' plays no part in classical Greek psychology, but it is all-important in the non-philosophical psychology of the ancient Jews. For them doing what you know to be bad, far from being puzzling, is the standard form of wrong-doing, and since it is will which has the function of ensuring that we do what we know we should, weakness of will is the standard form of failure. These points, though still sometimes overlooked, are not seriously contentious. For documentation see Albrecht Dihle, 1982, especially chapter 1.

David Kipp (1985) writes as if this way of thinking were a Christian invention. In fact it is an inheritance. St Paul was not challenging the Greek tradition but writing in his own when he made the famous avowal of akrasia quoted above. Temptation, which is what from apostolic times (e.g. James 1.12–24) has given spice to the Christian moral life, is a wholly familiar phenomenon to the author of Job. What is true is that the Jews had no academic philosophy of their own, and the earliest Jewish and Christian philosophers tended to reproduce Greek ideas about the psychology of action without noticing the discrepancy. The first person to introduce the notion of the will into philosophy does indeed appear to have been a Christian bishop, St Augustine of Hippo.

Augustine writes of the will sometimes as a faculty of the mind, sometimes as the mind itself in its role as a thing which issues commands. For him weakness of will is not entirely unproblematic, but the difficulty he sees is different from the one seen by the Greeks. Where they asked how an act could be intentional if it was not done because the agent thought it good, Augustine asks how the mind can give itself orders which are not obeyed.

> The mind orders the hand to move, and it moves so readily that we can hardly distinguish between the command and its execution . . . The mind orders the mind to will, and it is no different from itself, but it does not do it. How can this be? It orders itself to will, it could not have given the order unless it were willing, yet what it orders it does not do. (*Confessions* VIII.9; cf. Hare, 1963, p. 81)

The solution is that part of the mind wills and part resists, and hence that we have two wills, one complete and one incomplete. Since Augustine rightly refuses to assign these wills to two distinct minds, we might here look forward to quite a sophisticated discussion, particularly as he has earlier (II.5) argued at some length that it is incredible that anyone should do evil – kill a man or even steal a pear – simply because it is evil. But Augustine falls back on a Pauline dictum: 'When I act against my own will, that means I have a self that acknowledges that the Law is good, and so the thing behaving in that way is not my self but sin living in me' (Romans 7.16).

As a result of the fall of the Roman Empire in the West, Western thinkers had little direct contact with Greek thought until the first Latin translations of Plato and Aristotle appeared in the thirteenth century. When the *Nicomachean Ethics* was translated it was learnt that the Greeks had asked: 'Can reason be conquered by passion acting contrary to what it knows?' But for Aquinas (*Summa Theologiae* I–II.77.2) the answer is obvious: 'It is clear to experience that many people act against what they know, and this is confirmed by divine revelation in a passage of Luke: ''The servant who knew the will of his master and did not do it will be beaten with many blows''.'

The concept of the will continued to be taken for granted long after more theological elements in the Judaeo-Christian tradition had been called in question. It is accepted in one guise or another by all philosophers down to the 1930s, and as recently as in 1980 the Cambridge University Press published a monumental two-volume defence of it by Brian O'Shaughnessy. I shall examine modern ideas about the will in chapter 4.

The philosopher who thinks that how we act is determined by our will is almost bound to ask what determines the will. If it were determined directly by our view of what is best, the Greek problem would reappear (and the will itself would become fair game for Ockham's Razor). The Judaeo-Christian tradition, however, is firm that it is not so determined, and modern philosophical volitionists agree. They hold it is determined by motivational factors such as desires, intentions or what Locke calls 'uneasinesses'. Since thinking a course good plainly has some influence on our behaviour, a course which appears good must therein have a certain motivational appeal; but there is not the slightest guarantee that it will determine the will. Hume describes benevolence and 'a general appetite to good' as 'calm desires and tendencies which, tho' they be real passions, produce little emotion in the mind' (1888, p. 417). He distinguishes them from 'violent emotions of the same kind' and says:

> The common error of metaphysicians has lain in ascribing the direction of

the will entirely to one of these principles, and supposing the other to have no influence. Men often act knowingly against their interest; for which reason the view of the greatest possible good does not always influence them. Men often counter-act a violent passion in prosecution of their interests and designs: 'tis not therefore the present uneasiness alone which determines them. In general we may observe that both these principles operate on the will; and where they are contrary, that either of them prevails according to the *general* character or *present* disposition of the person. What we call strength of mind implies the prevalence of the calm passions above the violent. (1888, p. 418)

Given Hume's Judaeo-Christian conception of the will, this is all the philosopher needs to say about akrasia.

It is not surprising, then, that (with the exception of a thoughtful essay by Sidgwick in *Mind*, 1893) Western European philosophy has little to show on the subject of weakness of will before the present century. Descartes in *Passions of the Soul* I.45–50 speaks of strength and weakness, 'force' and 'faiblesse' of soul, and means by this what others would call 'strength' and 'weakness of will'. 'Those,' he says, 'in whom the will can most easily conquer the passions and arrest the movements of the body which accompany the passions, clearly have the strongest souls' (I.48). But weakness of soul is for him not a theoretical but a practical problem (and one for which, I.50, he believes he has a solution, though he regrettably omits to spell it out in detail). Alexander Broadie and Elizabeth Pybus declare that 'Kant has an extensively developed and far reaching theory of weakness of will' (1982, p. 406), but I do not find that the slender bundle of citations they supply goes any way at all to substantiating this bold claim.

Although the prime cause of this neglect was undoubtedly the prevailing conception of the will, a couple of contributory factors deserve mention. First, the Greeks conceived the state of mind of the human agent as one in which thought and appetition are logically inseparable; we might say that they viewed the agent's desire as a kind of cognition and his cognition as a kind of desire. When the will was given the task of making our behaviour conform to what we think best, desire was separated sharply from cognitive thought. From the seventeenth century onwards, philosophers tended to conceive it on the model of an unpleasant bodily sensation, like pain. When I experience pain I think about how to get rid of it, but the pain itself is not a kind of thought about anything. Neither, in the opinion of some philosophers, is desire. Russell's *The Analysis of Mind*, chapter 3, is a good illustration of this view. Men and other animals, according to Russell, exhibit 'behaviour cycles', that is, series of movements 'tending to a certain result, and continuing until that result occurs'. Desire is 'the initial stimulus to a behaviour-cycle', and a desire is of, or for, whatever state terminates the cycle it initiates. It is not (as people have wrongly supposed) an idea of this state; it is simply 'some sensation of the sort we call disagreeable' (1921 p. 67). Hence we can be aware of a desire without knowing what it is for, and when we do know what we desire, this knowledge consists in a true belief (based, no doubt, on past experience) 'as to the state of affairs that will bring quiescence with cessation of the discomfort'. I desire to go to Paris if I have a disagreeable sensation which keeps me moving till I reach the Gare du Nord, and then stops.

The significance of this railway-train theory of desire is obvious. Weakness of will is puzzling only if there is some logical connection between desiring to do something and thinking it would be good to do it. No such connection can exist if desire is a kind of sensation. We may still as a rule desire the things we think good and be averse to the things we think bad, but this is a fortunate regularity, just as Hume makes it out to be a lucky fact that we usually desire to benefit the people we love: 'This order of things, abstractedly considered, is not necessary . . . I see no contradiction in supposing a desire of producing misery annexed to love, and of happiness to hatred' (1888, p. 368).

Secondly, weakness of will is puzzling insofar as we think our behaviour is determined by our view of what is best; it is not so puzzling if we think our behaviour is determined mechanistically by our physical environment. Since the seventeenth century philosophers have been attracted to what might be described as a grandfather clock view of human beings. Just as an old-fashioned clock is so constructed that the simple downward pull of its weights causes its hands to rotate, its bell to chime, and sometimes other spectacular effects, so (it was thought) our brains, nerves and bones are so constructed that when our eyes and ears are stimulated by light and sound, our limbs move in so-called voluntary actions. Descartes held that 'beasts' are natural machines: 'Nature acts in them according to the disposition of their organs just as we see that a clock, which consists solely of wheels and weights, can count the hours and measure time better than we can with all our intelligence' (*Discourse* V, *Oeuvres* VI.59). Spinoza extended the sphere of mechanistic explanation to human beings; in *Ethics* III.2.Sch. he puts forward what would now be classed as a token-identity theory of mental and physical events. Now some of the ablest modern exponents of such theories, such as Donald Davidson, are also keenly interested in weakness of will, and the current orthodoxy is that all the problems of the libertarian are available to the determinist if he wants them. The fact remains that if a philosopher is satisfied that we could never have refrained from doing any of the things we do, it is unlikely to seem urgent to him to investigate the psychologist's or magistrate's distinction between deliberate villainy, weakness of will and compulsiveness. Spinoza himself, at least, betrays no sense of urgency. He recognizes a kind of 'fortitude' which saves people from being the slaves of their passions and ensures that they follow reason. But, he says,

> It would be as absurd for a man to complain that God has denied him fortitude . . . and given him so weak a nature that he cannot control or moderate his desires, as it would be for a circle to complain that God has not given it the properties of a sphere, or a child tormented by gall-stones that God has not given him a healthy body . . . That it does not belong to everyone's nature to have a strong mind (animus fortis), no one can deny who is not willing to contradict experience and reason alike. (Letter LXXVIII, IV.326–7)

Weakness of will is as unperplexing as gall-stones.

Perplexity revived only with the revival of philosophical interest in Greek philosophy. Down to the 1930s both in English-speaking countries and on the Continent Plato and Aristotle were studied primarily by classical scholars, and people doing original work in philosophy paid little more attention to them than did original thinkers in physics or biology. The University of Oxford, however, offered a course vaguely entitled Literae Humaniores (Humaner Letters) which carried great prestige and attracted some of the cleverest Arts students in Britain. This had on its syllabus Plato's *Republic* and Aristotle's *Nicomachean Ethics*. In the 1930s people started reading these ancient texts critically as philosophy. Some students of this generation, such as A.J. Ayer, found them unsuggestive, but others, like Gilbert Ryle and J.L. Austin, not only preferred them for their informal, jargon-free style to the philosophy in the German Idealist tradition which prevailed on the Continent; they also found them pointing the way round difficulties and mistakes which philosophers in the British Empiricist tradition, like Russell and Ayer, were unable to avoid. The analytical type of philosophy which is now dominant in English-speaking countries may be viewed as the result of a fertilization of these Oxford studies in ancient philosophy by the potent if slightly Delphic ejaculations of the Cambridge philosopher Wittgenstein.

In 1949 Ryle published *The Concept of Mind*, which contained an extremely forceful attack on the traditional concept of the will. In the following decade G. E. M. Anscombe developed a positive account of intentional action which dispenses with acts of will and instead appeals to reasons for acting and refraining. The work of Ryle and Anscombe on intention, desire and other notions closely pertinent to weakness of will was carried forward by Anthony Kenny in *Action, Emotion and Will* (1963). At about the same time R. M. Hare (1952, 1963) put forward an ethical theory which in temper is closer to Kant than to the Greeks but which re-establishes the Greek 'forward' connection between judging a course good and pursuing it.

Hare explicitly denied that clear-eyed akrasia is possible, and thereby provoked a good deal of discussion of that issue (well represented in a collection entitled *Weakness of Will* edited by Geoffrey Mortimore in 1971). Meanwhile a new generation of philosophically sophisticated classicists was taking up the Greek treatments of akrasia and offering discussions which aimed at shedding light not only on what Socrates, Plato and Aristotle thought but on the truth. Specimens to which I shall refer below include R. Robinson (1954), G. Santas (1964, 1966, 1969) and A. Kenny (1966).

This sort of work is still being continued by a later generation (witness C. C. W. Taylor, 1976, 1980; D. Charles 1984). But in 1970 a new impetus was given to philosophical discussion of weakness of will by Donald Davidson's paper 'How is Weakness of Will Possible?'. Davidson tries to show that we can adopt a Greek rather than a Judaeo-Christian psychology of action, that we can dispense with acts of will and connect acting intentionally with thinking one's line of action good, while still allowing the possibility of absolutely clear-eyed akrasia. His paper has been followed by a flood of writing on weakness of will which, after nearly twenty years, shows no sign yet of abating. I shall discuss his account and some attempts to improve on it in chapter 7.

Professional academics are creatures of fashion and Davidson is a writer who can do for a philosophical topic what the Prince Regent could do for a seaside town. If he were to raise the question 'How is climbing the Matterhorn possible?' the philosophical journals would soon be bursting with articles on oreology. But interest in weakness of will has proved too hardy and too fruitful to be attributed simply to fashion. I suggest that there are at least three reasons why, despite its long period of neglect, weakness of will should be regarded as one of the central and perennial topics of philosophical discussion.

First, the phenomenon of akratic behaviour forces us to consider together two distinct fields of philosophical enquiry, ethics and the philosophy of action. Philosophers from the seventeenth century onwards tended to treat them separately, often (we may think) with poor results. The Greeks, especially Aristotle, treated them together. If it is true that developments in either of these fields has implications for the other, to study weakness of will is to adopt a vantage-point from which these interactions can very conveniently be observed.

But it is a vantage-point which commands more than this internal dividing line. Philosophy as a whole marches with other disciplines. Weakness of will gives rise to questions which are treated not only by philosophers but also by economists and psychologists. It is a kind of irrationality, and economists in recent years have given much attention to rationality and irrationality in choice and deliberation. Irrationality has also been studied from a different angle by cognitive psychologists. At the same time clinical psychologists and psychoanalytical theorists have investigated other topics germane to weakness of will: compulsiveness, self-deception, unconscious motivation, and the possibility of dividing the human agent into a plurality of interacting subsystems. I believe that just as the various branches of philosophy cannot successfully be pursued without regard to one another, so philosophy as a whole cannot flourish in isolation from other academic disciplines. Weakness of will is of central importance because it straddles the frontiers between philosophy, psychology and economics.

Third, philosophy has its history as well as its geography; it must keep in touch with its past as well as with its neighbours. I have said that weakness of will is a topic which, perhaps more than any other, obliges us to compare ancient Greek with Judaeo-Christian thinking about ethics and action. But for the present-day philosopher who is unable to read Plato and Aristotle in their own tongue it has a further advantage. Many of the topics which are discussed both by the Greeks and by us are discussed by the Greeks in works which are either highly compressed, or couched in idioms which do not turn smoothly into modern languages, or both. I am thinking in particular of Plato's *Parmenides, Theaetetus* and *Sophist*, of Aristotle's *De Anima* and *Physics* III and IV. These works are not inaccessible to the Greekless reader, but they make painful demands on his concentration. The discussions of akrasia in Plato's *Protagoras* and Aristotle's *Ethics* are relatively easy to follow in translation, and give the reader a sense of making contact with the founders of his discipline across a huge and dizzy cultural gap.

2

Socrates and Plato

I

Weakness of will has been a topic of philosophical discussion since the time of Socrates (c.469–399 BC). That it does not or cannot occur is one of a group of doctrines known as 'the Socratic Paradoxes'.

While everyone agrees that there are such doctrines, there is less agreement as to what exactly and how many exactly they are. David Gallop speaks of 'the Socratic paradox' as if there were only one: apparently that 'one who knows good and evil will necessarily do the good and avoid the evil if he can' (1964, p. 117). Gerasimos Santas in his *Socrates* (1979) discusses two: the prudential paradox, as he calls it, that 'no one desires evil things and that all who pursue evil things do so involuntarily', and the ethical paradox 'that virtue is knowledge and that all who do injustice or wrong do so involuntarily'. Norman Gulley (1968) lists three: virtue is knowledge; no one does wrong willingly; and all the virtues are one. M. O'Brien (1967) goes up to six: no one does wrong willingly; no one wishes evil; virtue can be taught; virtue is an art like medicine or carpentry; virtue is knowledge; vice is ignorance. Evidently the Socratic Paradoxes as a body of doctrine is fuzzy at the edges. I shall be suggesting that such unity as it has is derived from a certain idea about the nature of voluntary action.

The unclarity about what doctrines should be included among the Paradoxes is matched by an ambiguity in one doctrine which must be accepted as central. This is usually formulated (cf. Plato, *Protagoras* 345d–e) 'oudeis hekon hamartanei', 'no one goes wrong willingly'. The verb 'hamartanein', here translated 'to go wrong', can be used either for wrong-doing or for missing a mark, failing to achieve an objective. The corresponding noun 'hamartia' can mean either a mistake or a sin. (Words in other languages like the English 'err' have the same ambivalence.) A cynic might wonder if the philosophical problem about weakness of will arises from a simple confusion of these senses. It is logically impossible to fail intentionally to achieve an objective you really have; it is neither logically nor psychologically impossible to do evil intentionally. In fact it does not appear that any philosopher has ever been guilty of this crude confusion, and the deeper we go into the notions of good and evil the more the initially clear distinction between evil-doing and failure becomes obscured.

Not only 'hamartanein' but also 'hekon' can express more things than one. 'Hekon' and the opposite term 'akon' are perhaps best translated 'of the agent's own free will' and 'not of the agent's own free will', but there are at least three ways (distinguished with care by Aristotle in *Eudemian Ethics* II.7–9) in which I may do something or bring something about without doing it of my own free will. First, I may do it in ignorance. If I put cyanide in the soup thinking it is salt, I put cyanide in the soup unintentionally, even though the causal action of sprinkling by which I cause the soup to become lethal is intentional. Secondly, I may not be in control of my causal action. If you push me out of the window and in falling I break a flower-pot underneath, even if I know that I am causing the pot to become fragmented, my causal action on the pot is unintentional, and hence my breaking of it is unintentional. In general A intentionally causes B to become f only if A both causes this change knowingly and causes it by causal action which is intentional. Thirdly I may do something knowingly, and my action may be intentional, but I still do not do it of my own free will if I do it unwillingly, reluctantly, against my wishes. The standard example is acting under threat. I hand over my wallet against my will when I cause this transfer at gun-point. When it is said, then, that no one does wrong willingly, the claim may be either that when someone does evil he is acting in ignorance, or that his causal action is not under his control, or that he acts against his desires. Each claim can be paradoxical, but the three are different, and in considering Socratic texts we must take care to see which precisely is being made. I shall suggest that whereas Socrates chiefly upholds the first, Plato eventually moves to something like the second.

Although it is hard to deny that Socrates held some form of the Paradoxes, no writings from his hand survive, and we depend for our knowledge of his views chiefly on reports by three people who knew him personally, Aristophanes (*c*.450–385), Xenophon (*c*.430–354) and

Plato (*c*.429–347). Aristophanes offers a not ill-natured caricature of Socrates in his comedy *The Clouds*, but this is no help to us here because Aristophanes does not attribute to Socrates any serious views on ethics or action at all. Xenophon and Plato both wrote dialogues in which Socrates appears as a speaker and puts forward ethical paradoxes. Not only, however, does Socrates' personality appear rather different in Plato's dialogues and in Xenophon's; the views the two authors ascribe to him also differ at several points.

Most scholars today prefer the testimony of Plato. The grounds, however, which Terence Irwin, not the least authoritative of these scholars, gives for the preference (1974) are dubious. One of Irwin's complaints rests on a simple misunderstanding. He says that Xenophon's Socrates does not deny that akrasia is possible at all; instead he denounces it in a way which implies it is all too common. Since we have to suppose that the historical Socrates denied the possibility of akrasia, we are forced to the conclusion that Xenophon had no understanding of his philosophy of action whatever. Irwin's argument here fails because though Xenophon's Socrates does in *Memorabilia* IV.v denounce something he calls 'akrasia' he uses this word not for action against one's better judgement but simply for dissoluteness or intemperance. It is true that he says 'by confusing people who perceive what is good and bad, it makes them choose the worse instead of the better' (IV.v.6); he is emphatic, however, that these intemperate people are not free to act otherwise; they are forced to behave shamefully; and the verb I have translated 'confuse' ('explettein', a verb also used for striking panic into people) strongly suggests that the 'perception' of good and evil is obscured (cf. Plato, *Protagoras*, 355b).

Irwin also suggests that Xenophon's personality was such that he cannot be taken seriously as a philosophical biographer: 'Xenophon quite closely resembled a familiar British figure: the retired general, staunch Tory and Anglican, firm defender of the Establishment in Church and State, and at the same time a reflective man with ambitions to write edifying literature' (1974 p. 410). I find this an amazing statement. Perhaps a few generals in the Indian Army were like Xenophon in making their fortunes out of plunder and marrying their native concubines, but this is not what our field officers are most famous for, and apart from this it is hard to see what resemblances Irwin can have in mind. Xenophon was not a professional soldier. He accompanied Cyrus' army of Greek mercenaries to Babylonia not as a soldier at all but as a civilian adventurer, and he was elected general by the mercenaries

only when the official generals had all been massacred. The total period
for which he was under arms can hardly have been more than six years.
And how can he be regarded as a 'firm defender of the Establishment'
when he was exiled from his native state at the age of twenty-seven,
served for the rest of his brief military career with its enemies the
Spartans, and lived out the remainder of his life in the foreign states of
Sparta and Corinth?

Modern doubts about Xenophon's trustworthiness really rest on his
religious views, and go back to Macaulay. Macaulay compares him
unfavourably with 'the shrewd and incredulous Thucydides' and even
with Herodotus: 'He was as superstitious as Herodotus, but in a way far
more offensive' (1889, p. 141). Xenophon does seem to have believed
both in the existence of gods and in the utility of divination. It hardly
follows, however, that everything he says about Socrates must be false
even when it is intrinsically credible. His reports of Socrates' development of the paradoxes are clear and give Socrates a line of thought which
is easy to follow. I think they may well be more accurate than Plato's.
Even if they are not, they deserve to be studied as specimens of fourth
century thinking.

Xenophon's most important discussions are at *Memorabilia* III.ix
and IV.vi. The first may be translated as follows:

> 4 Asked whether he thought that those who know what they ought to do
> but do the opposite are wise and temperate, he [Socrates] replied: 'Not more
> than they are unwise and intemperate. For I think that all men, choosing out
> of courses open to them, do those things which they think most advanta-
> geous to themselves.'

> 5 He also said that justice and every other virtue is knowledge (sophia).
> For what is just, and everything else that virtue makes us do, is fine and
> good. Those who know what is fine and good will not choose anything else
> instead of this, and those who do not, cannot do this but even if they try they
> will go wrong. So men with knowledge do fine and good things, and men
> without knowledge cannot, but even if they try they go wrong. Since, then,
> just things and other fine and good things are all things which virtue makes
> us do, it is plain that justice and every other virtue is knowledge.

Put a little more formally, the argument is:

1 Everyone chooses what seems most advantageous to himself.
2 What is just or otherwise virtuous is fine and good.
3 (Therefore) those who know what things are virtuous will not choose other
   things in preference to them.

4 Those who do not know what things are virtuous or good will not do these things even if they try.
5 Knowledge of what things are virtuous and good is necessary and sufficient for doing them.
6 But that which is necessary and sufficient for doing what is virtuous and good is virtue.
7 So virtue is knowledge.

It will be observed that (3) hardly follows from (1) and (2) without further premises. One is that deeds which are 'fine and good' are also advantageous to the doer, and another is that knowing that something is good involves thinking it is good. The latter, less problematic premise is included in the arguments in IV.vi to show that piety, justice and courage are all forms of knowledge. I give the argument concerning piety:

SOCRATES   What sort of man is the pious man?
EUTHYDEMUS   The man, I think, who honours the gods.
SOCRATES   Is it all right to honour the gods in any way you like?
EUTHYDEMUS   No. There are laws saying how you ought to do it.
SOCRATES   So the man who knows these laws knows how one ought to honour the gods?
EUTHYDEMUS   I think so.
SOCRATES   Does the man who knows how to honour the gods *think* he ought to honour them in any way other than the way in which he *knows* he ought to honour them?
EUTHYDEMUS   No.
SOCRATES   And does he honour them in any way other than that in which he thinks he ought to honour them?
EUTHYDEMUS   I think not.
SOCRATES   The man, then, who knows the law-enjoined things about the gods will honour them in the law-enjoined way?
EUTHYDEMUS   Certainly.
SOCRATES   And if in the law-enjoined way, then as he ought?
EUTHYDEMUS   Of course.
SOCRATES   And the man who honours the gods as he ought is pious?
EUTHYDEMUS   Certainly.
SOCRATES   So we may correctly define the pious man as the one who knows the law-enjoined things about the gods.

One observation we may make about these passages is that while Xenophon's Socrates certainly holds that virtue is knowledge, he does not seem to think the virtues are one. Gulley claims he does (1968, p. 151), but his only evidence is the phrase in III.ix.5 which I translated 'and every other virtue is knowledge'. It is true that the Greek words Xenophon uses could be translated 'and all the rest of virtue'. The doctrine, however, must be understood in the light of the argumentation offered to support it, and what is established in IV.vi is plainly that the different virtues are different bits of knowledge: piety is knowledge concerning the gods, justice knowledge concerning men, and courage knowledge concerning frightening and dangerous things.

More important for our purposes is that the paradoxical identification of virtue with knowledge flows from a view about voluntary action. In III.ix this is formulated: 'All men, choosing out of courses open to them, do those things which they think most advantageous to themselves.' IN IV.vi we have: 'No one honours the gods in any way other than that in which he thinks he ought to honour them. The first formulation is axiological, the second deontological, and the first asserts a forward connection from thinking good to acting while the second asserts a backward connection from action to thought; though whether Xenophon or his Socrates is alive to these differences may be questioned.

Why does Xenophon's Socrates maintain these connections? Has he just observed them to hold as a matter of fact, or does he think them somehow logically necessary? The distinction between empirical and logically necessary truth will hardly have been clearly grasped at this stage in the evolution of philosophy. We are told, however (Aristotle, *Metaphysics M* 1078^{b}17–23), that the historical Socrates concerned himself with definitions, and I am the more inclined to think that (consciously or unconsciously) he saw these connections implicit in the definition of voluntary action, because that seems to have been the view of his principal philosophical heir Plato.

II

Although there is no external evidence for the dating of Plato's works, scholars generally divide them into three groups which they label 'early', 'middle' and 'late'; they also think that the earlier a dialogue is the more accurate a picture it is likely to give of the thought of the historical Socrates. If we follow this orthodoxy (and I know of no good reason for diverging) it looks as if the early Plato joined Socrates in a

total rejection of akrasia, whereas the later Plato came to a qualified
acceptance of it. Plato's treatment of akrasia presents a good example of
a philosopher's development.

The *Protagoras* and *Meno* are classed as early. At *Protagorus* 358 b–d
Plato's Socrates says:

> If the pleasant is good, no one who either knows or thinks that other
> things are better than the thing he does will then do that thing when the
> better things are open to him . . . Nobody of his own free will goes for
> evils or for things he thinks are evil, nor, apparently, is this in human
> nature, to wish to go for things you think evil instead of good things; and
> when forced to choose between two evils, no one will choose the greater
> when it is open to him to choose the less.

Socrates seems to be saying that all this follows from the premise that
what is pleasant is good; but it does not, and I think Plato has expressed
himself awkwardly, and really means here to present the doctrine that
no one chooses what he thinks evil as an obvious empirical truth about
human nature. In *Meno* 77 b–78 a (see also *Gorgias* 467–8), however,
there is a conceptual argument for the doctrine.

SOCRATES   Do you mean that some people desire evil things and others
   good things? Don't you think all men desire good things?
MENO   I do not.
SOCRATES   You think some desire bad?
MENO   Yes.
SOCRATES   Believing these bad things to be good, or do you say that
   when they know they are bad these people desire them all the same?
MENO   I think both cases occur.
SOCRATES   So you think a person can recognize evil things as evil and
   still desire them?
MENO   Absolutely.
SOCRATES   Desire them how? Desire them to come to him?
MENO   Of course.
SOCRATES   Does he think these evil things will benefit a person they
   come to, or does he recognize that they are harmful?
MENO   There are those who think the evil things are beneficial and
   those who recognize they are harmful.
SOCRATES   These people that think the evil things beneficial: do you
   conceive them as recognizing them as evil?
MENO   Not altogether.
SOCRATES   Clearly then these people who are ignorant do not desire

evil things; they desire things they think to be good, though they are evil. So those who are ignorant about these things and think they are good clearly desire good things?

MENO That's about it.

SOCRATES What about the others who, according to you, desire evil things believing that evil things harm the people to whom they come: do they know they will be harmed?

MENO They must.

SOCRATES But do they not think that harmed persons, insofar as they are harmed, are miserable?

MENO They think that too.

SOCRATES And that the miserable are unhappy?

MENO I suppose so.

SOCRATES But is there anyone who wants to be unhappy?

MENO I think not.

SOCRATES No one, then, wants evil things if he does not want to be such a person.

The argument might be stated more formally as follows:

1 If someone desires something evil, either he knows it is evil, or he thinks it is good.
2 If he thinks it is good, he does not desire something evil.
3 (Turning to the supposition that the agent knows the thing is evil.) Desiring is desiring to get.
4 Evil things harm those who get them and make them miserable.
5 If someone thinks a thing is evil he thinks getting it will make him miserable.
6 No one wants to be miserable.
7 Therefore no one desires what he thinks evil.

Taylor (1976, p. 203) seems to think that this argument by itself establishes the principle of *Protagores* 358 c–d. It does not. But if we add the not implausible:

8 No one does a thing of his own free will if he does not want to do it,

we may conclude:

9 No one of his own free will does what he thinks evil.

How good is this argument? Someone might feel a qualm about (2): surely the man who desires something evil under the illusion that it is good desires something evil. Plato, however, seems to think (1a) that it is correct to say that A desires x only if 'x' is a description under which A thinks of the object of his desire in desiring it. If we allow him this additional premise, (2) goes through, and (2) is not unreasonable: it would be perverse to say that I want to bring about my friend's death if I want to take him for a spin in my new car and by doing so bring about his death.

More serious doubts concern (5) and the transition from (5) and (6) to (7). (5) does not follow from (4). If I do not accept (4) then thinking a course evil I need not think it will make me miserable; and even if I do accept (4) I may fail to apply the knowledge on a particular occasion (a possibility fastened on by Aristotle and later writers). But suppose (5) granted; to smooth the transition to (7) we might try inserting:

5a If someone wants something he thinks evil he wants to get something that will make him miserable.
5b If someone wants to get something that will make him miserable, he wants to be miserable.

Because of (1a), however, (5a) will be correct only if the agent thinks of the object of his desire when he desires it as something getting which will make him miserable. Furthermore (5b) will be correct only if he wants the object of his desire precisely because getting it will make him miserable. The most, then, that can be established (so Taylor, 1980, pp. 510–11) is that no one desires evil things because they will make him miserable. There is nothing paradoxical in that; what needs to be shown is that nobody desires evil things in spite of the fact that, as he recognizes, they will make him miserable. (As examples of such things we might take injections of heroin or sexual intercourse with attractive but diseased persons.)

Plato's Socrates applies these considerations to the issue of weakness of will in *Protagoras* 352–7. He does not deny that when a possible course of action has both good and evil consequences for the agent the agent may pursue it even though the evil outweighs the good; but he rejects a popular explanation of this. Most people say that the agent's knowledge of what is good and evil for him:

> is not strong and does not take the lead or rule . . . but often when knowledge is present in a man it is not his knowledge which rules him but something else, anger, pleasure, pain, sometimes love, often fear; and they think of knowledge quite simply as being, like a slave, dragged to and fro by all these things . . . They say that many people who have got to know what is best do not wish to do it, though they are in a position to, but do something else, and when I ask why, they say that people who do

this do it because they are mastered by pleasure or pain or one of the other things I mentioned just now. (*Protagoras* 352 b–e)

The popular view is that the wrongdoer knows the proposed course is more harmful than beneficial, but pursues it in spite of its harmfulness under the influence of passion; in other words, he acts akratically. To combat this view Socrates starts by attributing to its holders a crude form of hedonism: they pursue pleasure as good, avoid pain as evil, and have nothing else with an eye to which they call things 'good' besides pleasure and pain (354 b–c). The question is sometimes asked whether the hedonism is ethical or psychological. As stated, the doctrine is clearly the ethical one that pleasure is the good, not the psychological one that pleasure is the only thing people in fact pursue; though it is hardly suggested that anyone might in fact pursue anything else. It is also sometimes asked why Socrates bases his argument on a doctrine which Protagoras, his main adversary, has already rejected (351 d) and which neither he himself nor Plato can have thought correct. I do not find that too puzzling. Socrates wants to deny that anyone can be led by passion to act against his knowledge of what is best for himself. Socrates personally believes that action which is conventionally considered virtuous is beneficial to the agent, but this is a highly controversial opinion, while there is no doubt that people are often led by passion to do what they know is conventionally considered vicious. To obviate, then, irrelevant disputes and to forestall confusion Socrates adopts the crudest and most cynical view of the good for man and identifies it with pleasure.

The argument which follows contains obscurities and has been much discussed. First Socrates restates the thesis to be attacked. It is that:

It often happens that a man recognizes evil things as evil, but still does them, though it is open to him not to, because he is driven and confused by pleasure.

He then proposes that instead of two pairs of terms, 'good' and 'evil', 'pleasant' and 'painful', we should use only one, and he starts with 'good' and 'evil'. The thesis then becomes:

A man does evil things, knowing they are evil, though he does not have to do them, because he is mastered by good things. (355 d)

This (says Socrates) sounds absurd, presumably (so Taylor, 1976, p. 183) because a person under the influence of good would be expected to do good things. Socrates proceeds to ask: 'Are the good things such that they deserve to conquer in us the bad? . . . Evidently not, or the person who, we say, is mastered by pleasure would not do wrong' (355 d). But the only grounds for saying the good things do not deserve to conquer are grounds of size. So by 'being mastered by' we must mean 'taking greater evils as the cost of lesser goods' (355 e).

At this point Plato's way of speaking may well confuse the modern reader. He speaks of the 'good things' as prevailing in two different ways, both obscure: they 'master' the agent, and they 'conquer' or 'deserve to conquer' the 'bad things'. The first way of prevailing is best explained in terms of the second. The good consequences of a possible course of action *deserve to conquer* the bad if they exceed the bad. Presumably they *do* conquer the bad if the agent pursues the course, whereas the bad conquer if he refrains from it. That being so we might think that the good master the agent if he pursues the course, and the bad (or fear of the bad) master him if he refrains. But the word 'master' (hettesthai) has pejorative overtones. Being mastered by passion contrasts with being master of oneself (cf. 358 c), and implies that one goes wrong. So the agent is mastered by good things if he pursues a course although the good consequences are less than the evil.

Socrates then makes the same point using the terms 'pleasure' and 'pain'. The thesis under attack becomes:

> A man does painful things, knowing they are painful, being mastered by pleasant things – pleasant things, that is, which do not deserve to prevail. (355 e–356 a)

No doubt 'there is a lot of difference betwen pleasure here and now and future pleasures and pains', but nonetheless you should:

> gather together the pleasant things, gather together the painful, and weigh the near and the far in the balance, and say which are the more. If you weigh pleasant things against pleasant, the greater and more numerous are to be taken; if painful against painful, the fewer and less; and if you weigh pleasant things against painful, if the painful are exceeded by the pleasant, whether nearer by further or further by nearer, that action is to be done in which this is the case; but if the pleasant things are outweighed by the painful, you should refrain. (356 b–c)

Finally, after some further discussion about weighing and measuring, Socrates concludes that:

> Those who go wrong in the choice of pleasures and pains do so through

lack of knowledge . . . and not just knowledge, but a knowledge of how
to measure. (357 d)

In other words, it is not the case that they know the bad consequences of
their action exceed the good, but act in spite of that; they mistakenly
believe that the good consequences exceed the bad.

What objection exactly is Socrates bringing against the popular view
(apart from its 'absurdity')? Gallop (1964) argues that on analysis the
explanation 'Men do evil things knowing they are evil because they are
overcome by good' becomes 'Men do evil things knowing they are evil
because they do not know they are evil', and this is self-contradictory.
Although Taylor (1976 p. 185) accepts this interpretation, I find it very
strained. Plato nowhere gives a hint that there is any such latent contradiction. To persuade us he might think there is, Gallop gives him the
following line of argument:

1 Being overcome by good is choosing a course in which evil consequences
   predominate.
2 But men always do what they calculate to be most beneficial (Gallop, 1964,
   p. 127).
3 So if you are overcome by good you cannot know that the things you do are
   evil.

As Santas points out, once we recognize that the argument has (2) as one
of its premises, a much simpler interpretation is open to us. The thesis
under attack has been shown to be: 'Men do evil knowingly because
they choose greater evils as the price of (doubtless short-term) good.' (2)
makes such choosing impossible.

Taylor (1976, p. 182) urges against this inerpretation that it depends
on taking 356 b–c (quoted above) as a statement of psychological
hedonism. I agree that 356 b–c should not be so taken. Rather, it
explains what is meant by 'deserving to conquer' when one is comparing pleasures and pains which will occur at different times. But (2) is
essential to Gallop's interpretation which Taylor himself accepts, and it
does not have to be derived from 356 b–c. It is supported by the argument in the *Meno*, and it is implicit in what a historian of philosophy
might claim as the most important single passage in Plato.

At a dramatic point in the *Phaedo*, between replying to the first and
replying to the second of the two main arguments against his trust that
his imminent death will not be the end of him, Socrates makes a long
speech (96–101) about causes, explanations and methods of theoretical
enquiry. In the course of this he contrasts what later philosophers have

called explanations in terms of 'formal' with explanations in terms of 'material' and 'efficient' causes: saying, for instance, that beauty makes a thing beautiful and saying its shape or colour does. But he also contrasts what we might call 'causal' and 'teleological' explanations of human behaviour. He says it would be absurd:

> if someone were to say that Socrates does all that he does by mind, and then, endeavouring to give the factors responsible (*aitiai*) for each thing I do, were to say that I sit here now because my body consists of bones and sinews, and the bones are solid [etc.; there follows a primitive account of the physiology of sitting] . . . and were to ignore the truly responsible factors which are: that since it seemed better to the Athenians to condemn me, on that account it has seemed better to me to sit here, and more right to remain and undergo the sentence they impose . . . To call such things [as bones and sinews] responsible is too absurd. If someone were to say that without such things, bones, sinews and the rest, I should not be able to do the things that seem good to me, he would speak the truth; but that it is on account of these things that I do what I do, and not because of my choice of what is best, and that when I am acting by mind, is an extremely slovenly way of speaking. (98 c–99 b)

Throughout this passage linguistic considerations are at the front of Socrates' mind. A man's judgement of what is best can, and his physiological make-up cannot, correctly be called 'responsible' for his behaviour. But why is that? I suggest that it is because it is a further de dicto or conceptual necessity that if an agent acts 'by mind', that is, intentionally, he does what he does because it seems best. That is what differentiates intentional action from mindless change: it is, so to speak, the formal cause of acting intentionally. On this interpretation (I hope I do not excessively labour the obvious in saying) Socrates need not believe that the relationship between thinking it best to sit and acquiring (or holding) the sitting position is logical; for all he says to the contrary, it might be as causal as Davidson could wish. The view I impute to Socrates, or rather to Plato, is that the connection between sitting because you think it best to sit and sitting intentionally is logical: Øing intentionally and not mindlessly is Øing because it seems best. This is the true seed from which the Paradoxes spring.

Before moving on I should perhaps say that neither Plato's Socrates nor Xenophon's maintains on all occasions that we cannot do wrong intentionally. In *Memorabilia* IV.ii.19–20 Xenophon's Socrates argues that the man who injures his friends intentionally will have more knowledge of what is just than the man who injures them unintentionally. There is no suggestion that the man who knows what is just cannot fail to do it. A similar discussion occurs in Plato's *Hippias Minor*. When Hippias says that those who do bad acts intentionally are worse than those who do them unintentionally (371 e–372 a) Socrates does not say that intentional evil-doing never occurs; again he argues teasingly that it is better than unintentional. Nevertheless the impossibility of akrasia remains the official doctrine both of the *Memorabilia* and of the early Plato. Irwin (1977 pp. 191–6) claims Plato later discards it. That is an exaggeration; but we shall now see that Plato's treatment of cases of apparent akrasia undergoes a striking alteration.

III

The *Laws* is generally considered one of Plato's latest dialogues. It presents a completely different picture from the *Protagoras*. No longer is wrong-doing attributed solely to ignorance; no longer is action against one's better judgement an impossibility. In 734 b Plato introduces the word 'akrateia', a word with the same origin and connotations as Aristotle's 'akrasia', for a source of wrong-doing alternative to ignorance. In 875 a–b we are warned that even when a man has acquired knowledge of what is advantageous to the individual and to the state, if he achieves a position of power and immunity 'mortal nature will drive him' to rapacious pursuit of personal wealth and pleasure. That Plato has gone over to the opinion, rejected in *Protagoras* 352, that knowledge can be dragged about by passion, appears from 689 b and 863 e–864 a. He even seems to abandon the fundamental doctrine that we cannot desire evil things. At 689 a, a person can hate what he thinks good and embrace what seems bad. As a result, the remedy for evil-doing is not just instruction in a special measuring art (though that art apparently still exists: 644 d); before anything else it is educating people from infancy to like and dislike the right things so that when they grow up their reason and their passions will be in mutual accord (653 a–b).

How should we account for this change of view? Was it that as Plato got older, common sense prevailed and he came to see with Lemmon that since akrasia exists, any philosophical considerations that make it seem puzzling must be wrong? Rather the answer is to be sought in his mature speculations about the constitution of the human soul.

In *Republic* IV Plato argues that the human soul, at least in a mature adult, contains three elements. We learn things, feel anger and experience such passions as hunger and thirst not with the whole soul but with three distinct parts of it (436 a–b); it might even be correct to say that it is a different part which *does* each of these things (Plato uses a construction which can be used to introduce the *subject* of a mental activity or state: cf. *Theaetetus* 184 c 7, Aristotle, *De Anima* II.414ᵃ 4–14).

How does Plato hope to establish the existence and distinctness of these parts? According to Irwin (1977, p. 192), by distinguishing three kinds of desire. There are desires which are completely non-rational and independent of considerations about goodness and badness, desires which are completely rational and arise from 'considerations of what is best over-all', and desires which are partly rational and 'influenced by beliefs about some kinds of goods'. Desires of the first sort look like the blind 'drives' sometimes invoked in modern discussions of akrasia. I am not convinced that Plato thought there were any totally non-cognitive desires. Even a desire simply for drink (437 e) would surely involve the thought that drink would be *pleasant*. But in any case it is clear that Plato's main basis for his division is the phenomenon of internal conflict.

The same thing, he argues, cannot be affected in opposite ways at the same time (436 e). Desire involves a movement towards its object and aversion a movement from its object (437 b–c). There is a class of desires typified by thirst and hunger (437 d). But something springing from calculation often acts against these desires (439 b–c). Hence we must recognize distinct desirous and calculative elements. An example of what Plato has in mind might be this. I desire a drink of water in a tropical city but abstain because calculation tells me that water may give me typhoid. Someone might object that in this case there are not two conflicting forces; there is just a single desire for *safe* drinking. Plato seems to anticipate such an objection when he argues (at some length) that simple relatives have simple correlatives and complex complex. Thirst by itself is desire simply for drink; thirst for a cool drink would be a combination of desire for drink and desire for coolness (437 d–e). Presumably then desire for safe drinking would be a combination of desire for drink and rational desire for safety.

Plato goes on to show by further examples that 'thumos', a word which covers anger but also feelings of confidence, resolution and impetuosity, can conflict both with reason and with carnal desires. That it can conflict with calculation is obvious, and we can also be angry with ourselves for indulging base passions. So a third, 'spirited' part must be added to our psychic make-up.

Each of these parts has its own desires, pleasures and principles, and they compete for domination over one another (IX.580 d). This enables Plato to offer an explanation of akratic behaviour. It is only in the virtuous man that the calculative part is master. In some people the spirited part prevails, with the result that they are ambitious, competitive and fond of sport (548 c–549 a). And in many the desirous part rules, though its rule can take different forms depending on which desires predominate – in particular, whether desire for money or desire for bodily pleasure. The typical akrates would be a man in whom desires for food, drink and sex rule over calculation: Plato describes his situation as disastrous, but no more impossible than that of a country where an irresponsible tyrant rules over the intellectual elite.

Some readers in the past have found Plato's theory of the tripartite soul embarrassing. R.C. Cross and A.D. Woozley (1964, p. 128) say it is a metaphor which Plato nowhere tells us how to cash, and add patronizingly 'psychological talk nearly always is metaphorical'. Alas 'such use of metaphor has its dangers'. By personifying the elements in the soul Plato does away with personal moral responsibility, or if he tries to preserve it, he contradicts himself (pp. 129–30). Today this verdict seems over-hasty. Why not say that for a man's desirous part to prevail over his calculative is just what it is for him to be responsible for some akratic behaviour? Modern psychology has produced several serious partitionings of the psyche which cannot simply be swept aside as metaphorical. They admit of non-metaphorical interpretation, and if a particular model deprives us of personal responsibility, that needs to be shown by careful argument.

Colin Strang (1982) compares Plato's division of the soul with W.H. Sheldon's classification of traits of temperament: Sheldon finds these fall into three groups, the cerebrotonic, somatotonic and viscerotonic. This comparison is instructive if one concentrates on passages in which Plato is describing individuals in whom one or another of the three parts predominates. More relevant to our present concern, however, are the passages where Plato is considering conflicts between elements present in a single individual; and here it seems more fruitful to compare Plato with Freud. That Freud, like Plato, is a soul-divider is noticed by a number of writers on the *Republic*, for example Julia Annas (1981, p. 124). Her concrn, however, to defend Plato against the charge of making the parts of the soul into little men makes her prefer comparing

him with D.C. Dennett (see below pp. 172–3) and the comparison
with Freud has not, so far as I know, been worked out in any detail,
though Kenny discusses it briefly in his British Academy Lecture of
1969.

In *The Interpretation of Dreams* (1900) Freud makes a bipartite
division of the soul into Unconscious on the one hand and Preconscious
and Conscious on the other; his later work *The Ego and the Id* (1923)
contains a tripartite division into Id, Ego and Superego. A first resemblance between his work and Plato's lies in the nature of his elements.
They are conceived in a functional or dynamic way. In his paper 'The
Unconscious' (1915) he notes (XIV, p. 72) that the term 'conscious' has
a double use. A thought or feeling is conscious in one sense, which he
calls 'descriptive', if its possessor is currently aware of it, and unconscious in the same sense if he is not. He himself, however, wishes to use
the terms in a different sense which he calls 'systematic', to label distinct psychical systems. Freud seems to have started with the conception
of distinct physical systems of neurons in the brain, but the Unconscious
and Conscious systems at which he has arrived in 1915 are not located in
or related to distinct parts of the brain (XIV, p. 174); they are differentiated by their functions and dynamic behaviour; in particular by the
fact that the thoughts and feelings in the Unconscious are prevented
from becoming conscious in the descriptive sense.

The Id, Ego and Superego are not described as systems, but they too
are differentiated by functions and dynamic relations. The Id consists of
passions and tendencies which are normally unconscious. In 'The
Unconscious' these 'exist side by side without being influenced by one
another, and are exempt from mutual contradiction. When two wishful
impulses whose aims must appear to us incompatible become simul-
taneously active, the two impulses do not diminish each other or cancel
each other out, but combine to form an intermediate aim, a compromise' (XIV, p. 186). Processes in this region 'are timeless'; i.e. they
are not ordered temporally, are not altered by the passage of time . . .
[They] pay just as little regard to *reality*. They are subject to the pleasure
principle' (XIV, p. 187). It will be seen that the Id corresponds fairly
closely to Plato's desirous element in the soul. Desires in the Id, like
Plato's desires for drink and coolness, combine instead of conflicting,
and this is perhaps how Plato and Freud would both deal with a
question raised by Julia Annas (1981, p. 138): why not postulate as
many different parts of the soul as there are desires?

The correspondence between the Ego and the Superego in Freud and the superior parts of the soul in Plato is not quite so perfect. The Ego resembles the Calculative Part in that it 'seeks to bring the influence of the external world to bear upon the Id and its tendencies, and endeavours to substitute the reality principle for the pleasure principle which reigns unrestrictedly in the Id' (XIX, p. 25). In its relation to the Id it is like a man on horseback (XIX, p. 25; the simile may actually be borrowed from Plato, *Phaedrus* 246 a–b and ff.) On the other hand the Supergo watches the Ego and judges it in its first appearance as a distinct psychical agency in 'On Narcissism' (1914; XIV, pp. 95–7.), and in *The Ego and the Id* it is pitted against the Ego as the champion of the psychical against the purely physical (XIX, p. 36), whereas the Ego is 'first and foremost a bodily Ego' (XIX, p. 26). This makes the Superego seem like the Calculative Part and the Ego like the Spirited Part in Plato. But at any rate it is clear that the Ego and the Superego are entities of the same kind as the Platonic parts; they are part of a functional analysis, and to ask where they are or what they are composed of is to misunderstand their role in psychological theory.

A second point of resemblance is that Freud relies for his divisions on the same principle as Plato. He does not, indeed, say in so many words that the same thing cannot be affected in opposite ways at the same time. But the starting-point for his theories is the phenomenon he calls 'repression'. This is the preventing of an idea or impulse from taking effect by preventing it from becoming conscious in the descriptive sense, and it is chiefly to be observed in neurotic behaviour and dreams. In *The Interpretation of Dreams* he says we are 'only able to explain the formation of dreams by venturing on the hypothesis of there being two psychical agencies, one of which submitted the activity of the other to a criticism' (V, p. 540). These 'agencies' ('Instanzen'; a word soon to be replaced by 'systems') have to be conceived as acting against one another. Freud's paper 'Repression' (1915; XIV, p. 146) begins with the words 'One of the vicissitudes an instinctual impulse may undergo is to meet with *resistance* which seeks to render it inoperative' (my emphasis).

Freud also represents the Superego as struggling both with the the carnal desires of the Id and with the Ego. Its feelings of guilt force the Ego to self-punishment or even to self-destruction; Freud speaks of the Ego as 'suffering under the attacks of the Superego or perhaps even succumbing to them' (XIX, p. 56). In 'On Narcissism' the introduction of the Superego is justified on the grounds that we have the feeling of being watched. But the mere fact that the Ego is aware of itself is not a sufficient ground for postulating a second distinct agency; Descartes, for example, does not postulate a second ego to be aware of the first's cogitations; at the very least the Superego is distinct because it is a *critical* observer.

One reason why Freud's work is not much discussed by students of Plato may be that Freud puts great emphasis on the Conscious/Unconscious distinction; for him the chief psychical struggle seems to be less about what a person will do than which of his thoughts and feelings he will be aware of. The third point I wish to make is that this difference is less than it appears at first. I have already remarked that for Freud the Conscious/Unconscious distinction is primarily a distinction between dynamic systems, not between that of which an agent is and that of which he is not currently aware. At the same time Plato neither overlooks the Freudian Unconscious nor is indifferent to it. He argues for the existence of erotic and sadistic desires, desires to commit incest, murder and so on, in everyone, even those who appear most temperate, and he argues this precisely as Freud does, from dreams (*Republic* IX.571 b–d, 572 b). He may not say explicitly that the temperate-seeming people are themselves unaware of these desires when awake, but he surely thinks this. He also speaks of carnal desires as being sent into exile, breeding in secret and then returning (560 a–b). I do not think he means merely that these desires are hidden from the public; he is speaking at this point not of the individual as a member of society, but of the competing elements within the individual. His words fit the Freudian idea of desires being pushed out of consciousness, but continuing to enjoy a dynamic existence in the Unconscious.

Plato tackles the question 'How should we explain akratic behaviour?' by a partition of the psyche strikingly anticipatory of Freud's. Soul-dividing is a contentious project, but I do not think the difficulties are any greater for Plato than for modern psychologists. Hence I shall defer discussing them to chapter 9. But it remains here to say something about the mature Plato's handling of the other main question about akrasia, 'Is clear-eyed akrasia possible?'

When Irwin claims that Plato comes to allow 'incontinence' he may mean only (cf. 1977 pp. 24–5) that he allows that an agent can desire what he (or his Calculative Part) thinks bad. That is true, and it is a change from what is said in the *Meno*. But akrasia is not merely desiring what we think bad; it is not even simply doing what we think bad: it is doing what we think bad of our own free will, and that is generally taken to involve being able to refrain.

Davidson, indeed, denies this. He says (1980, p. 22 n. 1) that the akrates need only *believe* he could refrain. Davidson has to say this because he subscribes to a physicalism which makes all our behaviour causally determined; he thinks we are never able to behave otherwise than as we do. Plato, however, explicitly rejects this kinds of determinism (*Phaedo* 93–4). For Plato it appears that when we act intentionally or 'because of mind' we must be able to act otherwise. I shall not, in this book, consider whether he is right, whether freedom really is incompatible with physical determinism. That is partly because I think that so far as an enquiry into weakness of will is concerned the question is more verbal than substantive. The substantive question is whether a person can do what at the time he thinks bad without acting under some kind of compulsion, not whether such compulsion is compatible with acting intentionally. In general, however, I shall write as if action cannot be intentional unless the agent could act otherwise, and I suggest that it is because Plato thinks this that he would not agree with Irwin that he ever comes to allow akrasia.

That he would not agree is easily shown. He always retains the doctrine that no one is voluntarily bad (*Laws* 860 d, *Timaeus* 86 d–e). Neither will be accept the compromise position that people *are* vicious against their will but *do* vicious acts voluntarily (*Laws* 860 e): all unjust action is involuntary. Unfortunately he does not say clearly how he hopes to maintain this. Taylor (1976, p. 203) suggests that unjust action against the agent's better judgement is 'action under psychological compulsion'. I do not think this is a possible interpretation of *Laws* 863, the passage to which Taylor refers. For while Plato there says that one irrational force, anger, 'upsets many things with uncalculating violence', he says that another, pleasure, proceeds rather by trickery than by violence. According to 861–2 unjust action seems to be intentional harming which proceeds from an unjust character, and I think it is involuntary only inasmuch as nobody wants his actions to proceed from an unjust character.

If, however, we turn to the *Republic*, Taylor's interpretation gains in appeal. To say that a man's Desirous Part has gained tyrannical control of his Calculative (*Republic* IX) is precisely to represent his behaviour as in some degree compulsive. There are two ways in which apparently akratic behaviour can fail to be pure, clear-eyed akrasia. The agent can lose, at the moment of action, his grasp of the badness of what he is doing, or he can see it but be unable to refrain. Whereas the youthful Plato, like Socrates, thought that the failure is always one of intellect, the older Plato seems to have come round to the view that it is usually failure of ability. That, of course, would lead him to seek further insight into akrasia by using the methods of psychology.

The viability of this approach will be considered in chapter 9. In the next chapter, however, we shall se how Aristotle reverted to an approach which is at once more Socratic and more austerely philosophical.

3
Aristotle

Modern discussions of akrasia are still deeply influenced by Aristotle, and we have probably more to learn on the subject from him than from any other pre-twentieth-century philosopher. In the present section I shall say how he classifies different kinds of weak-willed behaviour and fits them into his general philosophy of action. I shall then consider his famous discussion in *Nicomachean Ethics* VII.3 of 'whether and in what way' the akrates knows that what he is doing is bad. Finally I shall say something about the general character of his philosophy of action as a whole. Katherine Wilkes (1978), Martha Nussbaum (1978) and, most elaborately, David Charles (1984) represent Aristotle as a kind of anticipator of modern physicalism. I shall challenge this interpretation and put forward an alternative.

Aristotle touches on akrasia at various places in his ethical and psychological writings, but his main treatment is in the book known as *Nicomachean Ethics* VII. Two full-scale ethical treatises have come down to us as Aristotle's work, the *Eudemian Ethics* and the *Nicomachean* hereafter referred to as *EE* and *EN*. The books usually printed as *EN* V-VII are common to both. Kenny (1978) argues vigorously that they originally belonged to the *EE*. For our present purposes I do not think we need decide about this, since it is now widely agreed that both treatises are really by Aristotle, and the differences between them seem to be more in emphasis than in substance.

Aristotle usually characterizes the akrates as one who acts contrary to the conclusions of thought, mind, reason or calculation in accordance with a certain kind of desire: so *De Anima* III.433 a 1–8, *EE* 1223ᵃ37–8, etc. His generic term for desire is 'orexis' and he distinguishes three varieties, 'boulesis', 'thumos' and 'epithumia'. How do these differ? According to J.J. Walsh (1963, p. 88; cf. Irwin, 1977, p. 192) in the degree to which they are obedient to reason. I should prefer to say they differ in their objects. Boulesis is desire for what reason presents as good; its non-technical meaning is 'wish' and no one wishes for what is bad (1223^{b}7). The central meaning of 'thumos' is 'anger'. Aristotle defines this as desire for vengeance (*Rhetoric*. II.1378^{a}31–3) and also uses 'thumos' to cover desire for fame, social status and the like. Epithumia is desire for pleasure (*De Anima* II.414^{b}5–6). Whatever the exact principle of division, it is fairly clear that Aristotle's three modes of desire are a residue of Plato's three parts of the soul, the Calculative, Spirited, and Desirous. Modern philosophers sometimes contrast rational preference, something not easily distinguished from thinking (on rational grounds) that something is better than alternatives, with sensations of craving and 'drives'. Aristotle's boulesis/epithumia contrast is not an anticipation of this since epithumia is not non-cognitive; it is a mode of awareness of its object (431^{a}8–16, discussed below pp. 54–6).

Pears (1984, pp. 235–40) finds an inconsistency between the treatments of akrasia in *EE* II–III and in *EN* VII.3. In the former reason and desire can conflict and 'being separate can be pushed out one by the other' (1224^{b}24–30) but without the agent's being thereby compelled. *EN* VII seems to imply that if the akrates sees clearly that his action is bad, he must be unable to refrain. Pears does not notice that at *EE* III.1229^{b}20ff Aristotle says that some emotions, like some sensations of heat and cold, are 'beyond what a person's nature is capable of bearing'. Aristotle allows, then, for psychological compulsion (see also 1225^{a}23–33 for compelling arguments). *EE* also introduces the distinctions between having knowledge and using it and between innocent and culpable cognitive failure (1225^{b}10–17) which are the basis of the *EN* VII account. The inconsistency between the two treatments, then, seems to me illusory.

In 1150^{a}9–15 Aristotle refers to a class of pleasant and unpleasant experiences connected with the sense of touch. Epithumia, temperance and intemperance and strength and weakness of will are defined in terms of these. The pleasant experiences are not so much pleasant sensations as activities which pleasant sensations render enjoyable, notably eating, drinking and making love. The unpleasant experiences include on the one hand feelings of distress or mortification at failing to satisfy epithumia for food, drink or sex, on the other unpleasant sensations of pain, strain, heat, cold, etc., and activities rendered unpleasant by such sensations. Equipped with the notions of these pleasant and unpleasant experiences, Aristotle distinguishes two main kinds of strength and weakness of will:

1 The akrates does wrong to obtain pleasure where most people would refrain.
2 The enkrates ('man of self-control') refrains in cases where most people, to obtain pleasure, would do wrong.
3 The malakos ('soft' man) omits to do what he should (cf. 1104^{b}10–11) in order to avoid pain or hardship which most people would endure.
4 The karterikos ('tough' man) does what is right in cases involving pain or hardship by which most people would be deterred.

Since temperance is a disposition to behave well in cases involving pleasant and unpleasant experiences, it may seem that the akrates and the enkrates are simply the man who is below average in temperance and the man who is above. In 1152^{a}1–5, however, Aristotle says that the enkratic have and the temperate do not have, bad epithumiai. The temperate man would not enjoy excessive drinking or adultery, whereas the enkrates would but resists the allurement. On the other hand the akrates differs from the intemperate man in that the latter thinks his undiscriminating pursuit of pleasure is right, whereas the former does not.

Aristotle's references to what most people would do might seem at first to involve a difficulty. If the enkrates refrains from misbehaviour where most people would misbehave, most people must have bad desires and be either akratic or intemperate. If the akrates misbehaves where most people would refrain, most people must be either temperature or enkratic. But if most people are temperate or enkratic, it is impossible that most people should be intemperate or akratic. The difficulty disappears, however, if we suppose (what is reasonable enough) that most people are neither very temperate nor very intemperate, but have bad desires on some occasions.

An objection less easily met, though it is not seriously damaging, is that if Aristotle wants to base the distinction between akrasia and malakia on the difference between pleasant and unpleasant experiences, he should not say that akrasia consists solely in action and malakia solely in omission. A pleasant experience is not just one in order to obtain which we act but one in order not to lose which we refrain from acting. Presumably the akrates fails to leave his bed or his table when most people would. Conversely the malakos takes trouble most people would not take to avoid unpleasant tasks.

Besides distinguishing between akrasia and malakia Aristotle distinguishes two varieties of akrasia, impetuosity (propeteia) and weakness (astheneia) (1150^{b}19ff). The impetuous man acts to satisfy his desire without thinking; the weak man deliberates but does not abide by the result. Presumably an analogous distinction could be drawn for malakia, though Aristotle does not draw it. Aristotle also distinguishes akrasia due to epithumia (the standard kind of akrasia) from akrasia due to thumos. This distinction will not apply to malakia, though people can, of course, through uxoriousness (Sir Geraint) or anger (Achilles) fail to do what they should.

What are we to make of all this psychological equipment? Wiggins (1978/9, p. 255) calls continence an 'executive' virtue. He takes the term from Pears (1978), but I am not sure he means to use it in Pears's way. An executive virtue for Pears is one which cannot be exercised purely for its own sake: some further goal is always needed. Temperance allegedly is not an executive virtue because I can act temperately just for the sake of acting temperately; courage is executive because to act courageously I have to have some further aim in view, say victory. I do not know if Pears would count enkrateia as executive in this way. If I can abstain from base pleasures merely for the sake of behaving temperately, why should I not abstain from base pleasures to which I am very strongly drawn just for the sake of behaving continently? Perhaps David Wiggins's idea is that whereas the temperate man abstains from base pleasures because they are base, the enkrates does not abstain from them because he is strongly drawn to them. But the word 'executive' and the example of courage suggest a slightly different contrast. Courage, it might be said, enables us to carry out plans in the face of danger; karteria enables us to carry them out in the face of hardship; and enkrateia enables us to refrain from courses we think bad when they appear extremely pleasant. Are enkrateia and karteria, then, executive virtues in that they are qualities which, though they do not tell us what things to pursue or shun, enable us to pursue some and shun others in spite of the unpleasant or pleasant sensations involved? I do not think Aristotle's account of human nature leaves room for such qualities.

Aristotle draws a broad distinction between 'dianoetic' qualities, qualities of intellect, and 'ethical' qualities, qualities of character (ethos). The former are capacities (or incapacities) for theoretical or technical as distinct from practical thinking, and include quick-wittedness, stupidity and various kinds of knowhow. Courage and cowardice, temperance and intemperance are states of character, and it belongs to a person's character to have general (virtuous or vicious) principles of conduct, to have specific objectives on specific occasions, to view situations in a certain way.

Aristotle speaks of our characters as dispositions with regard to action, to emotion, and to what English translators sometimes call 'pleasures and pains'. Of these three, emotion is the most important. It is because of our dispositions to be moved emotionally that we are disposed to act in certain ways and to find certain courses of action or inaction pleasant or unpleasant. Many philosophers in the past (Kenny, 1963, ch. 2) have conceived emotions on the model of bodily sensations like pain; they have conceived them as introspectible feelings differentiated by phenomenological qualities. An emotion might be caused by a belief and might cause a desire. The belief that you have slighted me might cause anger in me, and the anger might cause a desire to hit you. But there is no logical necessity for anger to be connected with any belief or desire, and what makes it anger is its being a feeling which, so to speak, *feels* a certain way to the person who experiences it. On such a view I can have a certain capacity for anger, fear or pity, a capacity which may be innate or modified by experience or training, like the capacity to differentiate notes of differing pitch; but I cannot have a disposition as regards the emotion distinct from such a capacity. Aristotle, however, makes it part of experiencing an emotion to have things appear in a certain way and to desire or be averse to some course of action. Anger essentially involves thinking there has been a slight and wanting to retaliate. Hector's fear of Achilles is not just a disagreeable feeling in the stomach: he thinks Achilles is going to kill him and is averse to standing and facing him. Since we can acquire dispositions to look at situations in particular ways, dispositions to attend to certain features, ignore others, etc., we can acquire dispositions to be affected emotionally. Aristotle equates moral virtues and vices, and even, it seems (cf. 1144^{a}8–9,^{a}20–2, 1227^{b}22–5), moral principles and general views of what is best, with such acquired dispositions.

We have seen that the akrates and the enkrates resemble the temperate man in their principles and view of situations, and the intemperate in their desires. Their principles and ways of looking at situations pertain to their acquired dispositions; where the desires are something different from principles I think they must pertain to capacities. The intemperate soldier, we may suppose, thinks it clever to drink on guard duty if he can escape detection, and watches for the duty officer as much as for the enemy. Off duty he seeks out taverns where he can get blind or fighting drunk without interference. The desires to find such taverns and to drink on duty are acquired and indistinguishable from his deplorable principles. Neither the akrates nor the enkrates share them: they want to be vigilant on duty and pleasantly convivial off. But they resemble the intemperate in that they enjoy drinking warm beer and sleeping with diseased *vivandières*. Even when drink or partner is unexceptionable they enjoy engaging in the activity to excess and in eccentric ways (1118^{b}25–7) and take it hard when gratification cannot be obtained (1119^{a}1–4). This is surely a matter of capacity, or what we should call 'temperament', natural or acquired. Our terms 'character' and 'temperament' mark the distinction Aristotle expresses by 'disposition' and 'capacity'.

The akrates and the enkrates are both people who present the combination of a good disposition with a bad temperament. But (if we ignore their intellectual qualities which are here irrelevant) their dispositions and their temperaments exhaust their personalities. There is no room for any further quality of psyche to differentiate them. If they had wills, the will of the enkrates might be qualitatively different from that of the akrates; but a will is not part of the equipment of an Aristotelian psyche.

Aristotle's treatment of karteria is briefer and less careful than his treatment of enkrateia, but similar considerations apply. I might endure hardship and pain which other people could not because I was insensitive to unpleasant sensations, but that sort of insensitivity belongs more to physical make-up than to character, and I doubt if the karterikos *is* insensitive. Apsley Cherry-Garrard displayed karteria, surely, on his winter journey in the Antarctic, but it is not suggested that he did not feel the cold. A close analogy with akrasia would require the karterikos to have above-average sensitivity, but that is absurd. Karteria is not, in fact, like enkrateia closely related to temperance. Rather it is a kind of courage. La Valette at the siege of Malta put up with hardship most septuagenarians could not have borne. His aversion to fighting all day in full armour was due to his advanced age and the August heat; his belief that it was possible to defeat the besiegers, but that to effect this he would have to fight personally in the breach, like his belief that it was a fine thing to face death in this cause, should be ascribed to courage. There is no distinct virtue of karteria.

Gary Watson (1977, p. 323) says 'the virtue of self-control is the capacity to counteract recalcitrant motivation'; that is, to resist strong desire for what the agent thinks bad. Watson seems to identify this capacity with 'capacities and skills of resistance which are generally acquired in the normal course of socialisation and practice'. Aristotle says we can steel ourselves in advance against passion as we can steel ourselves against being made to laugh by tickling (1150^{b}21–5) and a good deal of work has been done recently on techniques for fighting cravings and urges (for some references see Mele, 1987, pp. 23–4 and 77 nn). Such techniques or skills, however, cannot of themselves constitute a virtue of enkrateia. The notions of a virtue and a skill are radically different. If there are skills of desire-resisting the virtuous man will use them when and as he should, whereas the akrates will akratically fail to apply them.

This point is taken by Alfred R. Mele. He observes that if I am to have a *trait* of self-control, not only do I need skills but I must be motivated to exercise them (1987, pp. 59–60). Mele provides more argument than other recent writers for recognizing a special virtue of self-control, but in the end I remain unconvinced.

First, although Mele uses the word 'enkrateia' for his supposed virtue, his conception is much wider than Aristotle's conception of enkrateia. Self-control for Mele includes mastering fear (p. 54); for Aristotle that would pertain not to enkrateia but to courage. Mele's self-control also embraces not being soft-hearted (pp. 19–20); having good mental habits of the kind Nisbett and Ross (1980: see below p. 140) show to be rarer than is commonly assumed; and what Elster (1979) calls 'binding oneself'. We may indeed have a broad concept of self-control which covers all these things, but it is neither Aristotle's enkrateia nor the notion of a character-trait.

Secondly, Mele says that the self-controlled man must be 'appropriately motivated to act' as he 'judges best'. What is the appropriate motivation? There seem to be two possibilities. Any Aristotelian virtue is a disposition to be moved emotionally to certain ways of behaving. The appropriate motivation, then, to courageous, temperate or generous action might be the emotions which would be experienced by the courageous, temperate or generous person. The temperate Odysseus is motivated to refrain from abducting Helen by feelings of friendship and gratitude towards Menelaus, by aversion to imperilling Ithaca by irresponsible behaviour, by love for Penelope, and by concern for Helen's own long-term happiness. Alternatively the appropriate motivation might be a kind of second-order passion for controlling one's passions. The second kind of motivation might provide the basis for a special character-trait, but it is a little bizarre, and the trait sounds

more like priggishness than self-control. Mele mostly (1987, see especially his ch. 5) takes the motivational base for exercising self-control in
performing a virtuous act to be the same as the motivational base for
that act. If that is so, the man who 'is appropriately motivated to
conduct himself as he judges best' (p. 60) is simply the man with the
appropriate virtue.

I conclude that, as applied to persons, the terms 'akratic' and
'enkratic' are descriptive and statistical rather than explanatory. They
are like 'large' and 'small', not like 'dropsical' and 'anorectic'. Enkratic
behaviour is abstaining from a bad act most people would do although
you have intemperate desires; akratic behaviour is doing a bad act from
which most people would refrain although you have the temperate
man's outlook. The akratic man regularly behaves akratically and the
enkratic man regularly behaves enkratically. But what is it in a person
which is responsible for his behaving one way or the other, either
regularly or now and then? If Aristotle has an answer to that, it must be
found in *EN* VII.3.

II

Although everything Aristotle says about akrasia has been very carefully
studied in recent years, scholars continue to dispute about whether he
thinks that clear-eyed akrasia is possible. He usually writes as if it is, but
EN VII.3 seems to conclude that it is not. J. Cook Wilson in 1879 was so
unhappy about the discrepancy that he argued *EN* VII.3 is not by
Aristotle at all. Later scholars line up in opposing sides: Kenny, Charles
and Pears say Aristotle allows clear-eyed akrasia; Walsh, Anscombe
(1965), Davidson and Wiggins say he does not. This unedifying
division persists because scholars suppose that the question 'Does the
akrates know that what he is doing is wrong?' should have a clear
answer. On a natural reading the chapter is designed precisely to
challenge that supposition.

The general view, says Aristotle, is that 'the akrates, though he knows
certain things are bad, does them because of passion' ($1145^b12–13$); 'it
is a problem in what way he understands correctly when he behaves
akratically' ($1145^b21–2$; for the translation, see Hardie, 1968,
pp. 266–7). Some people think he cannot have knowledge in the strict
sense. Socrates, for instance, thought it would be strange indeed if anything could 'drag knowledge about like a slave' – Aristotle echoes the

wording of *Protagoras* 352. According to Socrates, wrong-doing is due
to ignorance; but that sounds absurd, and we must enquire what kind
of ignorance this can be: 'for that the man does not think [that what he
is doing is all right] before passion comes over him is plain.' So we must
see whether people who do what is bad 'know [that it is bad] and in
what way they know'.

Aristotle starts with a negative point: no help can be got from distinguishing between knowledge and belief, since people can put as much
confidence in their beliefs as in their knowledge (1146^{b}24–31). He then
makes four positive points. First:

> A person is said to know in two ways. Both the man who has knowledge
> and does not use it and the man who uses it are said to know. There will
> be a big difference between doing what you should not do when you
> possess the knowledge but are not contemplating, and doing it when you
> are contemplating. The latter seems strange, but it is not strange if you
> are not contemplating. (1146^{b}31–5)

What is the contrast between having knowledge and using it? We
ourselves might say that a man uses knowledge if he acts upon it, but as
Kenny (1966, p. 169) observes, that cannot be the meaning here since it
goes without saying that the akrates does not act on the knowledge that
what he does is bad. The use of the word 'contemplate' (theorein)
suggests that Aristotle is contrasting knowing something dispositionally
with actually thinking it on a particular occasion. Having once learnt
and not subsequently forgotten that William I came to England in
1066, I know this dispositionally even when I am not thinking about
English history at all. I know it, we might say, occurrently when
someone asks me, or when, going round Durham Cathedral, I am
surprised to hear someone say, 'This building is a thousand years old.'

This distinction is unproblematic for knowledge of particular facts or
obligations like 'William came in 1066', 'I have to go to London on
Tuesday'. But what exactly is it to have an occurent general thought like
'Petrol is explosive' or 'Parents ought to cherish their children'? Does
the mind somehow directly contemplate universal truths? Plato and
Russell may have thought so, but Aristotle sometimes seems more
hesitant. In *Metaphysics* M 1087^{a}15–25 and *De Anima* III.431^{b}24–6
there is a suggestion that while universals can be known dispositionally,
the exercise of this dispositional knowledge is not actual contemplating
of anything universal but rather contemplation of particulars which
instantiate (or fail to instantiate) universals. If that is right, contem-

plating a general principle will be applying it, if not in action, at least in judgement about particulars. I should contemplate the general thoughts about petrol and parents if I occurrently thought 'This stuff is petrol so it'll do for my Molotov cocktail' or 'I dare say Oedipus is my son, but I can hardly be expected to cherish him after what the Delphic Oracle has said about him'.

Aristotle's next point is consistent with this conception of 'contemplation' or 'use':

> There are two kinds of premise. There is no difficulty about acting against your knowledge if you possess both and use the universal but not the particular. And there is a difference about the universal: part of it relates to the agent, part to the thing. For instance [a man may think] that dry food benefits every human being, and that he himself is a human being or that a certain sort of food is dry; but that this food here is of that sort is something he does not possess or something that is not actually operative. These differences are enormously important, and to know in the one way seems nothing remarkable, whereas to know in the other seems amazing. (1146^{b}35–1147^{a}10)

To flesh out Aristotle's example a little, we might take the universal or major premise 'Unfatty food benefits men with high blood pressure'. This contains two terms, 'unfatty food' and 'men with high blood pressure'. 'Using' or 'contemplating' the major premise would be applying one or the other of these terms, either to an individual or to a type. 'Haddock is unfatty' and 'most stockbrokers have high blood pressure' apply them to types; 'I have high blood pressure', 'This food is unfatty' apply them to particulars. Aristotle's schema here in fact fits the case, not of doing something one knows to be bad but of failing to do something one knows to be good. A slight alteration of the example, however, yields doing something known to be bad. I know that I ought not to eat fatty food and I know that pork is fatty, but I eat this dish not knowing it contains pork.

If I do that I can certainly be said to do something I know to be bad; but my behaviour can hardly be classed as akratic. It is not due in the required way to passion or desire for pleasure, and it may well be wholly blameless. Although some readers, such as Hardie, try to understand 1146^{b}35–1147^{a}10 as describing a possible case of akrasia, Aristotle's next words show that he thinks the akrates does what he knows to be bad in a different way:

> There is another way in which human beings can have knowledge,

different from those just described. Under the heading of having and not using, we see a different kind of having: a person can both have in a way and not have, like those who are asleep, mad or drunk. And that is just how people are when they are in the grip of passion. Rage, erotic love and the like manifestly cause changes in the body and even make some people mad. Clearly we should say that the akratic are in a similar state to these. That they utter the words of people who know proves nothing. People in the states just mentioned utter proofs and the verses of Empedocles, and when people start to learn something they string together words, but they do not yet have knowledge: the knowledge must become part of them, and that takes time. So the utterances of people behaving akratically must be understood in the same way as the utterances of actors. (1147ª10–24)

Aquinas in a discussion of akrasia commended by Davidson (*Summa Theologiae* I–II.77.3) says that passion, like sleep or drunkenness, 'binds up' (*ligat*) a disposition and 'prevents it from being freely exercised'. He follows Aristotle in taking, as evidence that passion can have this effect, the alleged fact that it can drive people mad. Cases of love- or rage-induced madness do not seem to occur today; but if desire for pleasure can prevent a person from applying moral knowledge in the way drunkenness prevents people from following complicated proofs they can follow when sober, the akrates might indeed, at the moment when he acts, know and not know in this way that what he is doing is bad.

Finally, and for ease of commentary I break this last passage down into parts, Aristotle says:

a   One might also look at the cause physically as follows.
b   One opinion is universal, the other concerns particulars, things about which perception has the deciding say. When one [opinion] arises from them the soul must, in the one case, affirm the conclusion, in cases to do with doing, act at once. For instance if one ought to taste everything sweet and this, one of the particular things, is sweet, a person who can do this and is not prevented must at once do it.
c   When, therefore, on the one hand there is the universal [opinion] forbidding to taste, and on the other, [the opinion] that everything sweet is pleasant, and this is pleasant (and it is this opinion which operates), and desire happens to be present, the one says to avoid this but desire drives; for it has the power to move each of the parts [sc. of the body]. So it turns out that the man who acts akratically does so under the influence in a way of reason and of opinion, opinion, however, which is not opposed in itself to

the right principle – it is the desire, not the opinion, which is opposed to that, – but opposed incidentally.

d That, by the way, is why beasts are not akratic: they have no understanding of what is universal, but only have particular things appear to them and remember them.

e How the ignorance is resolved and the akrates comes again to know is to be explained as we explain what happens with drunkenness and sleep; the explanation is not peculiar to akrasia and should be sought from the physical scientist.

f But since the last premise is both an opinion about an object of perception and decisive for action, either the man in the grip of emotion does not have this, or he does not have it in such a way as to know it, but he merely voices it as the drunken man might voice the theories of Empedocles. And since the last term is not universal and does not appear to be as much a matter of knowledge as the universal, the conclusion Socrates sought actually seems to result. It is not while what seems to be genuinely knowledge is present that the emotion occurs [or, perhaps better – certainly the text looks corrupt – 'It is not what seems to be genuinely knowledge that is overcome by emotion'] nor is it this that is dragged about through emotion, but perceptual knowledge. (1147^{a}24–^{b}17)

(a) Most commentators take the cause in question to be the cause of akrasia, but Aristotle might have in mind the cause of the akrates' temporary ignorance. The adverb 'physically' sounds strange because Aristotle does not go on to offer what we should call 'physical' or 'physiological' considerations. He uses the terms 'physically' and 'logically', however, to label two contrasting ways of treating a problem. A 'logical' treatment draws analogies from other fields – the field of human artistry, for example, if the problem concerns living organisms. The discussion of 1147^{a}10–24 was 'logical' because the akrates was compared first to a drunken geometer and then to an actor. A 'physical' treatment remains within the field of the problem and makes use of principles or premises peculiar to it. The proper starting-point for a discussion of akrasia is a general theory of intentional human action, and this is what Aristotle now proceeds to invoke.

(b) Intentional action results from a combination of a general principle about what is right or good and a belief about a particular thing or situation in much the way in which, when someone reasons syllogistically, the conclusion results from a combining of two non-practical premises.

Charles construes the opening words: 'One [protasis] is a universal opinion' and wants to supply 'protasis' where I supply 'opinion' ('doxa') in the second sentence. The point of this manoeuvre will appear when we consider (f). If what I say there is right, though Charles could be correct in his construal of the opening words of the first sentence, doxa and not protasis must be the noun Aristotle has in mind in the second sentence.

(c) There are two main views about this section. (1) According to Santas (1969), Gauthier and Jolif (1958–9) Burnet (1900) and, apparently, Aquinas, the major 'forbidding to taste' is 'Taste nothing sweet'. The akrates also holds a second general view: 'Everything sweet is pleasant'. The belief about a particular 'This is sweet' is therefore fitted to serve as a minor premise to both principles. The effect of desire is to make the akrates relate it to the second, not the first. As Aquinas puts it, 'passion prevents him from bringing it under the first principle, and he brings it under the second, which the inclination of passion has suggested, and he concludes under that.' On this interpretation the akrates not only has but contemplates both premises of the 'good' syllogism (as Robinson and others call it) which starts 'Human beings should taste nothing sweet'. The alternative view (2), preferred by Ross, Robinson, Walsh, Wiggins (1978/9, p. 261) and others is that the major premise of the good syllogism forbids the tasting of something other than merely what is sweet – Walsh suggests 'Do not taste an excessive number of sweets'. If this is right the akrates is prevented by passion, not from combining the minor of the good syllogism with its major, but from contemplating it at all.

(d) and (e) are parentheses which need not detain us, but (f), it seems to me, gives us reason to settle for the second of the two interpretations of (c). The word I translate 'premise' in the first sentence is the Greek word 'protasis'. If we adhere to interpretation (1) of (c), we must take it to mean 'proposition', and 'the last protasis' must be not the minor premise 'This is sweet', since that is certainly grasped, but the conclusion 'It is wrong to taste this'. Either the akrates does not draw this conclusion at all (so, perhaps, Aquinas) or, if he draws it (as the words 'the one says to avoid this' suggest but do not absolutely establish), it gets dragged about by desire. It is not genuine knowledge because it concerns a particular and genuine knowledge is of universals. Some readers may welcome the idea that the conclusion gets dragged about since Aristotle will then be acknowledding that there can be a genuine struggle between conscience and passion. But however that may be, there are several serious difficulties.

First, although 'protasis' does literally mean 'thing put forward', it seems to me misleading to translate it 'proposition'. For that word is used by modern logicians for any bearer of truth or falsity, whether it is a premise or a conclusion, whereas Aristotle uses 'protasis' only for things put forward as a basis for argument or discussion, not for propositions established by discussion. (I here follow Hardie, 1968, p. 278 and Ross, 1949, p. 288.) Hence 'the last protasis' ought to be the minor premise, not the conclusion.

Secondly, a conclusion like 'It is wrong to taste this' whether or not it is genuinely knowledge (I am not convinced that Aristotle thinks genuine knowledge is restricted to what is universal), is just the sort of judgement which is provided by the virtue of prudence or practical wisdom (phronesis), and Aristotle is explicit that this virtue is incompatible with akrasia: 1140^b11-12, 1146^a4-7, 1152^a6-7. It might be objected that prudence enables us not merely to arrive at the good conclusion but to stick to it. Aristotle says: 'A man is prudent not just through knowing but through doing' (1152^a8-9). But Aristotle also and regularly says that prudence is an intellectual quality, a kind of excellence at thinking (1140^b25-6, 1143^b21-4, etc.) It would not be an intellectual quality if it was a combination of an ability to arrive at truths of a certain kind with a disposition to act on them. The prudent man is a doer, I suggest, because phronesis is an ability to see what is right at the moment of action (cf. 1140^b11-12). The 'weak' akrates, in contrast, though he reaches the right conclusion in advance, fails to stick to it (1150^b20) because at the moment of action his intellectual powers are impaired.

It seems to me that the whole drift of the discussion from 1146^b35 is that there is something defective in the akrates' grasp of the minor premise; and there is also a further reason for accepting interpretation (2). As we have seen, Aristotle holds that both the akrates and the enkrates resemble the temperate man in their view of the situation and the intemperate man in the strength of their desires. It is natural to suppose that the strong desires of the akrates overcome, and those of the enkrates fail to overcome, the temperate view of the situation. But the temperate view is what would be expressed in the minor premise, not the conclusion. The temperate Odysseus does not think 'It would be bad to rape Nausicaa': the thought of raping her does not occur to him. But he does think 'She is the daughter of the one man who can send me home; she will make a nice wife for someone', etc.

A prolonged and spirited but eventually, I think, unsuccessful attempt to show that it is the conclusion of the good syllogism which is not properly grasped in *EN* VII.3 is made in Charles (1984). What seems to me his best argument may be stated as follows:

1 If an agent does something intentionally, he must do it knowingly, that is, any description under which it is intentional must be one he knows to apply.
2 The akrates does intentionally something he knows to be bad. Hence
3 There is some description such that (a) the akrates thinks that acts satisfying this description are bad, and (b) the akrates knows that the act he is doing satisfies this description
4 But (a) and (b) are respectively the major and the minor of the good syllogism. So
5 The akrates must grasp the minor of the good syllogism.

Charles does not insist that the akrates must grasp the conclusion of the good syllogism. He thinks that sometimes the akrates grasps this but sometimes he fails to connect the minor with the good major; always, however, the minor of the good syllogism is grasped.

I agree that the argument is valid and that (1) and (2) hold in general. But in the present connection everything turns on how clearly the agent in (1) must know at the time of acting that every description under which his action is intentional applies to it. Charles appears to me to think that a question like 'Did the driver know he was drinking enough to slow his reactions?', 'Did Paris know he was making love to a queen while on a diplomatic mission? has a straight 'yes' or 'no' answer, and that if the answer is 'no' the action cannot be intentional or, therefore, akratic. He chiefly relies, however, on two passages outside of *EN* VII.3, 1136ª32–5 and 1152ª15–16. The first passage (which is about whether the akrates intentionally wrongs himself) does not seem to me to show more than that Paris, to act akratically, must know at the time of acting that he is making love to Helen: some kind of *mens rea* condition must be fulfilled. The second passage with its context runs as follows: 'He [the akrates] is not like one who knows and contemplates but like one asleep or drunk; and he acts intentionally (for he knows in a way both what he is doing and what the result will be) but he is not wicked.' This seems to me to tell against Charles, not for him; and if we confine ourselves to EN VII.3, the declared purpose of the chapter is to show how the answer to 'Does the akratic Øer know at the time of Øing that he is Øing;?' must be nuanced.

I conclude, then, that we should accept interpretation (2). The chief point commentators urge against it is that the text does not contain any indication of what a 'good' minor, as distinct from 'This is sweet', might be. I do not find that objection too grave, though something should certainly be said about the form a good minor and its corresponding major should take. If, as Walsh suggests, the good major were 'One ought not to consume too many sweets' the good minor would be 'This is one too many'. At first that sounds reasonable: surely the driver who drinks to excess against his better judgement fails precisely to realize 'This is one too many'. But 'This is one *too* many', as a value-judgement, is a judgement of phronesis and 'One ought not to consume an excessive quantity' is a tautology. 'Good' majors would be 'Drivers should not drink so much that their speed of reaction is impaired', 'Men with high blood pressure should not eat marrow-bones'. The akrates at the moment of decision then says 'I can take a third glass and my reactions will still be fine' or 'My blood pressure is not so *very* high'. The knowledge suppressed by desire here fails to be genuine knowledge not because it concerns particulars but because it is not evaluative or directly action-guiding.

On this interpretation Aristotle holds that the akrates in the grip of passion fails to understand properly that his action falls under a prohibition which in general he accepts. How good an account is this? Its severest critics must concede that it is an improvement on the account offered by Socrates in the *Protagoras*. By his distinctions between having and using and between ways in which knowledge can be had but not contemplated Aristotle undermines Lemmon's unqualified declaration that doing what one knows to be bad is a plain fact of experience. Ross (1923, p. 224) complains that Aristotle overlooks the obvious fact that akrasia is due to weakness of will, but Ross himself overlooks the fact that the will belongs to the Judaeo-Christian, not to the Greek tradition.

Aristotle's emphasis on kinds and quantities of food suggests that for him the paradigmatic cases of akrasia are failing to stick to a diet or even (see below p. 160) bulimia. That may have been natural for the son of a medical family but a satisfactory account needs to cover a wider range of examples. Paris while on an embassy to the court of Menelaus made love to Helen, Menelaus' wife. Let us suppose that he accepted the general principle that one ought not to make love to one's host's wife. Then Aristotle seems to be saying that he cannot, while yielding to passion, have clearly understood both 'I am staying with this lady's husband' and 'I am making love to her'. This does at first sound absurd. Even characters in Shakespeare like Angelo and Bertram hardly sleep with ladies inadvertently, and if Hector after the event asks Paris whether he knew Helen was his host's wife, Paris must say 'Of course'. But the case deserves to be considered more carefully.

In the first place there is room in an akratic love-affair for blindness and self-deception: the parties can fail or refuse to see that they have moved from companionship to love. Paris could think of what he is doing under the description 'wild-flower picking in the mountains with a charming woman' and not under the description 'flirting with my host's wife'. It is also possible to thrust an unwelcome thought out of one's mind or suspend belief in it for a short but crucial period. 'This is my host's wife' will be an unwelcome thought to the akratic adulterer at the moment of consummation; it functions (to borrow a phrase from William James) as 'the corpse-like finger of reason'; Aristotle might claim that if the akrates expresses it to himself it will be like reciting lines from a play.

Perhaps more important, the ancient Greeks did not, like the Jews and Christians, accept what are sometimes called 'moral absolutes', rules admitting of no exceptions. The rule against adultery is often interpreted in this way in the Judaeo-Christian tradition: to accept it is to hold that a lady's being married to someone else is in every possible situation an overriding reason for not making love to her, and renders sleeping with her absolutely wrong. If Paris' principle that adultery is bad were understood in this way, recognizing that Helen is married to Menelaus would in itself be sufficient to rule out intentional love-making. But Plato and Aristotle seem to have held that no moral principle is ever more than prima facie (see below p. 117); no general rule can ever determine what is right or wrong in every possible case. On that view Vronsky, for example, could really hold that adultery is wrong and still not consider the fact that Anna is married to Karenin an over-riding reason for not making love to her. The situation described by Tolstoy is complicated. Vronsky needs to balance a variety of morally relevant considerations, particularly once obligations of friendship and mutual dependence have grown up between him and Anna. Aristotle could hold that Vronsky is akratic even after he has realized that what he is doing is making love to another man's wife if his judgement of various factors is distorted by passion – for instance if passion makes him underrate the possibility of the Karenin marriage's being patched up. In chapters 8 and 9 we shall see some modern findings about how an agent's perceptions can be obscured or distorted.

But why does Aristotle think that such distorting or dulling must occur? Why should there not be absolutely clear-eyed akrasia? Santas (1969, pp. 187–8) suggests that Aristotle is making the following assumption:

> Given that a man is faced with doing or avoiding a course of action, and that he knows or believes that pursuing this course of action is bad for him, but also pleasant, and that he has a wish to avoid the harm contained in it and also a desire for the pleasure it affords; then if he knows or believes that the harm outweighs the pleasure (so that the course of action is bad on the whole) his wish to avoid the harm is stronger than his desire for the pleasure; and if he believes or knows that the pleasure outweighs the harm then his desire for the pleasure is stronger than his wish to avoid the harm.

Santas calls this the 'value-strength' principle and says it is an 'over-simplification'.

This is the main modern criticism of Aristotle and his predecessors. Modern writers declare that an agent's estimate of the relative goodness of two courses may be quite out of line with the relative strength of his motivations towards them, and think that they have thereby shown both that clear-eyed akrasia is possibile and why it occurs. Because such declarations have become increasingly frequent and confident since Hare and Davidson revived the doubt about akrasia, I shall defer a formal discussion to chapter 7. A couple of promissory remarks, however, may be made here. First, Santas omits to say what he means by the term 'stronger' as applied to desires. We shall see that when the various possible senses of 'stronger' have been distinguished (pp. 127–8 below) the words 'We can have a stronger desire for the course we think less good' sound rather less helpful. Secondly, the words appear to express an obvious truth only so long as we operate with concepts of evaluation and motivation which are very far from being above criticism.

Our present purpose is to understand why Aristotle thinks clear-eyed akrasia impossible. I believe we can best do this by seeing how he conceives desire and thinking good. I shall argue that he identified both desiring something and thinking it good with having it as an objective. Being an objective is not, strictly speaking, a matter of degree any more than being a cause. Hence for Aristotle the notion of relative strength does not apply in a straightforward way to desires at all. But I hope it will emerge that, independently of any value-strength principle, this view of desiring and thinking good makes it difficult to accept that there can be absolutely clear-eyed akrasia.

III

The most authoritative recent account of Aristotle's philosophy of action is probably that of David Charles (1984). If Charles is right, Aristotle held a sophisticated form of physicalism which some philosophers today might prefer to any of the varieties on offer from our contemporaries. I shall argue, however, that (for better or worse) Aristotle's account is less physicalist and more teleological than Charles takes it to be.

The foundation of Charles's interpretation is a theory about how Aristotle conceives desire. He claims that Aristotle sees it primarily as a mode of acceptance of a certain kind of proposition, a proposition that something is good. It is not identical with thinking that something is good because in *Metaphysics* Λ 1072ᵃ28–9 Aristotle says: 'The primary object of wish is the genuinely fine (kalon); and we desire because it seems [sc. fine] rather than it seems because we desire'. A person *S* desires to ∅, Charles says, if '*S* accepts the proposition that ∅ is good in the way appropriate if *S*'s aim is to do what is good' (1984, pp. 86, 229). At the same time Aristotle holds that desire is the efficient cause of human action (so, allegedly, *EN* 1111ᵃ22–4, 1139ᵃ31–3, *De Anima* III.10, *De Motu* 7, *Metaphysics* Θ 5). From this Charles deduces that Aristotle is an 'ontological materialist'. Roughly speaking, ontological materialism is the doctrine that for any psychological state there is some physical state such that the presence of the physical state is 'non-causally sufficient' for the presence of the psychological one (cf. 1984, p. 214). The model we are offered for the relationship of the physical to the mental is that of two telephone wires being in contact to there being an open line between two speakers (p. 246). Aristotle is committed to the doctrine, Charles argues, by the following line of thought. (1) Bodily movements have 'essential physical causes'. (2) Desires cannot be essential physical causes because they have physical properties only incidentally. (3) So for any bodily movement there must be some physical movement which causes it. (4) But desire *is* a cause of human actions. (5) So if there is not to be over-determination, the physical event which causes the agent's bodily movement to occur must be non-causally sufficient for the desire (1984, pp. 215–20; cf. p. 111 below).

But although Aristotle is in this way a materialist he does not, according to Charles, allow either that mental states are identical with physical or that they can be defined in purely physical terms. Mental states are not identical with the physical states which are non-causally sufficient for them (Charles wants to exclude identity both of types and of tokens) because the same physical state can be sufficient for two distinct mental states, say imagination and desire, and because different physical states can be sufficient for the same mental state. When Cato wants to destroy Carthage, blood boils near his heart; when a Dalek has the same desire-type, a wire glows near his batteries. And belief and desires have to be defined in terms of non-physical values. Desire, as we have seen, is the mode of proposition-accepting appropriate to persons seeking the good; belief, apparently, is the mode appropriate for seekers after truth; and the good and the true are values not definable in terms known to physical science.

Charles goes on to give an ingenious account of the mode of acceptance appropriate for good-seekers. Since desire is an efficient cause, it must not be so defined that its relation to action becomes logical. We must not say, for instance, that desiring to go to London is accepting 'It would be good to go' in a way that causes the accepter to go. 'He went because he did something that caused him to go' is less a causal explanation than a tautology. Charles defines appropriate acceptance as accepting in a way that validates a certain kind of inference. I accept 'It would be good to go' in the good-seeking way if I accept it in such a way that from 'It would be good to go' and 'The best way to go is to take the 2.15 train' I can validly infer 'It would be good to take the 2.15 train'.

This reconstruction of Aristotle's thinking has considerable intrinsic beauty, and its offer of materialism without reductionism or any kind of identity theory is one which many readers will find alluring. As an interpretation of Aristotle, however, I believe it is almost entirely baseless.

In the first place, it is far from clear that Aristotle thinks the bodily movements involved in purposive action do have 'essential physical causes'; it is unclear, at least, that he thinks they have an unbroken chain of causes stretching back to stimulation from outside of the agent's sense-organs and beyond. Some scholars, such as Martha Nussbaum (1978), think this; others, such as Allan Gotthelf (1976) and John Cooper (1982), think Aristotle regards this sort of causal explanation as incompatible with teleological explanation and, for reasons given elsewhere (Charlton, 1985), I prefer this latter interpretation.

Next, whether or not Aristotle thought the agent's limb-movements are caused, it seems plain to me that he did not think they were caused by desire, or any other psychological state. In 406^b22–5 he seems to reject the idea that the mental could affect the physical in an inter-actionist way. In *Metaphysics* Θ 5 he contrasts active powers like the power of a hot object to heat, which are necessarily exercised when any-thing with the corresponding passive power is at hand, with the powers of rational agents like doctors, which are not. Whether these rational powers are exercised, he says, depends on desire or choice (1048^a10–11). It is perverse to take him as presenting these as causal factors; the point is precisely that the exercise of these powers is determined in a way other than causally. 'He Øed voluntarily, from choice, because he wanted to' is naturally taken as a different kind of explanation from 'He Øed because this event caused him to'. The question in *De Anima* III.9–10 is not what causes movements of pursuit and avoidance but how responsi-bility for them is to be apportioned between the non-causal factors of desire and thought. In *De Motu* 700^b15–29 he says that the object of desire, that which appears good, fine or pleasant, 'moves' the agent just insofar as the agent's movement is *for the sake of it*. The *De Anima* III.10 doctrine that movement is due to desire is most easily understood as the doctrine that it is due to the object of desire in this way; in other words, movement is due to desire insofar as it is for the sake of some object of thought which appears good.

Charles and I are agreed that *De Anima* III.431^a8–16 is a crucial source for Aristotle's conception of desire, but we understand it in quite different ways. I translate it (there is no substantial dispute about the translation) as follows:

> Perceiving [sc. perceiving what Aristotle calls the 'proper', 'common' and 'incidental' objects of perception] is like bare saying and thinking; but when the soul is aware of something as pleasant or unpleasant, similarly to affirming or denying, it pursues or avoids. Experiencing pleasure and pain is being active with the perceptual mean in relation to the good or bad as such. Pursuit and avoidance are the same [sc. as this perceptual activity] when they are actual, and that which is appetitive and that which avoids are not different either from one another or from that which perceives, but the being is different. To the soul that thinks, appearances belong as do perceptions [to that which perceives]; and when the soul says or denies good or bad, it pursues or avoids.

It is fairly clear that the analogy offered is: as bare saying stands to affirming and denying so (with sub-rational agents) perceiving stands to pursuit and avoidance. But how *does* bare saying stand to affirming and denying? Charles says 'affirmation is a mode of accepting a proposition' (1984 p. 85), and infers that Aristotle is explaining desire too as a mode of proposition-acceptance; in the case of a sub-rational agent the proposition would be 'This is (or seems) pleasant'. I do not think either that affirmation and denial are well described as modes of accepting propositions, or that the analogues of bare saying are perceivings that something is pleasant or good; I understand these rather as analogues of affirming and denying – as explananda at 431ᵃ9.

If we think there is such a thing as expressing a proposition with no illocutionary force at all, that would be bare saying, and if there is such a thing as entertaining a proposition, that would be bare thinking. Affirming and denying would then be the acts of adding illocutionary force or adopting propositional attitudes. Elsewhere (Charlton 1983/4) I argue that there is no such thing as bare content-expressing (where the content is conceived as having a truth-value) or bare proposition-entertaining. I also argue, *contra* Frege, that when you believe that p and I believe that not-p, our thoughts are the same in content but differ in form. If these admittedly contentious theses can be sustained, the distinction Aristotle is offering as a model will be not between two mental or linguistic acts, but between the content and the form of such an act.

How does this apply to perception and desire? Aristotle has earlier distinguished three kinds of thing we perceive: things peculiar to a particular sense like colour, things perceived by more senses than one like shape and size, and things perceived 'incidentally' like aunts and botanists (these are perceived 'incidentally' because their botanical knowledge or blood relationship to the perceiver makes no difference to their effect on his sense-organs). Aristotle's account, I suggest, is that reports of someone's perception like 'George sees something red', George sees some Château Lafite' describe the content of an agent's mental state; and 'It looks nice to George', 'George thinks tasting it would be pleasant' describe not further thoughts but the *form* of his mental state. His perception of the stuff in the glass takes the form of thinking it would be pleasant to taste it. As any speech must have some form or other, that of an affirmation or denial or question or command or the like, so any actual perception or awareness of a thing must be awareness of it is as pleasant or unpleasant or in some other way practically significant.

According to the rest of the passage (about which Charles is silent) actual pursuit and avoidance are not separate from this perceptual activity in the way they would have to be if they were caused by it. Like later philosophers who will be discussed below, Aristotle sees a necessary connection between perception or belief and behaviour (Charlton, 1980). Rather than cause and effect they are two aspects (differing 'in being' or admitting of different descriptions) of a single vital activity. We might say that awareness of a thing, when it takes the form of thinking of the thing as somehow good, is expressed in pursuit; when it takes the form of thinking of the thing as bad, it is expressed in avoidance.

On this view, thinking something good is not accepting a proposition with the content 'x is good'; rather it is a special way of accepting a proposition with a different, relatively non-evaluative, content. But what way? Aristotle regularly (e.g. 195ª24–6) connects the notion of goodness with that of an objective; the good is 'that at which things aim' (1094ª3). If that is right, to think that an object like a glass of wine is good is to have it function in your life as that to obtain or preserve which you act, and to think a change such as your translation to London is good is to have it function as that to effect which you act (or that lest you prevent which you refrain from certain action). Putting this together with 431ª8–16 we could say that George's awareness of the glass of wine takes the form of thinking it would be pleasant to taste it if, when he is aware of its colour, spatial location, etc., he has the purpose of tasting it, or if it can be given as *that to drink which, that not to upset which*, etc., in an explanation of his purposive behaviour.

If thinking something good is not separate from pursuit, still less is it separate from desire. Pursuing and avoiding are expressions or fulfilments of desire and aversion. In 431ª8–16 Aristotle seems to me to represent thinking something good (in one way or another) and desiring it (in one way or another) as the same thing described in two ways. If we think of the agent's thought as expressed in action, we say it takes the form of desire or aversion; if we think of it simply as thought, we say it takes the form of thinking something good or bad. The only evidence Charles offers to show that Aristotle postulates a real gap between thinking good and desiring is the remark at 1072ª28–9 already quoted, 'We desire because it seems [sc. fine].' One passing remark should not be allowed to outweigh the mass of evidence to which I have been appealing, and in any case it is arbitrary to interpret the 'because' here as causal. It is surely more like the 'because' in 'His condemnation was unjust because he was innocent, not: he was innocent because his condemnation was unjust' (cf. Plato, *Euthyphro* 9–10).

That a report of the form 'A thought that B (or Øing) was good' rather describes the form of A's mental state than reports a complete mental state with form and content both specified; this seems to me an attractive idea and I shall return to it in discussing modern views on what it is to think something good. On the other hand Charles's idea that desiring to $\emptyset$ is a special way of accepting the proposition that $\emptyset$ing is good seems to me obscure at several crucial points. First, what for Charles is the content of the proposition that $\emptyset$ing is good? What do I think about $\emptyset$ing when I think it would be good to $\emptyset$? Secondly, can we really form any clear conception of Charles's two ways of accepting propositions, the truth-seeker's and the good-seeker's? Appparently I can accept 'It would be good to $\emptyset$' in the truth-seekers's way but not in the good-seeker's (in which case there is no dodging the question 'What is the content of this thought?'); could I accept a proposition like 'William came in 1066' in a good-seeker's as distinct from a truth-seeker's way? And however that may be, is it really possible that a mode of accepting a proposition should render valid an inference which would be invalid if the proposition were accepted in a different way? Have we a clear notion of validity which will allow the validity of inferences to depend like this on modes of acceptance? Finally, a major aim of Charles's enterprise seems to be make the concepts of belief and desire irreducible to purely physical concepts without making them concepts of connections in a special kind of non-causal teleological explanation. He says desire and belief 'would not be irreducible because they fit into a certain distinctive rational pattern of explanation' and adds 'Aristotelian irreducibility depends on the concepts in which desire is defined (goodness/well-being), and not on the absence of psycho-physical causal explanation' (pp. 229 and n.). It looks as if he wants to rule out an account like this:

> A desires that B should become f = there is some line of conduct $\emptyset$ing such that in order that B may become f, A $\emptyset$s

(where it is not possible to reduce 'In order that p, q' to any causal claim such as 'the desire that p causes q'). But this objectionable connective 'in order that' seems to be latent in Charles's own definition of desire:

> A desires that B should become f = A accepts that it would be good if B were to become f in a way appropriate for someone whose aim is the good.

For how does aiming at the good differ from acting and refraining from action *in order to* achieve it?

If to think something good is to have it as an objective, clear-eyed akrasia appears problematic independently of any theory which links thinking better with wanting more. If Paris thinks that because she is his host's wife, or because he is on a diplomatic mission, it would be better not to make love to Helen, making love to her is an object of aversion and must play the role of 'that to avoid which' in his behaviour. Of course, we are supposing that he also thinks it would be pleasant to make love to her. Love-making, though an object of aversion in one way, is an object of desire in another. But we can no longer say 'He makes love to her because his desire to do so is stronger than his aversion'. For no clear sense can be given to this claim. It does not make sense to say that making love to Helen is more something to effect which than something to prevent which he acts – unless we mean simply that he *does* make love to her.

We sometimes say that one objective is more important to a person than another. This is informative, however, only when we are talking about the person's long-term objectives – 'Domestic happiness means more to him than success in his career' – in which case we are really describing his character. If making love to attractive women was more important to Paris than observing the laws of hospitality or being a responsible prince, his act was not akratic but intemperate.

Aristotle holds that for agents that can perceive but not think rationally, what appears pleasant appears good absolutely and functions as an objective. I suggest that clear-eyed akrasia is impossible for Aristotle simply because he allows no idle cognitive states. If the akrates make what is pleasant his objective without judging that it is the best thing to pursue all things considered, he acts as a sub-rational agent and his intellectual powers must be for the moment, in suspense; if he actually thinks it best to refrain, this cognitive state must be reflected in his behaviour. That is not because intellect is somehow stronger than sense. Though Aristotle does sometimes speak of perceptual and intellectual parts of the soul, these parts are not, like Plato's, coordinate, and cannot conflict. The perceptual part is subordinated to the intellectual only in that intelligent agents apply intellectual concepts to objects of perception and are aware of them as objects of specific sorts with specific powers, useful or useless, harmful or harmless in specific ways. If perception is not subject to intellect in this way, intellect is not functioning at all; if it is functioning, the unity of the psyche requires the agent to have as his objects of pursuit or avoidance what seems good or bad.

How satisfactory is this theory which I am ascribing to Aristotle? I hope that an answer will emerge to that in chapters 5–7 when we consider modern theories of what it is to think something good, and some suggestions by Davidson which equally appear to rule out clear-eyed akrasia.

4
Do We Have Wills?

Aristotle's discussion of akrasia is the last which has come down to us from antiquity. Something might have been expected from the Stoics. For on the one hand they were inclined to accept some version of the Socratic Paradoxes: some kind of moral knowledge or wisdom is supposed to guarantee right conduct. But on the other they speak freely of strength and weakness of will and make out that virtue consists in the former and vice is an effect of the latter. How they reconciled these apparently conflicting views we cannot be sure because their most authoritative ethical writings are lost. It is possible, however, that they would have distinguished the kind of weakness of will which they allow from acting against absolutely clear-eyed perception of what is best. Epictetus, at least, seems to come down against the possibility of that. In *Dissertations* I.18.2 he says it is impossible 'to judge one thing advantageous and desire another, or judge one thing fitting and pursue another'; according to I.26.6 ignorance is the cause of all wrong-doing.

Whatever ideas the Stoics may have had about akrasia, they were superseded by the Judaeo-Christian view of human action which I contrasted with the classical in chapter 1. According to this we have a faculty, 'the will', distinct both from the ability to judge what it would be best to do and from the skill and physical strength needed to do this. The will plays two parts in the philosophy of action which are not always distinguished. First, an exercise of will is what differentiates an intentional or voluntary action from a mere bodily movement. Secondly, it mediates between judgement and behaviour. The second role is of more direct concern to us because if there is such a mediating faculty, akratic behaviour can be attributed to it. But if we ask whether there really is such a faculty, the need for something to play the first role may be felt to show there is.

Is the question whether we have wills (or whether there are volitions) empirical or conceptual? George S. Howard and Christine G. Conway (1986, pp. 1241–51) recently carried out some experiments which showed that the peanut-eating of their pupils depended more on whether they decided to indulge or tried to refrain than on whether available peanuts were in view. The visibility of the peanuts was taken to be a non-volitional (p. 1243) factor operating as an efficient cause (p. 1250). The experiments were interpreted as proving that pupils' behaviour was (at least partly) 'volitional' or under their 'self-control' (pp. 1243, 1244) and were claimed to 'make the case for the existence of a generative structure, human power or the capacity referred to herein as volition' (p. 1249).

The experimenters anticipated the objection that the pupils' behaviour was motivated in a causal, 'non-volitional' manner by their own instructions. To meet this they told the pupils to decide for themselves each day (and record the decision but keep it secret) whether they would eat or not eat. This device would hardly disarm the objection, but the objection and the whole project seem to be tainted by a confusion of three notions of the 'volitional'.

According to one, my peanut-eating is volitional if I eat peanuts voluntarily or intentionally, and could refrain if I so chose. This is what it is for the eating to be under my control. It is volitional in this sense if I eat because the peanuts are fresh and not stale, handy and not inaccessible, mine and not someone else's. Their being in view is not an efficient cause of my eating them but at most a causal condition of my eating them for these reasons.

My eating is volitional in a second way if I eat the peanuts not because they are fresh and handy but because I have more or less arbitrarily decided to, and as part of a study 'in which it would be possible to conclude something like the following: Subjects acted in a particular way because they wanted to, or they felt like it, or they wanted to see what would happen if they acted in a particular way' (pp. 1242–3). The objection seems to be that this is just a special case of action which is volitional in the first way; it can still be explained in terms of beliefs and desires, factors which some philosophers count as causal. This is true but not damaging. It is still a *special* case, and action which is volitional in the first way is under the agent's control.

Thirdly, someone might call my peanut-eating volitional only if it is caused by a special 'generative structure' known as the will. Behaviour which is volitional in the second way goes no distance at all towards proving the existence of such a structure. There is no more reason to think my behaviour is due to a special power of will when I act to measure or improve my self-control than when I act to measure or reduce my liability to income-tax. If we knew independently that to be in control of one's behaviour is to generate movements by a special mechanism, experiments with peanuts might show whether a given psychology student has or lacks this mechanism; but that this is what it is to have self-control or to act 'volitionally' would be shown rather by philosophical analysis than by experimentation.

We get a particularly clear view of the will in its first role, as that which distinguishes voluntary action from mere movement, in Mill's *System of Logic* I.iii.5:

> What is an action? Not one thing, but a series of two things; the state of mind called a volition, followed by an effect. The volition or intention to produce the effect, is one thing; the effect produced in consequence of the intention, is another thing; the two together constitute the action. I form the purpose of instantly moving my arm; that is a state of my mind: my arm (not being tied or paralytic) moves in obedience to my purpose; that is a physical fact, consequent on a state of mind. The intention followed by the fact, or (if we prefer the expression) the fact when preceded and caused by the intention, is called the action of moving my arm.

What, we may ask in turn, is a volition? Here it is convenient to turn back to Locke; we can hardly doubt that Mill's account of action is inspired by Locke's account of the will. Locke defines the will as the power 'to order the consideration of any idea . . . or to prefer the motion of any part of the body to its rest' (*Essay* II.xxi.5), and holds that by this mental act of preference a person begins, continues and puts an end to movements of the body (II.xxi.7, II.xxiii.28). For the rest,

> The act of volition . . . being a very simple act, whosoever desires to understand what it is, will better find it by reflecting on his own mind, and observing what it does when it wills, than by any variety of articulate sounds whatever. (II.xxi.30)

This crude theory is open to objection in various ways. First, though introspection is supposed to reveal what the mind 'does when it wills' (II.xxi.30), it is an unsatisfactory mode of observation. In science we dislike any mode of observation which cannot yield exact measurements. Even if introspection occurs (a contentious issue), it does not permit exact measurement of mental phenomena. Secondly, the theory is interactionist, and how a mental event of willing could cause a physical movement of a limb Locke himself admits to be 'obscure and unconceivable' (II.xxiii.28). Thirdly, the will's acts appear to be conceived on the model of the intentional actions they are supposed to explain. Although Locke talks of preferring, willing that my finger should move (his example, II.xxi.21) cannot be just preferring that it should be in a different position, and Locke has to appeal to the acts of commanding another person to do something (II.xxi.5) and 'suspending', i.e. holding something in check by a rope (II.xxi.52). Giving an order or holding on to a rope is supposed to be the effect of a volition. Is willing, then, also the effect of a volition? If so (as Ryle, 1949, p. 67 and other modern authors have pointed out at some length), we shall have a regress. If not, what does determine whether or not I will a finger-movement? A feeling of 'uneasiness' says Locke, and adds: 'There being a great many uneasinesses always soliciting and ready to determine the will, it is natural that the greatest and most pressing should determine the will to the next action' (II.xxi.47). But here an abyss of determinism opens at his feet. If our will is determined by the strongest feeling of the moment, where is our freedom? It lies in our ability to 'suspend' the operation of desire until we have considered what is best, and our will is then determined by 'the last result of our own minds, judging of the good or evil of any action' (II.xxi.48). In these words Locke abruptly crosses over to the Socratic position on intentional action. But while he thereby exposes himself to the difficulties about akrasia which that position involves, he does not get clear of the difficulties of his own position. For what determines whether and for how long I 'suspend'? Is it the strength of the uneasiness or my view of what is best?

Unsatisfactory as Locke's account is, until recently philosophers were unable to make any substantial improvement on it. In *The Analysis of Mind* (1921) Russell refers his readers to a 100-page chapter in James's *Principles of Psychology*, vol. II (1907). 'I see no reason,' Russell says (p. 285), 'to doubt the correctness' of James's view. James tries to dispense with non-physical acts of will. To act intentionally I must, James believes, have a mental image of the bodily movement involved, but in many cases that is all I need on the psychological side (1907, pp. 487–92). On the physical, of course, we need 'a special current of energy going out from the brain into the appropriate muscles', but no feeling accompanies this (p. 493). But then James reintroduces a 'fiat', an 'element of consent', and concedes that this 'constitutes the essence of the voluntariness of the act' (p. 501). What is this *fiat*? The agent, it appears, is able to attend to the idea of a possible movement or to a 'reason to the contrary' (p. 559). '*The essential achievement of the will . . . when it is at its most 'voluntary' is to ATTEND to a difficult object and hold it before the mind*. The so-doing is the *fiat*' (p. 561, James's emphasis), and at p. 567 it is 'the only internal volitional act which we ever perform'. But a page later we find that besides attending we may have to make 'the effort to consent' and that '*express consent to the reality of what is attended to* is often an additional and quite distinct phenomenon involved.' James's handling of behaviour at odds with the agent's better judgement follows the outlines of Aristotle's *EN* VII treatment, but shows no sense that there is any philosophical problem involved. There is 'precipitate behaviour' where the agent acts before inhibiting influences have time to appear (p. 537); this corresponds to *propeteia*; the agent may follow a bad impulse because the impulse is too strong or the inhibiting factor too weak (pp. 537–46); this covers *akrasia* in the narrow sense and also alcoholism and neurosis; or the agent may have a clear vision of what is best but 'impulsion is insufficient' (*aboulia*) 'or inhibition is in excess', the case of *malakia*.

James avoids some of the difficulties of interactionism since holding an image before the mind's eye is conceived not as a purely psychological affair which causes events in the brain but rather as a psychosomatic affair which already includes a cerebral part. That, however, is the only respect in which he improves on Locke. Access to the crucial acts of attending and consenting is through introspection (p. 486). As Locke may be asked what determines whether and how long we 'suspend', so James must face the same questions about 'attending'. His reply is disarming: 'My own belief is that the question of free will is insoluble on strictly psychological grounds . . . Taking the risk of error on our head we must project upon one of the alternative views the attribute of reality for us . . . The present writer does this for the alternative of freedom' (pp. 572–3). Since James clearly identifies freedom with indeterminacy we must conclude that whether, as he puts it (p. 563), the 'corpse-like finger' of Reason lies on our heart long enough to extinguish the fires of passion is, in the end, as luck would have it.

Besides these familiar objections James's account is open to a special one of its own because of its reliance on mental images. 'Will,' says

James (p. 559), 'is a relation between the mind and its "ideas"'; it is a 'peculiar attitude of consciousness' corresponding to the imperative mood in grammar (p. 569). But you can decide *not* to crook your finger (James's example, p. 527) as much as to crook it. James says, '*Its not really moving* is part of what you have in mind.' But there can be no mental image of not crooking a finger distinct from the image of crooking it. James also says, 'What checks our impulses is the mere thinking of reasons to the contrary' (p. 559), and he probably has in mind images of possible consequences or attendant circumstances which are reasons pro and con. But what determines whether a particular imagined circumstance is a reason pro or a reason con? Alice, who is married to Bernard, is contemplating a weekend with Charles. She imagines Charles's style of love-making and Bernard's distress on learning of the episode. But is Bernard's distress a reason against weekending with Charles and Charles's mode of embracing a reason for it, or is it the other way round? That depends on whether she wants to spare Bernard pain or to wound him by infidelity with the most unattractive person they know; but the images will be the same in either case. It is impossible to explain an agent's decision whether or not to do something in terms of mental imagery.

II

Ryle (1949) argued very persuasively that acts of will cannot be used to define intentional action, and Anscombe (1957/1963) showed that intentional action can be defined in terms of reasons. Many philosophers, however, (see, for instance, Hardie 1971) retained a belief in volitions as intermediaries between thought and action. H.P. Grice (1971) argued for a psychological state of 'willing' (which is not restricted to things which the person who wills can do: we can 'will' a footballer to run faster, p. 276). And in 1980 Jennifer Hornsby and Brian O'Shaughnessy published full-length books (*Actions* and *The Will*) in which acts of will are reincarnated, so to speak, in modern flesh. The styles and modes of presentation of these two writers are very different. O'Shaughnessy flaunts the similarity of his view to traditional volitionism. He calls his book *The Will* because 'I actually believe in the existence of the phenomenon it purports to designate' (vol. I, p. lxi) and describes the activity of willing in the language of German Romanticism: 'Willing is spirit in motion' (vol. I, p. l); it is 'the unique phenomenon of 'going before' a psychic force [sc. 'act-desire'] in the psychic domain' (vol. I, p. 1ii). Hornsby, in contrast, though she accepts the word 'conation', is reluctant to call her conations 'acts of will' and is at pains to distance herself from thinkers like Locke. She relies, however, on some of O'Shaughnessy's early work and the accounts they give, at least so far as they are relevant to weakness of will, are largely the same.

They point out that a regress of volitions arises only if we hold *both* (1) every voluntary act is caused by an act of will, *and* (2) every act of will is a voluntary act. Locke, who uses acts of will to define voluntary action, rejects (2); O'Shaughnessy and Hornsby reject (1). They claim there are acts of trying: we try to cause changes in the things around us and, still more, we try to cause movements in our own limbs. These tryings are what O'Shaughnessy calls 'acts of will' and Hornsby 'conations'. They are voluntary actions, and therefore cannot be employed to explain what makes action voluntary; but they stand between judgement and action and they sound at first as if they are just the factors which in pre-philosophical common sense distinguish strong- from weak-willed action. Do they really exist, and can they play this role?

Both writers are aware that the verb 'to try' is expressive of doubt and denial. We should not say 'Macbeth tried to kill Duncan' if we can say 'Macbeth killed Duncan' or 'Balbus is trying to build a ten-foot wall' unless we doubt if he will succeed. They argue, however, that from this fact about our speech-habits it cannot be inferred that Macbeth does not in fact try to kill a kinsman when he succeeds in killing one. On the contrary, if A intentionally causes B to become f it follows that (in their sense of 'try') A *does* try to make B f.

That all intentional action involves trying is argued in two ways. First, they appeal to an experiment, either the one described in James, vol. II, p. 490 (Hornsby, 1980, p. 40) or an imaginary one of the same type (O'Shaughnessy, vol. II, pp. 93–4). A man believes he can move his arm but, because he is blindfolded and partly anaesthetised, he cannot actually tell whether or not he is doing so. Unknown to himself, he has been made unable to move it. Asked to move it, he believes he does. Surely in this case he has *tried* to move it. But if he tries in this case surely he does so on the (to him indistinguishable) occasions when he in fact moves it.

Secondly, an analogy is drawn with experiencing visual sense-data. Grice (1961) tries to show that perceiving involves sensing sense-data (he tries, it might be less contentious to say, to justify the conception of 'sentire' we find in Descartes' *Meditation* II) by arguing that not only when we experience an illusion or a hallucination but when we perceive something correctly by sight we have an experience describable as 'seeming to see' or 'thinking we see' the thing we in fact see. He considers the objection that we should not say 'It seemed to George that he was seeing a table' when George saw a table that was in plain view; and he meets it by distinguishing conditions under which it is *appropriate* or *usual* to say that *p* from conditions under which saying that *p* is saying something *true*. Even when the table is in plain view, to say 'It seemed to George just as if he were seeing a table' is to say something true. Its seeming to me as if I were seeing a material object is 'what is left over if I subtract from the fact that I see a material object the fact that the object is present' (Hornsby, 1980, p. 112). Anyone who has swallowed Grice's argument that all perception involves seeming to perceive will not strain at the idea that all intentional action involves trying to act.

We often operate with a notion of trying according to which I try, for example, to start the lawnmower if I act causally in order that it may start; I try to secure the nomination for Parliament if I canvass my friends, write letters, etc., with this end in view; I try to lift a heavy stone if I pull upwards on it in order that it may rise. Such trying occurs whenever we act purposively because it is identical with purposive action, but for the same reason it is not an intermediary between judgement and observable behaviour: for that we need the sense-datum-like tryings of Hornsby and O'Shaughnessy.

Their notion derives from Arthur Danto's notion of a basic action. Danto's original (1965) presentation of the argument for basic actions is notoriously unsatisfactory, and later writers, notably Hornsby herself, have felt it necessary to improve on it. The following version is, I hope, reasonably charitable. When an agent *M* performs the action of moving a boulder, he causes the boulder to move, and does so by doing something else, say causing the end of a crowbar to move. But if everything which he does, he does by doing something prior, he will never do anything. Hence there must be things *M* does, actions he performs, which he does not do by doing anything prior. 'These actions', says Danto, 'performed by *M* which he cannot be said to have caused to happen . . . I shall designate as *basic actions*' (1965, pp. 141–2). Danto goes on to give moving an arm as a paradigm of a basic action and says that it is not the result of an act of will so much as itself an act of will; and trying to

move your arm is not a cause of moving it (if it were, moving it would
not be a basic action), but the action of moving it 'being performed in
untoward circumstances' (p. 148).

O'Shaughnessy follows Danto in taking 'familiar cases of moving
one's limbs' (Vol. I, p. xiii) as the standard examples of basic actions.
He argues that (with minor exceptions) only limb-movements can be
willed; and an act of will, for him, is a trying to move a limb. It differs
from Mill's volitions only in two ways (vol. II, pp. 269–70). First, it is
not quite accurate to say that it causes movements in limbs. Trying to
move my arm, when the effort is successful, is the same thing as moving
it or causing it to move, so to say 'I caused it to move by trying to move
it' would be as vacuous as to say 'I caused it to move by causing it to
move'. Second, and more substantial, because trying successfully to
move a limb is the same action as moving it, trying is not, as Mill took
volitions to be, purely mental.

O'Shaughnessy in fact presents tryings as a thrilling bridge between
mind and body. Though physical in one aspect (he calls his whole
theory a 'dual aspect theory') and not mental, they are nevertheless
psychological. O'Shaughnessy's book contains an extremely elaborate
attempt to arrive at a non-idealist account of man from idealist
premises. The effect, however, seems to me to be that tryings are neither
physical nor psychological rather than both. On the one hand,
O'Shaughnessy has a Cartesian or phenomenological vision of the mind
as infallibly contemplating sensations, working overtime in dreams and
so forth. That being so, it is not too easy for him to hang on to the
objective reality of the body and the 'material basis' of trying, the
'power line' of mechanisms stretching from the brain to the limb we try
to move (Vol. I, p. 130). When we dream that we try to move a limb,
while we do not really try to move that limb, we do really try to move a
seeming-limb (Vol. II, pp. 85–6, cf. pp. 159–66). What guarantee the
existence of our bodies are Jamesian images of the limbs to be moved.
These are different from visual sense-data in that while the latter are
'genuine non-pictorial naturalistic images' (Vol. II, p. 141) interposing
themselves between us and reality, the body-images we get in tactile
sensation give us 'immediate' (Vol. I, p. 146), even if not infallible
(Vol. I, pp. 204–5) access to our limbs. This sounds like having one's
sense-data and eating them. On the other hand, given that our bodies
really exist, O'Shaughnessy needs to show that tryings are not purely
physical. His argument for classing them as psychological is that we have
priviledged access to them: 'We stand epistemologically to bodily

strivings as we do to psychological items like sensations, i.e. imme-
diately/authoritatively/on pain of the unavailability of the attention'
(Vol. II, p. 194). But how do we know that we have this immediate
access? Apparently because they are 'experienced psychological events'
(Vol. I, p. 128); it is in consequence of this that arm-raising is
'mentalistically and therefore also simply or criteria-lessly given to the
subject'. There is at least an appearance here of circularity.

I am doubtful, then, about the soundness of O'Shaughnessy's notion
of psychological but non-mental tryings and my doubt cannot be met
by his insistence that he is aware of them by a kind of introspection. As
Alan Donegan pointed out in his review of *The Will* in *The Journal of
Philosophy* (1983, p. 303), those who think that there are no such
things as tryings and that beliefs and desires by themselves suffice to
explain behaviour have an easy reply open to them. They can say that
O'Shaughnessy 'has mistaken confidence in the causal efficacy of desire
and belief for immediate awareness of an additional event'.

Hornsby starts by distinguishing a transitive and an intransitive use of
verbs like 'move'. These could be illustrated, respectively, by 'George
moved the boulder an inch' and 'The boulder moved an inch'. She
argues that a limb's moving (intransitive) is never an action, but she
does not question the idea that (if we ignore such purely mental acts as
forming a mental image of something) to perform an action is always to
move (transitive) a limb. Since moving a limb is causing a change either
in its position relatively to the rest of the body or in its parts' positions
relatively to one another, and since the events that cause these changes
'presumably occur inside the body', she reaches the arresting conclusion
that all actions 'occur inside the body' (1980, p. 13); and it is these
actions that are her tryings. If building a shed or crossing the Atlantic is
trying to do anything, it is not the sort of trying with which she is concerned. For her as for O'Shaughnessy a trying is what is left over from a
basic limb-movement when the actual change in the limb has been
subtracted.

Hornsby arrives at this notion, I suspect, through failing to eliminate
confusions in current philosophical conceptions of an action and a
bodily movement. She is aware that both notions involve difficulties. In
connection with the first she writes:

> The phrase 'do something' can mislead, because it can sound as if it
> reported both an event which is a *doing* and a separate event that is a
> *something* done. But that cannot be how it [sc. the phrase 'do some-
> thing'] behaves. If I raise my arm at some time, raise my arm is something

I do then, and my doing something then is my raising my arm then. But *what* I do – raise my arm – is not a particular event that happens at a time: the only event here is my raising of my arm! (1980, p. 3)

Her thought here is that a 'thing done' is a kind of universal and a 'doing' of it is a particular occurrence or event. She then declares that she will use the word 'action' not for things done but only for doings.

I agree that when a person performs an action he 'does something', and that the thing done stands to his doing of it as universal to particular. I do not think, however, that either the thing done or the doing should be spoken of as 'an action'. We have a notion of performing an action according to which I perform an action if I build a shed, murder an aunt or (the favoured example) intentionally raise my arm from where it hangs at my side to a position of being extended straight up above my head. But there is nothing in these cases that can be identified as *the action I perform* or *an action done by me*. In each I intentionally cause a change in something: in my arm, in the body of my aunt, in the materials out of which I build the shed. It is possible in theory to specify with some accuracy the objects in which I intentionally cause changes, the changes I cause in them, and the intentional causal action by which I cause it. Hornsby is right that the change I bring about is not the action I perform, not the action for which, perhaps, I am praised or censured. Still less, however, is the action by which I cause the change an action I perform. The English word 'action' is used in two grammatically different ways, which may be illustrated by (1) 'George did one good action this afternoon: he moved the boulder off the drive' and (2) 'George moved the boulder off the drive by action on it with a crowbar'. In (2) 'action' may be replaced by 'acting': A's action on B, or the action by which A causes B to become f, is A's causal acting.

The words 'movement' and 'change' have something of the same ambivalence. We might say (3) 'Suppose a body M moves from a place P_1 to another place a mile away P_2: that's a movement, isn't it?' But we can also say (4) 'M's movement was an hour long, and during it I smoked a cigar'. In (3) 'movement' is used for something in which we can distinguish two elements or aspects: a change, starting at P_1 and ending at P_2, which takes place, and a taking place or going on of that change. In (4) 'movement' is used for the second of those two aspects; M's hour-long movement is M's hour-long undergoing of the change which, in turn, is the change's taking place. An action, similarly, is something in which we can distinguish a change effected and a causing of that change, whereas action in the sense of acting is the second of these distinguenda. It stands to the change effected, as Hornsby observes, in the relation of token to type or particular to universal; but it is not an action.

If Danto had noticed that 'action' has these two uses both he and his followers might have been spared some difficulties. He says:

> Suppose every action were a case of the agent causing something to happen. This means, each time he does a, he must independently do b, which causes a to happen. But then, in order to do b, he must first independently do c, which causes b to happen.

And he infers that:

> There must be actions which are not caused to happen by the person who performs them. And these are basic actions. (1965, p. 145)

To say that every action is a case of the agent causing something to happen is surely just to say it is a case of the agent causing some change in something. This does not entail that if A causes B to become f there must be some x such that A causes B to become f by causing x to become g. And even if there is such an x, A's causing it to become g is not his causing his causal action. When in thinking that A Øed we attribute some mode of causal action to A we do not in general think of A's Øing as caused either by A or by anything else. Danto's insight was that if A (whether intentionally or unintentionally) causes B to become f, there must be some mode of causal action expressible otherwise than as the causing of a definite prior change, some mode of action like moving for a time or pushing or heating, by which A makes $B f$. What this shows is that we need to recognize not basic actions but periods of causal acting.

But is there any significant difference between a Dantonian basic action and a period of basic acting? Can we not say that, at least for us, the basic mode of acting is moving limbs? Not without drawing distinctions both about basicness and about bodily movement. Hornsby distinguishes two kinds of basicness which she labels 'causal' and 'teleological'. Suppose that A by the same causal action causes B to become f and C to become g, and suppose that C becomes g because B becomes f, that the change in B is causally prior. Then the report 'A caused B to become f' is causally more basic than the report 'A caused C to become g'. 'George contracted an arm-muscle' is more basic in this causal way than 'George bent his arm at the elbow'. On the other hand suppose George can bend his arm at will, and knows that if he so bends it his biceps will bulge, and there is no prior change he can effect at will such that if he effects it his biceps will bulge. In that case we might say 'He made his biceps bulge by bending his arm', and 'He caused his arm to bend' might be teleologically more basic than 'He caused his biceps to bulge'. Now reports of actions in terms of contracting muscles and sending impulses along nerves will be causally more basic than reports in terms of moving arms or wielding axes. But we do not, in general, intentionally contract muscles or send impulses along nerves unless we do so by moving limbs or tools. If we are looking, then, for basic intentional action, we shall be more concerned with teleological than with causal basicness. Are teleologically basic action-reports reports in terms of limb-movements?

Hornsby distinguishes, as I said earlier, between a transitive and an intransitive use of 'move' and she holds that reports of the form 'A transitively moved limb L' or 'A tried to move L' are teleologically basic. But there is a distinction between transitive uses which she overlooks. She takes it that 'A moved B' must mean 'A caused a change in B's place or position'; in fact, it could mean rather 'A used B'.

We talk of using an instrument like a pen or a needle. Using an instrument is acting causally with it in a more or less skilful fashion. To say I used a pen is not to say that I caused a change in the pen, but rather than I caused a change in something unspecified (perhaps a piece of paper) with the pen. It might be argued that if I cause a change in B with C I necessarily also cause a change in C. I am not sure that is true; irrigating my vegetables, might I not use a spade to deflect the course of a small stream by holding the spade motionless? But in any case, 'A used a spade' surely does not mean the same as 'A (intentionally) caused a change in a spade'. Now we often use 'move' instead of 'use' in connection with instruments and still more in connection with limbs. The boatman holds the boat in position by moving the oars; the hostess communicates with her daughter by moving her eyes; the leader of the deaf-mutes gives orders to his followers by moving his hands. Moving a limb in this sense of 'move' is an acquired skill like writing or swimming; indeed, to learn to sew or to play the piano is precisely to learn a specific way of using your fingers.

It is, I think, roughly correct to say that teleologically basic action-reports are of the form 'A moved limb L' where 'moved' means 'used' and expresses an acquired skill. I say 'roughly correct' because when a man is a real artist with an oboe or a pencil it seems more natural to speak of him as using that instrument than as using his fingers or lips. But the important point is that when 'He moved his arm' is teleologically basic, it reports not a conation responsible for an unspecified change in the arm but a period of causal action with the arm. Even when the policeman directing traffic causes the traffic to stop by causing his arm to take up the 'stop' position, he causes this change in his arm by exercising the art of arm-signalling, by using his arm in one of the ways in which he has learnt to use it.

It seems, then, that we have no notion of a trying which is a notion of something more basic than a piece of purposive causal action. Purposive action with an organic part of the body is causally prior to purposive action with tools, and may generally be teleologically prior too. But it does not normally take place inside the body. Perhaps the only purposive causal action which takes place inside the body is the skilful use of tongue, teeth or dentures.

The question with which we are concerned here about putative acts of will is whether they intervene between practical judgement and action, and ensure that we act as we judge best unless they are so weak that they cannot prevail over contrary emotions and desires. It is plain that pieces of purposive causal action cannot play this role.

They can be relevant, indeed, to praise and blame in some cases. You praise me for trying hard to lift the heavy stone if I pull on it with great force; you blame me for not trying hard enough to start the lawnmower if I do not act long enough or zealously enough on appropriate parts of it. But this kind of trying is not relevant to weakness of will. For akrasia typically consists in doing what is bad, not in failing to do what is good. The akrates does not refrain from drinking, smoking, embracing or what not. We may say he should have tried to refrain, but accounts of trying to do something are not easily transferred to trying not to do something. If trying successfully to do something is doing it intentionally, can we say that refraining intentionally from doing something is trying successfully to refrain? I might refrain intentionally for weeks from passing on a piece of information, but you would hardly say I tried successfully for weeks to refrain. If trying to hit the bull's-eye, when the effort is successful, is the same action as hitting it or causing it to be perforated, is trying not to hit your exasperating husband, when the effort is successful, the same action as not hitting him, not causing his eye to become black? The trouble is that there are no criteria of identity for inactions. Neither, of course, is there anything left over from not moving your arm when its remaining motionless has been subtracted.

There are occasions when the akrates fails to act. The akratic knight omits to go questing after adventures in order not to lose the embraces of his lady-love. But here we should not say that he did not try hard enough to leave his castle. The action does not require an active effort; if it did, the knight's failing would be not akrasia but malakia.

It may be added that neither Hornsby nor O'Shaughnessy cast tryings for the role we are interested in. O'Shaughnessy is far from making trying a locus of spontaneity. He maintains the following 'entailment law': 'If I know *of* an instant that it is correctly indexically singled out as "now" and *at* that instant that it is the intended time of a presently intended action 0, then necessarily that instant is one in which a striving-to-0 is occurring' (Vol. II, p. 333). The argument for this law is that if striving does not necessarily occur, then whether or not I strive will be as luck would have it and 'one *really* acts for no reason . . . every act turns out to be a Gidean *acte gratuit.*' (Vol. II, p. 339). Whether I can judge it best to do one thing and intend to do something different is unclear; but given intentions, tryings are not a new factor that can shed any light on apparently akratic or irrational behaviour. Nothing in *Actions* suggests that Hornsby thinks anything different.

III

It will be seen that O'Shaughnessy has intentions as well as tryings. When I $\emptyset$ intentionally my (successful) trying to $\emptyset$ is caused by an intention of $\emptyset$ing (Vol. II, p. 327). This intention is itself caused by desires and beliefs; it is a 'device whereby these latter two items can non-accidentally fuse as causal forces *in such a way that* the very fact that they *convert* one's reason is causally operative' (Vol. II, pp. 318–20). A number of other philosophers who do not postulate tryings nevertheless hold fast to intentions.

Gilbert Harman is an example. He declares (1975/6, p. 441) that 'Actions cannot be explained in terms of beliefs and desires alone; these attitudes must be translated into intentions before one can act.' Intentions are 'a real part of the explanatory order'. They are 'real attitudes' but also, it appears, cognitive states: 'an intention is an idea of the future for which one has one sort of reason' (p. 451) – sc. a reason related to an unmotivated desire for something for its own sake. Grice (1971) had suggested that when X intends to do A X 'wills' that he should do A (or that some limb-movement should occur) and believes that his doing A will result from his so willing. Harman, developing this idea, says: 'The intention to do A is the intention that, because of that very intention, it is guaranteed that one will do A' (p. 441). Mele (1987) obtains a notion of 'brute resistance' in this way. In general intention 'mediates between overall motivation and intentional action' (p. 106); 'brute resistance', or what non-philosophers call 'sheer effort of will' is forming or retaining an intention 'to do X *in order to bring it about* [my emphasis] that, rather than succumbing to temptation, one X-s' (p. 26).

Peacocke agrees (1979, p. 15 n.) with Harman about the need for intentions and maintains (1985, pp. 68–9) that the intention to $\emptyset$ is a disposition caused by the agent's reasons for $\emptyset$ing and resulting under appropriate conditions in his $\emptyset$ing or trying to $\emptyset$. Wiggins belongs to the same camp. He offers the following long and eventful scenario (1978/9, pp. 253–4): (1) Faced with a choice between courses of action x and y we appraise and evaluate each; (2) we decide that x is better; (3) we decide *to* follow x: this is forming an intention and may be preceded by (2 ½) '*Finding*' x better; (4) we stick to our intention or we change it.

What arguments are there for thus casting conceptual economy to the winds? Peacocke (1979, p. 15 n.) says we need intentions to deliver us from the predicament of Buridan's Ass: when we think two objects equally good and have equal desires for each, belief and desire are insufficient to explain our reaching for one rather than the other. Wiggins may have this in mind when he distinguishes his (2) and (3) on the ground that 'one can decide for x rather than for y without thinking either of them the better' (1978/9, pp. 253–4; cf. Bratman, 1979 p. 161). If we are not allowed to say that the Ass thought it best to spin a coin and abide by the result (no impossible feat for a Houyhnhnm); if there is a genuine problem about why it eats bundle X and not bundle Y, I do not think the problem can be solved by interposing intentions or decisions between thought and action. For why does the Ass *intend* to eat X and not Y? If we are told 'It just does', we might as well say this at the beginning when asked why it *eats* X and not Y.

It might nevertheless be wondered if the case of the Ass destroys the Backward Connection which causes the problem about whether clear-eyed akrasia can occur. Certainly it is awkward for anyone who holds that if A $\emptyset$s intentionally A must think $\emptyset$ing better than any alternative he thinks open to him. But we shall find akrasia puzzling so long as we hold that if A $\emptyset$s intentionally he must think it at least as good as any alternative, or must not think any alternative better; the Ass constitutes no objection to this more modest thesis.

Suppose I believe on Monday that there will be a concert on

Thursday, and want to go, and judge after reflection that it would be best if I did. That forming the intention of going is different from reaching this practical judgement might be argued as follows. On Wednesday I might give up the judgement that it will be best for me to go (I hear bad reports of the soloist; I catch cold); but I might retain the intention of going: I say to myself 'I'll stick to my intention'.

This cannot show that *forming* the intention is different from *reaching* the practical judgement; at most it will show that retaining the intention is different from retaining the judgement. Does it even show that? Surely I should not retain the intention of going unless I still thought it best to go. 'But now', it will be objected, 'your reason for judging it best to go has changed. Formerly it was the excellence of the soloist; now it is Monday's decision'. I would reply that judgements are individuated by their content, not their reasons; my judgement that it is best to attend Thursday's concert is not altered because my reasons for it have altered. But in any case it is too simple to say that on Wednesday my reason for thinking it best to go is Monday's decision. If I form the intention at t_1 of $\emptyset$ing at t_2 I plan the interval on the assumption that I shall $\emptyset$ at t_2. If $\emptyset$ing requires substantial preparations (not going to a concert, say, but going to China), I start preparing. This planning and preparing constitutes a reason for $\emptyset$ing at t_2 independently of whether other reasons still hold. Indeed, planning and preparing is already starting to carry out the intention to $\emptyset$, and by Wednesday I both think it best to continue and intend to continue in the course on which I originally thought it best and intended to enter.

I find myself sympathetic, then, towards the line taken by Davidson in his 1978 paper 'Intending' (1980, pp. 83ff). He concedes that there are cases where an agent forms, and perhaps retains, the intention of $\emptyset$ing without $\emptyset$ing, but he suggests that here 'the intention simply is an all-out judgement' that it is best to $\emptyset$. In the case where the agent does not merely intend to $\emptyset$ but $\emptyset$s, his judgement that it is good to $\emptyset$, and hence his intending to $\emptyset$, may be identical with the $\emptyset$ing: 'nothing seems to stand in the way of an Aristotelian identification of the action with a judgement of a certain kind' (p. 99).

5
Thinking Good

The Judaeo-Christian contribution to ethics is not unlike its contribution to the philosophy of action. As the Bible represents events in the world as due to acts of the Divine will, but offers no theory of what an act of will is, so it represents God as knowing infallibly what actions are good and what bad, but omits to say what kind of knowledge this is. Some simple believers may have thought that goodness and badness are intrinsic, non-relational properties of actions rather as yellowness and blueness are of objects, and that recognizing that an act is good is purely cognitive. This view would go well with the view that we need wills to ensure that we do the acts we think good, but it has not, so far as I know, been defended by any Jewish or Christian philosopher (unless one counts Moore as a Christian *malgré soi*). Locke suggests that moral goodness is a kind of relational property: an act is good if it conforms to a law (and bad if it conflicts with one) which is sanctioned by rewards and punishments (II.xxviii.5; this was a deduction from ethical hedonism). But some passages of the Bible suggest that God's knowledge is knowledge of what he likes and dislikes: behaviour is good if it is pleasing in his eyes and bad if it excites his anger or disgust. If we replace God by philosophers (a move foreshadowed by Locke in II.xxviii.10), we get the kind of ethical theory put forward by Shaftesbury (*Inquiry concerning Virtue* I.ii.3) and Hume: actions and qualities of mind are good if they cause sentiments of pleasure and approval in discriminating people who contemplate them without prejudice.

Hume does not, of course, support this theory by appeal to scripture. He argues that the judgement that an action is good or bad has 'an influence on the actions and affections' (1888, p. 457). But the only thing that can have such an influence is a feeling or other motivational state. A purely cognitive state, recognition that an object has a certain intrinsic or relational property, can move us only if we already have a favourable or hostile attitude towards that property. The conclusion should be that thinking something good is a motivational state. Hume sometimes writes as if goodness were a kind of causal property, a power to cause pleasant feelings in those who contemplate what has it. If that were so, thinking that truth-telling is good (a favourite example with British philosophers) would be like thinking that whisky is intoxicating; it would be holding a factual belief with a truth-value, though one determined by human reactions. But what Hume's premises imply is that thinking truth-telling good is like being intoxicated by whisky: it is not holding a true or false belief about veracity, but feeling pleasure at the thought of it.

Modern moral philosophers mostly accept the substance of Hume's argument. They think that if our moral views are to guide our conduct holding a moral view cannot be a purely cognitive affair; and they seek theories which exhibit it as involving a pro-attitude or which in some other way ensure that the agent who thinks a course good will be at least inclined to pursue it. Any theory of this kind makes akrasia in some degree anomalous. One theory, prescriptivism, is admitted by its author to make akrasia impossible. In this chapter we shall see that there are formidable objections both to prescriptivism and to its main rival emotivism, but I shall suggest that the objections do not apply to the kind of purposivist theory attributed to Aristotle in chapter 3.

I

Prescriptivism is the theory put forward by R. M. Hare in *The Language of Morals* (1952). Hare assimilates using words like 'good' to commanding. The sentence 'This is a good motor-car' is similar in meaning to 'If you are choosing motor-cars, choose one like this'; and 'One ought not to repay evil with evil' is close or even equivalent in meaning to the prohibition, addressed to all rational beings without exception: 'Never repay evil with evil' (p. 178). The marks of a moral pronouncement (says Hare) are prescriptivity and universality; moral pronouncements entail imperatives, and the imperatives have unrestricted generality, applying even to the persons uttering them. If I say 'Promise-breaking is (morally) bad' I express a veto on promise-breaking which applies to me no less than to you.

This theory leads Hare to deny the possibility of akrasia. Since to say that one ought to keep promises is to express a kind of universal prescription, to *think* such a thing, to accept a moral judgement, is to assent to such a prescription. But to assent to a prescription is to obey it. So it follows at once that any kind of action against one's convictions, including akratic action, is impossible.

Having made clear-eyed akrasia impossible (at least when the agent's better judgement is judgement of what is *morally* best), in *Freedom and Reason* (1963) Hare addresses himself to cases where it seems to occur. Sometimes (Hare tells us) when a man says he ought to do something but does not do it, his pronouncement is lacking in universality: he does not apply it to himself. Sometimes it is lacking in prescriptivity: 'I ought' means simply 'People would say I ought'. The meaning of 'ought' has a convenient elasticity which allows the hard-pressed moral philosopher to say that using it in this way is abusing it, but doing so legitimately. The more conscious an agent is of talking like this, the more fairly we describe him as hypocritical (p. 77). But 'typical cases of "moral weakness" are cases where a man *cannot* do what he thinks he ought' (pp. 68, 80). As typical cases Hare gives us St Paul's description of his plight in Romans 7 and a speech which Ovid puts into the mouth of the legendary enchantress Medea at *Metamorphoses* VII.20ff: Ovid represents Medea, Paul represents himself, as psychologically unable to do what is right.

This treatment has attracted a good deal of criticism. One objection (urged by Lukes, 1965; Neil Cooper, 1968; Kenny, 1975) is that Hare's notion of psychological impossibility is unclear or unconvincing. How does Hare conceive psychological impossibility, and how does he suppose it to differ from physical impossibility? Lukes suggests the notion is the result of confusing the logical with the empirical. Hare's theory makes it logically impossible for a person while accepting a moral judgement to act against it, but Hare represents the inability as due to the contingent impact of emotion. Is it really impossible in any way for the akrates to act otherwise? A man who has been hypnotized perhaps cannot help doing at least some of the things the hypnotist suggests; a neurotic person may be unable to stop himself from washing his hands; but the ordinary man who acts against his moral principles is not like a hypnotic or neurotic subject, and the onus is on Hare to show that he could not have behaved as he thinks he ought. And suppose he succeeds in showing this: will he not have excluded akrasia only at the cost of embracing a depressing determinism? If the akrates cannot help doing what he does, what of the enkrates? What of the amorous young wife who is attracted by her new stepson's advances but resists them? Does her desire to behave temperately or her aversion to incest make it psychologically impossible for her to yield?

Although I do not know that Hare anywhere takes up these points, I think they can be answered. The objectors assume that there is a big discontinuity between akratic and compulsive behaviour; in chapter 9 I shall argue there is not. As will also appear in chapter 9, a clear notion of psychological impossibility can be defined in terms of the unconscious. We can say that an agent is *psychologically* unable to $\emptyset$ insofar as he has reasons for not $\emptyset$ing which are unconscious. As for the charge of determinism, the standard parry is to say that people are free agents insofar as their behaviour is determined by beliefs they are aware of and can test, and desires they are aware of and can modify (for a more technical statement, see H.J. Eysenck, 1982, pp. 370–3).

Pears argues (1984, pp. 240–7) that Hare could give a prescriptivist account of moral judgement without ruling out akrasia. On Hare's view, it is part of thinking that I ought to $\emptyset$ to address a command to $\emptyset$ to myself. Hare says that if 'we assent to a second-person command addressed to ourselves, we are said to be sincere in our assent if and only if we do or resolve to do what the speaker has told us to do; if we do not do it but only resolve to do it later, then if, when the occasion arises for doing it, we do not do it, we are said to have changed our mind' (1952, p. 20). Pears shows that this is erroneous. If A orders B to $\emptyset$ (and A is sincere; he is not trading on the fact that B is counter-suggestible), he must intend that B should $\emptyset$. But it does not follow that if he orders himself to $\emptyset$ he must himself intend to $\emptyset$. All that follows is that he must intend *that he should $\emptyset$*, which is not the same as intending *to $\emptyset$*. Rather (where the $\emptyset$ing is conceived as intentional) it is intending that he should intend to $\emptyset$. Noticing Dido's interest in him, Aeneas says to himself 'If she suggests that you make love to her, say "No"'. To be sincere he does not need to form any resolution at the moment; it is enough if he intends that if she makes advances he will then be resolute. What if they are already alone together in the cave? He can still sincerely say to himself 'Stop!' in the hope that this will generate the resolution to stop; if the resolution fails to well up and he yields, it does not follow that he changes his mind.

Hare talks not of sincerely issuing a command but of sincerely assenting to one. But this exposes him to a further criticism. He is able to say that assenting to a command is obeying it because the notion of assenting to a command is unclear. I agree with P. L. Gardiner (1954/5, p. 24) that 'the expression "assent to a command" . . . is not one in common use' and 'seems to me peculiar'. When a colonel gives his regiment the order 'Charge' he wants his men to obey it, but he would certainly not say he wanted them to assent to it, and it might be held that it simply does not make sense to talk of assenting to an order. The *Oxford English Dictionary* reminds us that laws in England require royal assent, but for the Queen to give her assent to a law is for her to give her approval or to ratify it, not to obey it. Hare might complain that this objection is merely verbal and ask what stands to an order as belief stands to a declaration. But it is not clear that the only answer is 'obedience'. When you make a declaration and I believe it, I think it is true. If there is any analogue for orders it is surely thinking that the order is right or good. But of course Hare cannot say that assenting to an order is thinking it right because he wants to explain what thinking something right is in terms of assenting to orders.

These objections are directed against that part of Hare's theory which explains the agent's commitment to do what he thinks best specifically in terms of commands. It is sometimes objected that he conceives this commitment too strictly in any case. Taylor (1980, p. 514) points out that Hare accepts a form of the value-strength principle; like Davidson (see below p. 114) he holds:

> If an agent judges that it would be better to do x than to do y, then he wants to do x more than he wants to do y.

Taylor suggests that he should hold instead:

> If an agent judges that it would be better to do x than to do y he ranks the doing of x by him on this occasion higher than he ranks the doing of y by him on this occasion.

The truth of the consequent, 'A ranks the doing of x by him on this occasion higher than he ranks the doing of y', is explained as follows:

> [It] is loosely linked, in the way characteristic of cluster-concepts, to the satisfaction of an open disjunction of conditions of which the following are typical: A does x spontaneously and unhesitatingly in preference to y; A feels pleased that he has done x in preference to y; A feels remorse that he has not done x in preference to y; A regards this as a typical case of choice between doing x and doing y, and admires people who in such cases do x in preference to doing y. No single condition is either necessary or sufficient, since any condition may be absent provided that some other

is satisfied, or may be present but be overriden by some contrary condition. Yet the satisfaction of some disjunction of conjunctions of those conditions is sufficient, and that of the disjunction of conditions necessary, for the truth of '*A* ranks the doing of *x* by him on this occasion higher . . .'. (p. 516)

On this showing *A* can judge it better to do *x* than *y* but still do *y*: there is no obstacle to akrasia.

Taylor's variables *x* and *y* clearly range over types of action, not individual actions. I think he gives a plausible account of what it is to hold dispositionally that one type of action is better than another – giving money to charity, say, than spending it on expensive wine. With only minor modification it will do as an account of what it is to hold dispositionally that some type of action (hospital-visiting, abortion) is good or bad. But the akrates acts not just against a general principle but against a judgement on how he should behave here and now. Taylor's account seems to me quite implausible for the man who thinks 'It would be better to give this money I have just won on the Derby to the Famine Relief Fund than to order this item from this new wine-list'; or for Taylor's own man (p. 501) who suddenly has an opportunity to sleep with a friend's wife, and judges it better not to.

II

There are further objections to Hare's theory, but before coming to them I should like to look at the second twentieth-century theory I mentioned, emotivism. Chronologically this comes before prescriptivism. In *The Meaning of Meaning* (1923) G. K. Ogden and I. A. Richards distinguished between what they called 'symbolic' and 'emotive' uses of words. 'Symbolic' was not a luckily chosen term because it suggests allegory or metaphor, and what Ogden and Richards had in mind was, on the contrary, the use of words in the exact sciences. 'Circle' and 'equilateral' would be used 'symbolically' in geometry. A word is used 'emotively', in contrast, 'to express or excite feelings and attitudes'. Ogden and Richards (rightly) thought their distinction important for the philosophy of literary criticism: 'Very much poetry consists of statements, symbolic arrangements capable of truth or falsity, which are not used for the sake of truth or falsity but for the sake of the attitudes which their acceptance will evoke' (1923, p. 150). In *Language, Truth and Logic*, however, A. J. Ayer suggests (1936, ch. 6) that moral terms have emotive meaning, and this suggestion is developed at considerable length by C. L. Stevenson in *Ethics and Language* (1945).

The emotivist theory is that although 'good' and 'bad' may have some non-emotive, some 'symbolic' or 'descriptive' (so Stevenson) meaning, we give a central part of their meaning in saying they are used to express, arouse or preserve favourable and adverse feelings and attitudes. 'Promise-keeping is good' does not mean 'Promise-keeping has the property of causing feelings of approval'; rather it is an expression of approval in the sort of way in which 'Ouch!' is an expression of pain. To the extent to which he uses 'good' emotively, a person saying 'Promise-keeping is good' does not say anything true or false, but if he speaks sincerely he must *have* an approving attitude towards promise-keeping, and anyone who sincerely assents to his pronouncement must share the attitude. Roger Scruton (1974) uses the emotivist theory to explain the meaning of aesthetic terms: we explain the emotive meaning of a predicate term 'F' by giving a specification of 'the acceptance condition of "$F(a)$"' rather than a specification of the state of affairs which determines the truth of "$F(a)$"' (pp. 64–5). The acceptance condition is experiencing the mental state expressed.

It follows from the emotivist theory that an agent who thinks it would be good to $\emptyset$ (where $\emptyset$ing is something he can do straightaway) will have some motive, some internal impulse to $\emptyset$. For our purposes, however, we are interested in the thought that a course is better than any alternative or that it is morally obligatory or bad. The classical statements of emotivism are not explicit here and seem to leave room for two possibilities. Ayer and Stevenson write admiringly about Hume and may have thought that 'It is best to $\emptyset$' or 'It would be morally wrong to ψ' express Humean calm passions which could be overcome by violent desires. On the other hand Stevenson emphasizes that moral terms are used in order to direct behaviour. If 'You ought to visit your aunt' is to direct your behaviour it will have to arouse in you a motivational state which actually results in your visiting your aunt. Presumably, then, what Scruton calls the 'acceptance condition' will be having a motivational state which so results.

As a theory of the meaning of moral terms, emotivism leaves the possibility of clear-eyed akrasia an open question; what view the emotivist takes will depend on whether he accepts anything like the value-strength principle. It may look, therefore, as if emotivism has the advantages of prescriptivism without the disadvantages: it makes it intelligible that a person who thinks it good to $\emptyset$ should $\emptyset$ without making it inevitable. But unfortunately there are grounds for thinking emotivism incorrigibly mistaken.

In his paper 'The Thought' (which came out five years before *The Meaning of Meaning*) Frege distinguishes three kinds of thing which may be 'contained in' a sentence. His followers call these the 'propositional content' or 'proposition' expressed, the 'illocutionary force' and the 'tone', and suggest that a word, phrase or grammatical construction can have three kinds of meaning, one corresponding to each. It can determine what proposition is expressed; it can determine whether the utterance in which it is used has the force of an assertion, a question, a command or the like; or it can contribute to the aptitude of the utterance to affect someone's state of mind – usually the hearer's but occasionally that of the speaker himself. We do not speak, any more than we drive or sew, without some reason or purpose. We speak to rouse or quiet an emotion, to make something clear or to confuse someone, to implant, uproot or activate a belief. A word or construction contributes to the tone of a speech insofar as it makes the speech apt or inept to effect some such practical aim. What emotivists call the 'emotive meaning' of a word is part of its contribution to tone.

Clearly a certain aptitude to affect people's states of mind does attach both to type-speeches, i.e. sentences or sequences of sentences which can be uttered on many occasions, and to token-speeches, i.e. particular utterances. Clearly too the aptitude of a type-speech depends almost entirely, and the aptitude of a token-speech depends largely, on the words and constructions used. The practical effectiveness of a speech, of course, is mainly determined by what the speaker says, and the words and constructions he uses go a long way to determining this. But they also have features like being long or short, simple or complicated, archaic or slangy, which are non-semantic in that they make no difference to what the speaker says, but which make a difference to the emotive power or the intelligibility of the speech. That being so, the notions of tone and of a word's contribution to tone are sound. But Frege himself issues a warning: 'What is essential depends on one's purpose. To a mind concerned with what is beautiful in language what is indifferent to the logician can appear as just what is important.' Conversely what is important to the literary critic may be irrelevant to an enquiry into the meaning of moral terms.

Tone attaches to sentences and to longer compositions like the *Iliad*, not to words. The type-sentence 'A large spider is climbing up your collar' may have an aptitude to unnerve or disconcert someone; none of the words used in it has that aptitude in itself. The words do contribute to the aptitude of the sentence, and contribute by virtue of their non-semantic properties. If my aim is to disconcert you by telling you that there is a large spider climbing up your collar, I will probably prefer the short, low-key adjective 'large' to 'gigantic', 'colossal' or 'gargantuan', and the simple noun 'spider' to the scientific phrase 'a member of a species of arachnids'. But these words have an aptitude to disconcert only in this sentence, along with the other words used. No word has an aptitude of this kind in itself, independent of context. It cannot, then, be a kind of meaning 'good' has that it excites approbation or guides choice.

But surely (it may be protested) a word can be *expressive* of a feeling or attitude. In Spanish the third person or *usted* is expressive of respect; 'nigger' expresses feelings of superiority or contempt. It would be unrealistic to claim that 'good' or 'bad' is expressive in this way of any particular feeling, but in any case two distinctions must be drawn. First there is a distinction between expressing, say, respect, and using a word like '*usted*' which is called a 'respectful form' or a word 'expressive of' respect. The judicious use of respectful forms can be highly effective in expressing disdain. It is not true of any word taken by itself that it is used to express any particular mental state. Secondly we should distinguish between facts about a language and facts about language-users. That 'nigger' has become a term of contempt or abuse is a fact about our society, just as it is (or used to be) a fact about French Polynesia that you can address strangers as '*tu*' without familiarity. But the meaning of a word should be something about which we consult a linguist, not a social historian.

This point may be pressed further. There is a broad sense of 'say' which covers not only asserting and denying but also asking, ordering, expressing wishes. To ask what a speaker says, in this broad sense, is to ask what statement he makes, what question he asks, what order he issues, as the case may be. What he says is normally determined partly by his intentions and the time and place of utterance (since most speeches are token-reflexive) and partly by the words and constructions he uses. To grasp the meaning of a word, it is natural to suppose, is to know what difference it makes to what a person using it says. The emotivists make no pretence to tell us what a person using 'good' or 'bad' says; rather they claim (mistakenly, I have just argued) to tell us what he means to *do*, what practical result he means to achieve.

Criticisms to this effect have been proposed by John Searle (1962) and

Paul Ziff (1960). In *The Emotive Theory of Ethics* (1968) J. O. Urmson attempts a reply. He distinguishes between central and peripheral illocutionary forces:

> I call an illocutionary force central if anyone who assented to the utterance with any illocutionary force could not consistently dissent from it when used with that illocutionary force. An illocutionary force is peripheral if not central. (p. 138)

If I say 'Oedipus married his mother', Urmson would probably regard the force of factual narration as central and the force of horrified exclamation as peripheral. He proceeds to claim that the force of commendation is central to any utterance of the form 'That is a good X', and that this is due to the meaning of the word 'good'. Hence '"Good" has comendatory force' or '"Good" is used to commend' does tell us something about the meaning of the word.

Urmson's defence fails, in my opinion, because of the unsatisfactoriness of the notions of commendation and assent. What is commending? Hare (who wants the notion for reasons we shall see in a moment) says 'To commend . . . is to guide choices' (1952, p. 129). He probably means it is to *try* to guide choices. But if commending is either, we can no more assent to it than we can assent to ordering or forbidding. In point of fact 'to commend' (and this is even truer of the Greek verb *epainein* which Urmson and Hare probably have at the back of their minds when they use 'commend') means 'to say something is good' or 'to say "good"'. It is true that to use 'good' is to commend, but this tells us the meaning of 'commend', not of 'good', just as 'To say something is great is to magnify it' tells us the meaning of 'magnify' and 'To speak of an abstraction or an inanimate object as a person is to personify it' tells us the meaning of 'personify'.

The emotivist theory is untenable because emotive meaning is not a kind of meaning that can attach to words. This objection does not apply againt prescriptivism, at least as I stated it above. Although prescriptivism and emotivism are similar in spirit, from the technical standpoint of the philosopher of language they are profoundly different. According to Hare, moral pronouncements contain implicit in them universal commands. Followers of Frege would say that the difference between the assertion 'My children obey my orders' and the command 'My children, obey my orders!' is one not of tone but of illocutionary force; and the difference between the universal 'All men are deceivers' and the particular 'Some men are deceivers' is one not of tone but of propositional content. Whether a declaration is universal or particular is determined by the words and construction used and so, it may be argued (though not all philosophers agree) is whether a speaker declares, asks or orders. It looks as if Hare, then, is assigning to 'good' and 'bad' the sort of meaning we assign to 'all' and 'some', to the imperative mood-inflections, and to particles like the Latin 'ne', the Polynesian ''a'.

This is a perfectly respectable kind of meaning. But if Hare really wished to assign it to 'good' he would have to say that 'good' can really be used both as a universal quantifier and as an imperative particle. Plainly it cannot. That is why Hare falls back on the notion of commending. Instead of saying that using 'good' is giving a universal order he says it is guiding or trying to guide choices. But then his theory becomes a variant of emotivism and is open to the same objection. Prescriptive meaning is something that some words have, though 'good' is not among them; emotive meaning is something no word at all can have.

III

Can we derive a non-cognitivist account better than either prescriptivism or emotivism from the Aristotelian idea that the basic notion of goodness is that of an objective? How would such an account go?

In general, to think something good is to have it as an objective. Both material objects and changes can be counted as objectives. Vandeleur's objective is the Rajah's Diamond; the sunbather's is a change from white to brown in his skin. But an object can be an objective only if a change is: Vandeleur has as an objective the diamond's coming into his possession. Hence we may concentrate on changes. For these, the following definition suggests itself:

> A thinks it would be good if B became f = there is something A does, or something A refrains from doing, in order that B may become f.

The 'something' need not be very dynamic. A may merely cast about in his mind for ways of promoting the change. What the definition excludes is A's actually or occurrently thinking it would be good if B became f, and this thought's being totally idle.

If we use 'T' as a symbol for 'in order that' (and 'N' for 'not'), we may formulate the definiens:

There is some Ø such that either $TfBØA$ or $TfBNØA$

The definiens is not, of course:

There is some Ø such that TfB either ØA or NØA

We have no purpose in obeying the Law of Excluded Middle.

This definition is of thinking a particular course good, thinking it would be good if a specific change occurred in a particular individual – e.g. good if *I* were translated to the hospital where *my* aunt Augusta is immobilized with a broken leg. But we also think kinds of action, like hospital-visiting or uxoricide, good or bad, and it seems that sometimes an agent thinks a particular course good because it is of a type he thinks good. If my thinking it would be good if I visited Aunt Augusta in the Brighton Infirmary is my having this translation as an objective, what is it for me to hold the general principle that it is good for nephews to visit hospitalized aunts?

An emotivist could give either of two answers. He could say that it is to have a pro-attitude towards a maximization of aunt-visiting through-out the world, or that it is to be the sort of person who, when an aunt is hospitalized, has a favourable attitude towards visiting her. The second answer is preferable (the first might lead to the maxim 'First hospitalize your aunt') and someone offering the purposivist theory we are exa-mining should answer similarly. To think that nephews should visit aunts in hospital (if you are male; the analysis is more complicated if you are female) is to be the sort of person who, when he knows or thinks an aunt of his is hospitalized, has visiting her as an objective.

It is convenient at this point to introduce a restricted notion of a reason. The word 'reason' is used very widely in ordinary speech. It covers purposes, motives and grounds for belief: 'His reason for going to the village was to buy cigarettes', 'The real reason why Macbeth did the murder was that he was afraid of his wife', 'My reason for ordering rum on the aeroplane was that rum had mitigated my travel-sickness on cross-Channel ferries'. In the first of these explanations I would use 'purpose' not 'reason' – the village-goer's purpose was to buy cigarettes. I shall keep 'reason' for something that can be introduced into an explanation of someone's behaviour by a conjunction with the sense 'for the reason that'. Anything that does function as an explanans in this way must do so as an object of knowledge or belief. If for the reason that p, A $\emptyset$s (which we might express symbolically: $Rp\emptyset A$ A knows, perceives or at least thinks that p. If for the reason that p A $\emptyset$s or tries to $\emptyset$, that p is on that occasion a reason to A for $\emptyset$ing; we may say that in general that p is a reason to A for $\emptyset$ing if it is the case that if or when A knows or thinks that p, $Rp\emptyset A$. To use the terminology of p. 56 above, that p is in general a reason to A for $\emptyset$ing if A has a disposition such that for him the cognitive state of knowing or believing that p takes the form of a desire to $\emptyset$.

In the light of this we can say that A believes dispositionally that it is good to visit aunts in hospital if A is a person to whom an aunt's being in hospital, or a hospitalized lady's being an aunt, is in general a reason for visiting.

Is this theory open to the same objections as emotivism? I have been considering sentences of the form 'A thinks it would be good if B became f'. It is not these which give trouble to the emotivist: he can offer as a paraphrase 'A has a pro-attitude towards fB'. The difficulties arise over sentences of the form 'It would be a good thing if B became f', e.g. 'It would be good if your room became tidier'. The emotivist says that a speaker uttering this has the practical purpose that his hearer should cause B to become f, and that an important way in which 'good' is significant is that it helps the speaker to achieve this objective. We, in contrast, can say that 'It would be good if B became f' is equivalent to 'There is something which is a reason for action or inaction TfB'. We say nothing about the practical objective of the speaker, but we attribute to him a certain mode of expression. He expresses a certain change in B (the room's becoming tidier) as a possible purpose or teleological explanans of unspecified action by undesignated agents. The construction with 'good' enables him to express the change – we might even say it enables him to express f-ness – in this way. This is to attribute to 'good' the sort of meaning it has in the prescriptivist theory. We say it has meaning in the same way as mood-inflections, imperative particles (or, I would argue, inflections of tense). But it does not have the same meaning as any of these items. Expressing a change as a possible objective is not the same as ordering anyone, much less everyone, to effect it.

Since this use of 'good' is so problematic, perhaps I should say as little more about it. If I say to my daughter 'It would be good if your room became tidier' I may well want her to tidy it, but I do not say that there is something which (in the way explained above) is a reason to her for tidying it. There may be nothing such that if she were aware of it, her awareness would take the form of a desire to tidy. Even if I say 'You would do well to tidy your room' I still do not say that there is a reason to her for tidying. Rather I say that there are circumstances (expected visitors; present disarray) such that action by her which *tended towards* its becoming tidier could be understood as action *that it might* become tidier. If she is moving books about, 'She's trying to make her room tidier' is not a non-starter as a teleological explanation. No doubt expressing a change as something which could play the explanatory role of 'that to effect which' is a linguistic act which calls for further study. (I suspect that if I say '*A* ought to $\emptyset$' I commit myself to a favourable attitude towards *A*'s trying to $\emptyset$). But I do not think the investigation is likely to reveal any fundamental objection to the purposivist analysis.

If a purposivist account can be upheld, what obstacle does it present to clear-eyed akrasia? Like Taylor and unlike Hare, a purposivist can allow us to act against our general moral principles. I said that thinking it is good to visit aunts in hospital is being a person to whom an aunt's being in hospital is in general a reason for visiting her. The conditions for being such a person can be quite liberal.

In the first place, an aunt's being in hospital need not be an over-riding reason. It need only be a prima facie reason which can be over-ridden by others which to a third party might appear slight. Could a person be said to hold a general principle if he never acted on it at all? Perhaps even that is not impossible. For there are other ways of applying a principle besides acting on it oneself. One can apply it to other people. Though I am bad about visiting my own sick relatives, when I hear that an aunt of yours is sick I think that is a reason for action to you, and my awareness of her sickness takes the form of wanting you to visit. This desire may be expressed in telling you your aunt is sick; urging you to visit her; if you are an employee, giving you time off for the purpose; if you have no transport, offering to help. It is characteristic of the weak-willed man that though poor at behaving as he thinks right himself, he wants others to refrain from excessive drinking, adultery, etc. That should not be considered hypocritical; rather (see below p. 106) it is friendly.

Another way in which we can apply principles which moral philosophers often overlook is in reading a book or watching a play. To be interested, to be engaged with the characters, we must want the 'good' ones to obtain benefits and escape harm, and the 'bad' ones to come to grief (or perhaps to undergo a reformation). But in particular we want the sympathetic characters to behave well. In *Measure for*

Measure, when they hear the proposals of Angelo and the pleas of Claudio, most people want Isabella not to yield. In so wanting they are applying quite subtle moral principles which they must therefore possess, though they might not act on them themselves.

Not only, on a purposivist view, can we act against our general principles; of two positive courses we think open to us, we can judge one better but pursue the other. At a party I think I could win either the approval of a certain powerful but jealous man or the smiles of his flirtatious wife but not both. If I think it would be better all things considered to please the husband, does it follow that, if I try to please either, I must try to please him? Not if I also think pleasing him would be extremely difficult and pleasing his wife would be a cinch.

My flirting with the wife would be akratic only if I thought it better not to do it than to do it. On a purposivist view that would be to have flirting with her rather as an object of aversion than as one of desire; rather as something which plays an explanatory role as 'that lest I do which' than as 'that in order to do which'. Under these circumstances it seems impossible for me to flirt. Purposivism makes clear-eyed akratic action more problematic than emotivism or, if Pears is right, prescriptivism. But what about akratic inaction? Suppose I am in the bath, and although the water is pleasant, because I have dinner-guests to greet I think it would be best to get out now: can the purposivist allow me to linger? It sounds paradoxical to say he cannot, but the question is a difficult one to which I shall return below p. 109.

6

Intentional Action

In chapter 4 we saw some of the difficulties in defining intentional action in terms of volitions. G. E. M. Anscombe (1956/7, 1957) developed an alternative account which rests on the idea that acting intentionally is acting for reasons. I shall defend and elaborate this, and also discuss the currently orthodox view that reasons are causes.

Anscombe begins her study (1957/1963) by distinguishing three uses of 'intention' and its cognates (§ 1). We speak of (1) expressions of intention for the future: 'I intend' may, but need not, be used in such expressions; (2) intentional action or actions; a man has the intention *of* doing what he does intentionally; (3) an agent's intention *in* doing something, i.e. the intention *with which* it is done. Our concern here is with intentional action. Anscombe points out that it is not necessary for my acting intentionally on a particular occasion that I could beforehand have expressed an intention so to act in the future, or even that I should have any specific intention in acting; though we should not have our present concept of intentional action if there were no expressions of future intention or if it were impossible to ask with what intention someone acted (§ 20).

On the positive side she has two intertwined lines of speculation. First, when I act intentionally I have knowledge of my action which is not derived from observation or hearsay. That I have knowledge of my action is shown as follows. In acting intentionally I directly or indirectly cause many changes, and my action may be described as causing any of them. But it is not intentional under every description but only under a description I know to apply. A intentionally causes B to become f only if he knows or thinks he is causing B to become f. And he knows he is causing it without having to perceive or infer he is (§ 8). This does not suffice, however, to define intentional action since there are also involuntary movements we know we make without knowing this by perception or inference.

The second and more important line is this. Action is intentional insofar as it calls for a certain kind of explanation viz. explanation in terms not of a cause but a reason. What is the difference between a cause and a reason? The cyanide in your cocktail (or your drinking it) is the cause of your crashing to the floor and not the reason for it. Here you are unaware of the cyanide and its causing of your collapse, and a reason must be an object of awareness. But it is possible for me to be aware of the cause of my doing something and even to be aware, without observation or inference, that it makes me do it. For instance, if while I am placidly reading you fire a pistol behind me, I know that I jump and I know that it is the bang that makes me jump. In cases like these (Anscombe calls them cases of 'mental causality', using that phrase in a different way from O'Shaughnessy in *The Will*, Vol. II. pp. 289–91), there can be genuine and irresoluble doubt whether an explanans is a reason or a cause: 'That reason and cause are everywhere sharply distinct notions is not true' (§ 15). In general, however, mental causes are to be distinguished from motives. Anscombe distinguishes three sorts of motive: forward-looking motives, among which are included intentions and desires; backward-looking motives such as gratitude and revenge; and what she calls 'motives in general'. Insofar as I act under a forward-looking motive my action can be explained as being for some purpose: I act in order that (or lest) some change occur. Insofar as I act under a backward-looking motive my action can be explained by something which has (supposedly) happened. Hamlet acts out of revenge when he kills Claudius because Claudius had killed his father. Insofar as my action springs from a 'motive in general' it is to be explained by being 'put in a certain light' or interpreted as an action of a certain kind. 'The motives admiration, curiosity, spite, friendship, fear, love of truth, despair and a host of others are either of this extremely complicated kind or are forward-looking or mixed' (§ 13). It appears that supporting a motion because I admire the proposer would be an example.

An explanation of any of these kinds will be in terms of a reason (§ 16), and if my action can be explained in any of these ways it is intentional. But it can be intentional even if no explanation of this kind is available, provided the request for such an explanation is in order (§§ 17, 21). Anscombe has in mind idle trivial acts like kicking a stone which one does 'for no particular reason', but there are other more important cases and I think that what she says needs amendment.

Like many writers she uses 'reason' widely to cover both what I above called 'reasons' – factors introduced by 'for the reason that' – and also purposes introduced by 'in order that' or 'lest'. We often exercise an acquired skill, and hence act intentionally, for a time without having any definite single purpose in view, without acting to bring about or prevent any particular change. For example, I may talk to a friend for a time without having the aim of learning anything from him or persuading him to do anything. We may walk, sing or read the papers in this purposeless way. But we cannot so easily act intentionally without a reason. In general action needs explanation whereas inaction does not. It is silly to ask me why I did not go to Bridlington, at least if I had no reason for going there. It is not so silly to ask me why I walked or talked for ten minutes. Sometimes, of course, we act in order not to become bored; then we have a definite purpose. But if I act, and there is no threat of boredom, and I have no other objective, my action calls for explanation. What will explain it is something which renders the activity pleasant or enjoyable. Good weather explains walking in this way, a lady's wit or beauty our talking to her. While it is possible, then, to act intentionally without acting for any purpose, I do not think it is possible to act intentionally without acting for any reason. If there were a change I effected for no reason whatever, why should I consider the effecting mine?

The characterization of intentional acting as acting for a reason is more important than its characterization as acting of which the agent is aware without observation. That is partly because our knowledge of our actions is more complicated and problematic than Anscombe recognizes, but also because, as she does recognize, we have knowledge of our actions precisely because they are for reasons. She argues that when I act intentionally I am aware of my action as the conclusion of an Aristotelian practical syllogism; or, since I need not go through a process of practical reasoning, as something the rationale of which can be explained in the Aristotelian way. Aristotle's account 'describes an order which is there whenever actions are done with intentions' (§ 42). Wanting a certain vitamin, and believing it to be contained in *tripes à la mode de Caen*, I think of ordering *tripes à la mode de Caen* as the thing to do (§ 33). Of course, I may inadvertently order the item next to it on the menu. But if (to vary the example) I write intentionally on the blackboard, and I mean to write 'This sentence is ungrammatical' but in fact I write 'This sentences ungrammatical', it is not my knowledge of what I am doing which is at fault but my performance. It is, in fact, impossible to do certain things – Anscombe suggests telephoning and marrying; writing an English sentence might be another example – without knowing you are doing them. The knowledge, she quotes from Aquinas, 'is the cause of what it understands' (§§ 47–8). Someone might object that all the same if I write 'This sentences ungrammatical' I do not know, but only believe, that I am writing 'This sentence is ungrammatical'. True, but then I do not intentionally write 'This sentences ungrammatical'. I *write* intentionally, and I know that I am writing and what I am trying to write.

Anyone who defines acting intentionally as acting for reasons and purposes will have to meet challenges concerning both purposes and reasons. If A's purpose in Øing is that B should become f, A must desire that B should become f (either as an end in itself or for some further purpose); surely, then, he is motivated by that desire, and the desire may be said to cause his Øing. If this is to be a challenge desire must be conceived in the old-fashioned way as an internal feeling, recognizable by introspection, distinct from the action it is supposed to cause. Anscombe does not deny that there are such mental states: a feeling of desire for an apple might make me go to a cupboard where I think there are some (§ 11). But she denies that such feelings are always present or, when present, always operative, and she distinguishes them from a kind of wanting which perhaps *is* always present in intentional action and of which 'the primitive sign . . . is trying to get' (§ 36). When she wrote, some philosophers held it to be logically possible for anyone to want anything. 'There are no logical limits,' said P. H. Nowell-Smith (1954, p. 115) 'to the possible objects of pro- and con-attitudes'. Anscombe argues that (in her sense of 'want') it is possible to want something only if it appears to satisfy some 'desirability characterisation', some description like 'pleasant', 'suitable', 'should be done' (§ 37). Her main argument is that if a person claims to want something and cannot say or show in what way it seems to him good, his claim is unintelligible.

I agree. Indeed, I do not see how an agent could himself think he wanted something unless he could see some reason for wanting it or some purpose it served. The image of a hedgehog might come often into my mind, accompanied by a feeling of 'uneasiness', and my disquiet might diminish if I went into the English countryside and become more insistent if I stayed in central London or went yachting. But these introspectible phenomena would not make me think I wanted a hedgehog if there was nothing I wanted a hedgehog for; I should merely think I had a mental disorder. For further argument on this issue see pp. 109–11 below.

The challenge concerning reasons is that the whole notion of a reason for action is unsound. We can have reasons for thinking things; opinions can be reasonable or unreasonable. And if we already have a goal or desire, reason can tell us what is necessary or sufficient to achieve it, and it is unreasonable to do what is neither. But no action can be reasonable or unreasonable in itself, independently of our desires. If I want to go to Paris, the fact that this train is going there is a reason to me for taking it, and even, in a way, for being eager to take it; but it is not a reason for taking it, and still less for wanting to take it, independently of the desire to get to Paris. The classic development of this view is by Hume in *Treatise* II.iii.3 and III.i.1, but to many people it seems obviously true, and it is one of the bases of the holistic theory developed by Christopher Peacocke (1979). Peacocke says: 'If a person possesses a particular belief, this seems to have no consequences for his action that are consequences independently of his desires' (p. 3). He seems to mean that, in itself, a real or supposed circumstance is not a reason either for doing anything or for refraining from doing anything. In *The Possibility of Altruism* (1970) Thomas Nagel introduces the term 'a practical reason': it is 'a reason to do or want something as a theoretical reason is a reason to conclude or believe something' (p. 64). Neither Hume nor, it seems, Peacocke believes that there are any practical reasons.

Does Anscombe? She says we can think food good for us without wanting to eat it (§ 36), think something our duty and not want to do it (§ 41). She is not merely pointing out that we can have reasons for not wanting to discharge a duty (it involves toil or danger) or to eat something our health requires (it tastes nasty). In her account of practical reasoning, though the starting-point must involve something wanted, that the agent wants something is not itself, strictly speaking, a premise of his reasoning. 'The role of "wanting" in the practical syllogism is quite different from that of a premise. It is that whatever is described in the proposition that is the starting-point of the argument must be wanted in order for the reasoning to lead to any action' (§ 35). In itself the fact that Helen wonderfully resembles the immortal gods will not lead anyone to consort with her or the fact that the pool contains crocodiles lead swimmers to vacate it; these will be reasons only to persons who desire charming companions or are averse to being eaten.

If that is so, Hume is surely right that reason 'only directs' our impulses (*Treatise* II.iii.1; 1888, p. 414), somewhat as a pipe directs the flow of water through it, and intentional action will at best be action directed in this way. Anscombe is on record as questioning whether there is a problem about weakness of will (1965), and the account in *Intention* certainly leaves it an open question whether 'a man need ever prefer the greater [good] to the less' (§ 39). It looks as if Anscombe is offering us a theory of intentional action half-way between those of Aristotle and Hume. She agrees with Aristotle that desire cannot motivate us independently of thought, but with Hume that even thought of what is advantageous has in itself no motivational power. The racist implications apart, she could echo Hume's declaration that 'Tis not contrary to reason for me to chuse my total ruin to prevent the least uneasiness to an *Indian* or person wholly unknown to me' (1888, p. 416).

Perhaps that needs some qualification for reasons which are past events. Here she has good and evil enter explicitly into the conception both of the reason and of the action it explains. That Claudius killed Hamlet's father can be a reason to Hamlet for killing Claudius because killing someone's father is doing something bad, and so is killing the killer. 'What the agent reports in answer to the question "Why?" is a reason for acting if in treating it as a reason he conceives it as something good or bad, and his own action as doing good or harm' (§ 14). This suggests that the consideration 'He killed my father' might itself motivate Hamlet to kill Claudius. But several questions arise. Can an event or state of affairs be a reason for action to someone who does not 'conceive it as something good or bad'? How do we tell whether something is good, bad or indifferent? Anscombe takes it that my killing your father is injuring you; but if you are an impatient heir you might be grateful. And is being harmed a reason for harming?

Thomas Nagel (1970) argues for the existence of two sorts of practical reason, prudential reasons and reasons to do with the desires and needs of other persons. For our present purposes it is enough to consider what he says about the first. He uses the word 'reason' in a technical sense he explains as follows: 'Every reason is a predicate R such that for all persons p and events A, if R is true of A, then p has prima facie reason to promote A' (p. 47). Such predicates might be 'is in the interest of p', 'is pleasant'. This is a different usage from the one I introduced but (with some awkwardness to be noted below) it will cover the same cases. Where I should say 'That there was gold in Mexico was a reason to Cortés for going there' Nagel would say 'Going to Mexico's having the property of taking the goer to where there was gold was a reason to Cortés for going there'. Where Nagel says 'A route's being through beautiful scenery is a reason for taking it' (cf. 1970, p. 51) I should say 'Scenery's being beautiful is a reason for travelling through it'.

Nagel's argument for prudential reasons is an attempt to show that considerations about my future desires and needs have motivational power independently of my present desires. Hume allows that the fact that an action will satisfy a present desire has motivational power; that drinking this beer will satisfy my present thirst is a (prima facie) reason for drinking the beer. This being granted to him, Nagel claims that the fact that I shall in the future have a desire which $\emptyset$ing will assuage is a reason to me now for action to ensure that at the appropriate time I can $\emptyset$. That I will be thirsty on my transatlantic yacht is a reason to me for provisioning my yacht with water now, even if I do not now feel thirsty or experience any itch to put water in my yacht. If I do not regard it as a reason, I am failing to think of myself as identical with the person who will be thirsting in mid-Atlantic. To allow motivational power to considerations about the future is part of thinking of oneself as a being that exists through time. Nagel concedes that if, for the reason that drinking water will satisfy a future thirst, I lay in water now, I must now want to lay it in. But he distinguishes between motivated and unmotivated desires (1970, pp. 29–30). Thirst, or the thirsty man's desire for water, is unmotivated (though it is, of course, caused); but the yachtsman's desire to lay in water for his voyage is motivated by the consideration that this action is necessary to prevent death by thirst. Accordingly we cannot say that his action is caused by the desire; rather the desire itself, and hence the action, is due to the prudential consideration.

The distinction between motivated or rational and unmotivated or non-rational desires is important, and Nagel establishes that intentional action does not have to be motivated by a present unmotivated desire. Since Hume, however, rejects the notion of a practical reason altogether, he might be unwilling to say that the property of satisfying a present desire is a *reason* for promoting what has that porperty; doing what we want to do is natural rather than reasonable. Alternatively he might accept the notion of a prudential reason but insist that p has a prudential reason to promote A only if A will satisfy some unmotivated, brute desire, or cause some pleasant or prevent some unpleasant sensation. Nagel thinks this notion is too narrow, but he might have difficulty in persuading a determined Humean to widen it.

While, therefore, Nagel's defence of practical reasons is not ineffective, it would be comforting to see it supplemented. I think also that his terminology is cumbersome. The restriction of 'reason' to properties of actions, happenings and promotable situations does not correspond closely to ordinary usage and makes some kinds of rational explanation hard to express. That there are crocodiles in the pool is a reason for not swimming there in that it renders swimming there conducive to being eaten. This point is not well conveyed by: 'That swimming in the pool has the property of conducing to being eaten by crocodiles is a reason for not (promoting) swimming in the pool.' Desdemona's supposed promiscuity was a reason to Othello for killing her 'lest she betray more men' (V.ii.6). This is hardly conveyed at all by 'That killing her had the property of preventing her from betraying more men was a reason to Othello for killing her.' I shall adhere, then, to the usage of 'reason' and 'purpose' explained in chapter 4.

Besides holding that wanting involves thinking good, and therefore having knowledge of the thing wanted, Anscombe says: 'Knowledge itself cannot be described independently of volition; the ascription of sensible knowledge and volition go together' (§ 30). On a Humean view they need not: there is no logical connection between perceiving and wanting or between 'impressions' and 'ideas' of objects and 'impressions' of desire and other passions. The more Aristotelian position to which she here reverts provides, I think, the best basis for a defence of practical reasons.

An extreme version of the doctrine that cognition and volition are interdependent makes the concept of a reason enter into the concept of belief: A knows, perceives or thinks that p if and only if for some behaviour $\emptyset$, either $Rp\emptyset A$ or $RpN\emptyset A$: either he does something for the reason that (or in spite of the fact that) p or he refrains from some action because of (in spite of) this circumstance. In recent times some such thesis has been advanced by R. B. Braithwaite (1932/3; see also Ramsey 1926/1978, ch. 3) and spoken of sympathetically by D.H. Mellor (1977/8) and others. Hume may have sensed a threat from this quarter since he singles out for attack a writer, William Wollaston, who puts forward a similar thesis about speech. Wollaston does not say that it is part of thinking that p to act as if p, but he claims it is part of acting as if p to say that p:

> There are many acts [other than weeping, laughing, etc.] which have in nature, and would be taken by any indifferent judge to have a

signification, and to imply some proposition . . . Whoever acts as if
things were so, or not so, doth by his act declare, that they are so, or not
so; as plainly as he could by words, and with more reality. (1722/1897,
pp. 362, 364, §§ 1026, 1028)

Anscombe denies that 'every perception must be accompanied by
some action' (1957/1963, § 36) and would probably reject the extreme
view formulated above. But she thinks that a person could not discriminate objects perceptually if he did not do things with the objects
discriminated, if they did not play roles in his practical life, and this idea
gives us what we need for a reply to Hume.

> Though reason . . . be sufficient to instruct us in the pernicious or useful
> tendency of qualities and actions; it is not alone sufficient to produce any
> moral blame or approbation. Utility is only a tendency to a certain end;
> and were the end totally indifferent to us, we should feel the same
> indifference towards the means. It is requisite that a *sentiment* should
> here display itself, in order to give a preference to the useful above the
> pernicious tendencies. (1902, p. 286)

What Hume actually says here is quite untenable. 'Pernicious' means
harmful or bad, and if reason can establish that, say, selling contaminated food to the poor is pernicious, it is sufficient to produce blame.
Utility is not just a tendency to a certain end but a tendency to a desired
end; that is what distinguishes it from perniciousness. What Hume
should have said was that reason tells us in non-evaluative terms what
the results of certain action will be, and sentiment then pronounces
whether these results are useful or pernicious.

Is this true? Reason may tell me that bees produce a sweet substance
which is nourishing to human beings, and have stings which cause
sensations of pain. Would it really be possible to think the former
tendency pernicious and the latter useful? Reason says that if you act on
a boat in one way it will deposit you in the water and sink, and if you act
on it in another it will carry you dry to the further shore. Might a Martian
consider boats useful for depositing their occupants in the water and
dangerous in that they are liable to transfer their occupants across the
water's surface? It is not easy to see how there could be a concept of a
thing which was useful and pernicious in just these ways; and if there
were it would not be a concept of a boat, even if the same material
structures seemed to satisfy it as satisfy the concept of a boat. But surely
a suicide might prefer doing what will cause his boat to sink to doing
what will cause it to carry him to the further shore? If he did, we should

want to know why. If I see you doing what will cause your boat to sink (taking the cork out of the bottom; running it on to sharp rocks) my first thought is that you are acting in ignorance or against your will. If it seems you are acting intentionally, I can reasonably ask 'Why are you trying to make your boat sink?' – whereas it is not in general reasonable, but inane or insulting, to ask 'Why are you trying to prevent your boat from sinking?' The suicide who is not mad has some reason for pursuing a course which is pernicious.

If I did not already know whether the tendency of boats to drown their occupants was useful or pernicious, how could a sentiment tell me? The image of an outcome might occur in me accompanied by a feeling of contentment or uneasiness, but we have already seen the difficulty in supposing this could constitute desire or aversion. (We might add, in the words of Lucretius II.4, that 'it is pleasant to contemplate evils from which you yourself are free'.) But in point of fact it is only because we already want to be transported across water and are averse to being drowned that we notice a boat has these tendencies. A visitor from Mars, having different needs and aims from ours, might think our boats useful or dangerous in different ways; but Anscombe's point, I think, is that it is only insofar as an object has some practical significance, is capable of playing some part for better or worse in our lives, that we notice it at all. Do not scientists (it might be objected) take note of kinds of metal and species of butterfly which are completely useless and completely harmless? Yes, but once science is a going concern, a new metal or biological species has a high utility of an artificial kind: it will bring fame or promotion to the scientist who discovers and describes it, and confound his academic rivals.

In recent years there has been much discussion of sortal concepts. The term (which is taken from Locke III.iii.15) is applied to concepts of living organisms, of inanimate natural objects (the concept of a star would be a sortal concept), of artifacts, and of kinds of natural or artificial stuff – gold, wine, air, etc. All these concepts are problematic in various ways. As regards artifacts, it seems there is no definite property or set of properties common and peculiar to all tables, say, or all books; hence it has been suggested (R. Bambrough, 1960/1) that the words 'table' and 'book' are used on grounds of Wittgensteinian Family Resemblance. Scientists do sometimes have precise definitions for species of animal or plant and for natural substances. But these definitions are not, in general, known to non-scientists who happily use words like 'tiger' and 'gold'. Hence is is suggested that the ordinary man means by 'tiger' or 'gold' whatever a scientist would apply the word to; or perhaps whatever has the same real but to him unknown essence as some paradigm, a man-eater of Bengal or the material of his mother's wedding ring (H. Putnam 1975/1978, ch. 12). Without challenging these suggestions I offer a further one. Familiar sorts of material object and (though to a lesser extent) familiar sorts of material are all (however else we may conceive them as well) conceived as such as to benefit us in definite ways, to harm us in definite ways, and to be more or less useful in definite ways. A thing is useful in a simple way if it can be used as a tool or instrument to effect some kind of change; our hands and feet, of course, are useful in this way as well as our saws and our motor-cars. A thing is beneficial if like wine or an electric fire it can give us pleasant sensations, or if it renders other things more useful or beneficial. A thing is harmful it it can cause unpleasant sensations (pain, nausea, etc.) or render other things useless or harmful.

I suggest not only that we have these concepts but that to have them is to be disposed to act for reasons. If I conceive objects of sort s as such as to cause a harm h, I am the kind of person to whom the presence of an s, or a circumstance likely to make an s cause h, is a reason for action to prevent h. Since I conceive scorpions as causing pain by stinging, the presence of a scorpion near my bare foot is a reason to me for action to avoid being stung. If I conceive an s as such as to cause a benefit b, the presence of an s is to me a reason for action to secure b. Don Giovanni conceived girls as objects which give pleasure to those who embrace them, so to him the presence of a girl was a reason for action to obtain an embrace. Often there is little or nothing more to applying a sortal concept, thinking that an object in the neighbourhood satisfies it, than acting for such a reason. I think there are policemen in that car if, for the reason it is there, in order not to be stopped for speeding, I slow down. This notion of a reason is implicit in the notion of practical significance generally, and if we try to dispense with the notion of practical significance, our ideas of cognition and perceptual awareness become vacuous. We might as well say a cinema screen is aware of the film projected on it.

II

Reasons are of various kinds, and can play differing explanatory roles. Some taxonomy here will not only show precisely where I wish to part company with Hume; it will also enable us distinguish different ways of desiring and thinking good, and will give us a clearer view of the factors involved in rational deliberation.

The reasons we have been considering are all (in a non-pejorative sense of the word) egocentric. The benefit, harm or utility involved has been to the agent. Within the field of egocentric action we can draw certain distinctions. Reasons connected with pain, damage and other kinds of harm render action or inaction *necessary*. The hot, thundery weather makes it necessary to put the milk in the refrigerator; the presence of crocodiles makes it necessary to refrain from bathing. Reasons connected with benefits render action not so much necessary as advantageous. The presence of gold in Mexico made it advantageous for the Spaniards to go there but hardly necessary. It made it good to go rather than bad not to go.

The necessity here is neither logical nor causal (as in 'The action of the Sun made it necessary for the snow to melt') but practical. Is it, however, conditional? It is conditionally necessary to do something if doing it is causally required for achieving a purpose you did not have to have. Given the purpose of getting to London this evening, my being in Inverness makes it necessary for me to charter an aeroplane, but being in Inverness, or a town 600 miles from London, does not make plane-chartering necessary independently of any such purpose. Hume, it might be said, holds that all practical necessity is conditional. Given the objective of not being stung, the presence of of a scorpion near my bare foot may make foot-moving necessary, but it does not make it necessary otherwise. Similarly with benefits. Given a violent passion for gustatory pleasure, the presence of wine in the glass makes it advantageous to drink, but otherwise not.

As I said a moment ago, it is foolish or offensive to ask 'Why are you averse to being stung?' whereas it is at worst indiscreet to ask 'Why do you want to get to London this evening?' Hume might reply that that is just because it is *normal* for people to be averse to being stung, not because it is reasonable. But apart from the fact that it seems to be a conceptual truth (masochism notwithstanding) with pain is a sensation which is an object of aversion, it is part of my concept of a scorpion that the presence of a scorpion is a reason for acting to avoid a certain outcome, whereas acting to achieving a certain outcome does not seem to enter into the concept of a town 600 miles from London. There is, I suggest, a formal difference between the explanation of the plane-chartering and the explanation of the foot-movement. The first is of the form: $T\!fBRp\emptyset A$. I had the objective of getting to London that evening, and my being in Inverness made chartering an aeroplane (causally) necessary for achieving that objective. The second is of the form $Rp T\!fB\emptyset A$. There was a scorpion by my foot, and that made action in order to avoid being stung a (practical) necessity.

Knowing that if you are in Inverness in the afternoon, to reach London that evening you must fly, is a piece of quasi-technical knowledge; whereas knowing that if there is a scorpion at your feet it is necessary to take sting-avoiding action is practical knowledge. Hence I call being in Inverness a 'technical', as distinct from a 'practical' reason. Technical and practical reasons explain in different ways. A technical reason shows why an agent acted in one way rather than another (took an aeroplane, not a train) and exhibits it as more or less skilful (an exercise of knowledge of geography and modern means of transportation); it does not explain why the agent rather acted than refrained. A practical reason tells us just that.

I suspect that philosophers are sometimes led to doubt if there are any genuine practical reasons because they see the same circumstance functioning as a reason for opposed lines of conduct. To me, who wish to stay alive, the cocktail's containing cyanide is a reason for declining it; to you, who want to end it all, it is a reason for knocking it back. But if we distinguish between technical and practical reasons, we never find the same circumstance functioning as a reason of the same kind for opposed courses. The presence of cyanide in the cocktail is to me a practical reason rendering it practically necessary to decline. It is a technical reason to you. You want to effect your death, and the presence of cyanide makes downing the cocktail causally sufficient for your purpose.

Within the field of egocentric action, then, we have distinguished practical from technical reasons, and within each group we have found reasons which render necessary and reasons which render advantageous or sufficient. Further distinctions might usefully be drawn among the practical reasons. Some depend directly on our sensitivity to pleasant and unpleasant sensations. These can be reasons for what, perhaps unconsciously following Plato, we call 'gut' emotions: the presence of a source of pain can be a reason for fear, the presence of a source of pleasant sensations would be a reason for epithumia. On the other hand reasons which are connected with a thing's becoming less or more useful, and which are independent of our sensitivity, could be called (in a narrow sense of the word) 'prudential'. We noticed earlier that there is a class of reasons which are reasons for acting without being reasons for acting to secure any particular benefit or avoid any particular harm. I have suggested elsewhere (Charlton, 1983) that aesthetic reasons belong to this class. But it is time to look beyond the field of egocentric action.

The principle that it is good to visit hospitalized aunts (p. 88 above) concerns a class of persons, aunts, defined by a relationship to the agent. The relationship here is a causal one (being the sister of a parent) but the man who thinks it good to visit hospitalized *aunts*, as distinct from hospital-patients generally, must be understood to conceive this relationship as carrying with it a certain passive right against nephews, a right to some cherishing. I think we conceive nearly all human relations – parent and child, husband and wife, employer and employee, doctor and patient, etc. – as carrying rights and duties. Precisely what rights and duties they are thought to carry varies from society to society, and hence different societies have slightly different concepts of, say, a wife or a priest.

Insofar as a concept of a sort of person involves rights and duties in this way, I call it a 'social' concept. Corresponding to social concepts are social practical reasons. If Prospero conceives a father as having a duty to educate his children, then the fact that Miranda is his daughter will be a reason to him for educating her, and render his so doing socially obligatory. If Hippolytus conceives a father as having a right to have his son refrain from making love to his wife, the fact that Phaedra is his father's wife will be to him a reason for not yielding to her advances, and will render yielding socially impermissible.

We sometimes use the words 'necessary' and 'impossible' here, but the necessity is different in kind from the necessity of action to avoid harm. There the harm may be an object of aversion for its own sake, but the action is not an object of desire for its own sake. On the other hand doing what is socially impermissible is an object of aversion for its own sake. To Hippolytus sleeping with Phaedra is intrinsically bad, not bad because it is conducive to something further. We cannot say it is conducive to unfilial or incestuous behaviour: it *is* such behaviour; and that it may conduce to censure from other people in the society is irrelevant if Hippolytus thinks it is his duty to refrain. Of course, not everything which is an object of aversion for its own sake is an object of the same kind of aversion. Hippolytus is averse to sleeping with Phaedra in one way and to being gored by wild boars in another. Similarly educating Miranda is an object of desire for its own sake to Prospero, though not in the same way as listening to music. If, however, it turns out to be impossible to educate Miranda on the island, then he will have to send her to school in Milan, and this is not an end in itself but necessary to avoid the evil of not doing what is socially obligatory.

Although visiting hospitalized aunts, refraining from incest, etc., is hardly egocentric behaviour, neither is it strictly speaking altruistic. Suppose, however, that for the reason that there is a scorpion near your foot, instead of acting in order that *I* may not be stung, I act in order that *you* may not be stung; and suppose I act not by slaying the scorpion myself, but by directing your attention to it. Then the presence of the scorpion, which is, so to speak, a first-level reason for action to you, functions as a second-level reason to me: it is a reason to me for acting in order that you may act because of it. To put the case symbolically, $RpTRp\psi B \emptyset A$. Clearly a straightforward social reason to one person can also be a second-level reason to another. That Jocasta is Oedipus' mother is a reason to Oedipus for not marrying her; surely it might have been a reason to Teiresias for warning him not to marry her.

In these cases A acts in order that B may be aware of a reason and act accordingly. That is kind or friendly of A. In general if the circumstance that p makes it egocentrically or socially (or even altruistically) good for B to ψ, *it makes it friendly for A to act $TRp\psi B$*. But people have enmities as well as friendships. If B is an enemy, then that p will be a reason for action $TNRp\psi B$.

We distinguished between first-level reasons which render necessary and those which render advantageous. This distinction carries over to friendly and malignant action. If that p makes it necessary for B to ψ (there are crocodiles where B, or B's daughter, proposes to swim) it makes it necessary for B's friends to act $T\psi B$. If it renders it advantageous for B to ψ, B's friends do not have to act $T\psi B$, but it is kind if they do. The position over malignancy (a topic strangely neglected by philosophers, at least in print) is not quite so clear. Perhaps, however, what is necessary is to prevent benefits to our enemies, and causing harm to them is merely desirable. It is vital for the Spanish to prevent the English from learning there is gold in Peru; it is not necessary, but a good idea, to foster the illusion that there is a passage to the Pacific north of Greenland.

Corresponding to these different kinds of practical reason are different ways of thinking good and bad, different kinds of desire and aversion, for these, if I am right, are forms awareness of practical reasons takes. Awareness of a source of pleasant or unpleasant sensations, I suggested, often takes the form of a 'gut' emotion. The judgement that it would be better not to face a source of pain and bodily harm is fear to face it. Awareness of a book lying on the lawn as I come in at dusk is awareness that it is 'prudentially' necessary to fetch it, and this is a way of wanting to fetch it. 'Think it (practically) necessary to' should be regarded less as a combination of a verb of thinking and a predicate term than as a verb of wanting. If something renders your current activity enjoyable (the sun as you walk over the hills), and awareness of it takes the form of thinking it good to continue, this may be nothing different from enjoying the activity. 'Think it socially obligatory to' is another verb of wanting, and expresses the form which may be taken by awareness of someone as standing in a social relationship to you. Awareness of reasons to others as reasons to others must, I think, take either the form of thinking it would be good if they acted appropriately, or the form of thinking it would be bad. In the first case we have a benignant or 'altruistic' desire, and are aware of the other person as a friend; in the second we have a malignant desire and are aware of the other person as an enemy.

Naturally we do not and cannot act in accordance with all our reasons. We must act because of some and in spite of others. We might say that corresponding to the different kinds of reason, there are different dimensions of intentional action, different coordinates. To locate a piece of action precisely as intentional action is to locate it by these coordinates. Courageous action is action in spite of one sort of egocentric reason, temperate action is action in spite of another. People are classed as purposive agents of different sorts, ambitious, altruistic, compassionate, cruel, etc., according as they are disposed to give more or less weight to practical reasons of different kinds.

This is a convenient point at which to deal with one of the subordinate questions mentioned in chapter 1. Aristotle's akrates does what he (correctly) believes to be morally bad. The akratic behaviour which presents a problem to Hare, and which Hare eventually rules out, is explicitly limited to not behaving as the agent thinks he morally ought. Davidson, in contrast, says: 'As a first positive step in dealing with the problem of incontinence, I propose to divorce that problem entirely from the moralist's concern that our sense of the conventionally right may be lulled, dulled or duped by a lively pleasure' (1980, p. 30). If Davidson wishes to make a sharp distinction between what is conventionally right and what is morally right, it is unclear why his moralist is concerned with the former. If he does not wish to make the distinction, he seems to commit himself to the view that an agent might judge one course morally best and a different course best all things considered. Similarly Anscombe says: 'Whether there are orders of human goods, e.g. whether some are greater than others, and whether if this is so a man need ever prefer the greater to the less, and on pain of what; this question would belong to ethics, if there is such a science (1963/1957, pp. 75–6); and she adds a footnote: 'Following Hume, though without his animus, I of course deny that this preference can be as such "required by reason", in any sense.' This footnote seems to imply that there is no reason why moral considerations for or against a course should override others. Our question is whether this is correct.

As Mary Midgley observes (1972), the term 'moral' has broader and narrower uses. Our taxonomy of reasons enables us to differentiate these (perhaps more sharply than she would wish). One use of 'moral' is in connection with some, if not all, social relationships. Family duties in particular, duties to parents, children, spouse, master, servants and remoter members of families are reckoned moral. That Oliver is the secretary of a literary society of which you are a member may not be a moral reason for acting or refraining in any particular way, but that Polyneices is your brother, uncle or what not surely is. Secondly, action to benefit other persons simply as persons, regardless of their relationship to the agent, is considered to be morally good, and action to harm others when the agent thinks they have done, and threaten, no harm to him, is thought morally bad. We might try to assimilate this second use of 'moral' to the first, perhaps by talking of the duties of friendship or humanity, but this simplification would, I think, be more confusing than illuminating. The fields of social obligation and personal friendship or enmity are quite distinct. It is kind to help your friend to discharge his social obligations, and kind to discharge your own if your friend wants you to; but the same could be said about egocentric behaviour. Both these uses of 'moral' are relatively narrow and what Midgley calls 'classificatory'. They serve to contrast certain kinds of reason and certain ways of being good with others. A moral consideration of either kind, a consideration of social relationship or altruism, in itself establishes only what Ross (see below p. 116) calls 'prima facie' rightness or wrongness.

On the other hand there is a broad, inclusive use of 'moral' according to which the field of the moral is the field of the practical as a whole. Moral deliberation here is deliberation in which all kinds of consideration, including those of social duty and friendship, are weighed against one another; and moral judgement is judgement precisely of what is best all these things considered.

What is it exactly to judge that the reasons for a course of action outweigh those against it, or vice versa? The word 'outweigh' is metaphorical; I suggest the following way of cashing it. If I judge that p, a reason for $\emptyset$ing, outweighs q, a reason for not $\emptyset$ing, i.e. that it is better to $\emptyset$ because p and despite q than not to $\emptyset$ because q and despite p, then I desire to be the sort of person so to act. And if I desire to be that sort of agent then (unless I have some overriding reason to the contrary) I shall $\emptyset$ for the reason that p in order to be that sort of agent.

If this suggestion is correct it covers the case of akratic inaction which I left for further discussion in chapter 5. When an agent has reasons for and against doing something, we are readier to accept his not doing it, even though he thinks the reasons for for doing it are the better ones, than we are his doing it, even though he thinks the reasons for not doing it are the more weighty. That is because in general inaction calls for less explanation than action. If, however, the host in the bath would like to be the sort of person who puts his guests' pleasure above his own, and does not want to be the sort of person who is guilty of discourtesy through excessive attachment to sensuous pleasure, then akratic lingering becomes as problematic for him as positive akratic action.

III

Anscombe is at pains to distinguish reasons from causes, though she does not believe that the distinction can be sustained in all cases. In his paper 'Actions, Reasons and Causes' (1963/1980, pp. 3ff) Davidson argues that reasons *are* causes, and that explanation of action by beliefs and desires is a kind of causal explanation. That is at present the prevailing view, but it is not, of course, above being questioned, and in any case there may be debate about how it should be developed.

Spinoza in *Ethics* IV Preface suggests that if I build a house for the purpose of obtaining shelter, the desire for shelter is the efficient cause of my action. It might similarly be held that if the Spaniards go to Mexico for the reason that it contains gold, the belief that it contains gold is the efficient cause of their journey. The beliefs which Davidson identifies with causes are slightly different in character from that one. He says: 'Whenever someone does something for a reason, he can be characterised as (a) having some sort of pro-attitude towards actions of a certain kind and (b) believing . . . that his action is of that kind' (1980, pp. 3–4); and he calls the relevant pro-attitude and belief 'the *primary reason* why the agent performed the action'. Such beliefs would be not so much practical as instrumental or technical reasons. They would appear in explanations of the form $TfBRp\emptyset A$ ('in order to get the gold, for the reason that fighting the Mexicans was necessary for getting the gold, they fought the Mexicans'). This point, however, is not important for the evaluation of Davidson's account.

Why should we think that beliefs and desires are causes? Certainly if Macbeth kills Duncan in order to become King, Macbeth must want to become king, and we can say 'He killed Duncan because he wanted to become King'. We can equally say 'The Spaniards went to Mexico because they believed it contained gold'. But it is not possible to view 'because' in these sentences as playing the grammatical role it plays in a straightforward causal explanation like 'Duncan died because Macbeth stabbed him'. In the first two sentences, where 'because' introduces a verb of wanting or thinking, the verb can be replaced by a parenthesis. We can say 'Macbeth killed Duncan in order that, as was his ambition, he might become King'; 'The Spaniards went to Mexico because, as they believed, it contained gold'. When 'because' introduces a genuine verb of causing, this transformation is impossible. We cannot say 'Duncan died because, as Macbeth stabbed'.

Davidson argues that nevertheless 'because' followed by a verb of thinking or wanting is explanatory. We wish to say not just that Macbeth killed Duncan and wanted to become King, but that he killed Duncan because he wanted to become King and because he believed killing Duncan conducive to this aim. In effect, Davidson challenges his opponents to say how desires and beliefs account for action if they are not causes (1980, pp. 11–12).

If they are defined in terms of action, it seems impossible they should be causes. Suppose that to desire fB is to be disposed to do what conduces to fB, and to believe that p is to be disposed to act as if p. In that case we certainly could not give A's belief that p or his desire for fB as a cause of his doing what he does Rp or TfB. Davidson, however (following Spinoza, *Ethics* III.2.sch., and in the company of nearly everyone who holds reasons to be causes), takes a different view of belief and desire. Belief and desire (or, if these are states or dispositions, then coming to believe and coming to desire) are episodes which precede the action of which they are causes, and are therefore qualified to be Humean causes (cf. Mackie, 1974, p. 291).

If anything is to cause supposedly intentional causal action it must cause the bodily movements involved, and if anything is to cause a bodily movement it must itself be some form of physical action. Hence if desires and beliefs are such causes they must be identical with physical occurrences. This conclusion is not necessary on a strictly Humean view of causation. If there is no more to one event's causing another than the first's being regularly attended by the second, the causes of physical events need not be physical. Those, however, who hold reasons to be causes are happy to accept some version of physicalism. Davidson argues that if one event causes a second there must be a general causal law to the effect that events of some type to which the first belongs cause events of some type to which the second belongs. He also argues that there can be no psycho-physical laws. Since every mental event is the cause or effect of some physical event (this is an assumption or postulate), it follows that every mental event must be of a type which can be dealt with by some physical law; and hence it must be physical (1980, pp. 223–4).

Peacocke (1979, pp. 134–6) similarly assumes that mental events cause physical events (such as changes in limb-positions). He argues for an identity of mental and physical events as follows:

1 When a mental event $C\,\psi$ causes a movement of my hand e there is a physical event in my brain $C\,\phi$ simultaneous with $C\,\psi$ which causes e.
2 'We have a complete and wholly physical account of . . . the causal antecedents of $C\,\phi$'.
3 Hence if $C\,\phi$ is not identical with $C\,\psi$, e is over-determined.
4 But in that case e would have occurred even without $C\,\psi$, which 'we ordinarily take to be false'.
5 So '$C\,\psi = C\,\phi$'.

This argument differs from Davidson's in relying on considerations about over-determination, not on considerations about causal laws. No doubt further arguments could be produced too, and it seems undeniable (given a robust view of causality) that if reasons are causes, beliefs and desires must be identical with physical events.

I am concerned here only with the notion of a reason and not with the truth of the identity theory; I think it worthwhile, however, to point out that there are two alternatives to making reasons causes. One entails a different version of physicalism, the other is consistent with a rejection of physicalism.

In *Linguistic Behaviour* (1964) Jonathan Bennett suggests that desire and belief may be viewed as special cases of having a goal and what he calls 'registration'. Roughly speaking fB is a goal of A if A is so constructed that for any circumstance c and any change $\emptyset$ (both within certain ranges), if c renders it necessary for A to $\emptyset$ if B is to become f, then c causes A to $\emptyset$. For instance suppose A is a launched rocket with a radar screen, and B is an aeroplane which appears on the screen. If movements of B cause changes in A's radar screen which in turn cause A to undergo such changes in direction as are necessary for A to hit B, then hitting B is a goal of A. The suggestion is that my desiring, say, to get to Paris would be a special case of having arrival in Paris as a goal. One of its peculiarities is that the circumstances which are to cause changes in me which result in my getting to Paris do so not through affecting a radar screen (I am not equipped with radar) but through affecting my brain via my sense-organs.

Registration is to be explained in terms of goals. If fB is a goal of A, and the circumstance that p renders gA necessary for fB, and this circumstance causes A to become g in the appropriate way (there is no 'deviance' in the causal process), A *registers* that p. If the aeroplane B moves to the left, and this change causes a change in the radar screen in A, and thereby makes A turn to the left, A registers the movement of B. A can also be said to register a leftward movement of B if something else, say the leftward movement of a flock of wild geese C, affects A's screen as B's movement would have done with the same result. Perceiving that p or coming to believe that p can then be understood as a special case of registering that p. I register that train T goes to Dover if (1) getting to Paris is a goal of mine; (2) if T goes to Dover, my taking it is necessary for (conducive to) my getting to Paris; (3) I am caused to board it by a brain-event which could have been caused (or which actually is caused) by stimulation of my eye by a notice on T saying 'Dover'. If my boarding T is so caused I may also be said to take T for the reason that it goes to Dover and for the purpose of getting to Paris.

If this account is on the right lines we can say that all my bodily movements are causally determined by a chain of prior physical events, and that I act intentionally insofar as I act for reasons and purposes, without saying that reasons and purposes or beliefs and desires are causes. Indeed, to say that wanting (or even coming to want) is a cause of behaviour will be inaccurate and misleading. It will not be illegitimate to say that acquiring the belief that p is the brain-event involved in registering that p, and that this event causes the behaviour which is for the reason that p; but there will be little point in saying this since the brain event is the acquiring of a belief only given the rest of the believer's structure and his goals. If we want to hold a physicalist view of man, I think it is better to interpret $TfB\emptyset A$ and $Rp\emptyset A$ along Bennett's lines than to say simply that A's $\emptyset$ing is caused by the desire for fB or the belief that p.

If, in contrast, we wish to leave it open whether physicalism is true, we may start by saying that the notions of desire and belief are notions of explanatory roles: I desire fB if it functions as an objective in my behaviour, and I believe that p if it functions as a reason. So far, the account is not very different from Bennett's. But instead of offering his causal analysis of $TfB\emptyset A$ and $Rp\emptyset A$ we say that these are explanations of a radically different kind. Whereas a causal explanation of the form 'because p, A $\emptyset$s' explains A's $\emptyset$ing by exhibiting it as necessary or inevitable, an explanation of A's $\emptyset$ing by means of a reason or purpose explains it by enabling it to be seen as voluntary, or intentional. This seems to be Aristotle's view. Peacocke objects by asking 'How can "explanation" be univocal in the two cases?' (1979, pp. 166-8). It is fairly clear that Aristotle does not suppose it is: his term 'aition', 'responsible factor', is not meant to apply univocally to the four kinds of thing which, he claims, can be held responsible for, or given in explanation of, explananda. Neither, however, does it seem to be used in either of the two other non-equivocal ways he distinguishes. It is not used 'by analogy' as 'matter' and 'form' are used of analogous elements in material objects; neither is it like 'healthy' applied to things (pinkness in the cheeks, appetites, modes of exercise, people) which are all related, though in different ways, to some single thing. Perhaps, however, we can say it is used by virtue of Wittgensteinian Family Resemblance. There are many connections between the various kinds of explanation and understanding, severally too slight but jointly sufficient to justify the use of the same word. At any rate, I do not think Peacocke's objection need stop anyone from holding that the relation of reasons and purposes to intentional action is sui generis and irreducible to any complex causal relation.

7

Davidson and his Critics

I

Donald Davidson in 'How Is Weakness of Will Possible?' (1980) represents the problem as arising from desire to maintain three principles
each of which is plausible when taken by itself but which taken together
appear inconsistent. They are:

P1   If an agent wants to do x more than he wants to do y and he believes himself
free to do either x or y, then he will intentionally do x if he does either x or y
intentionally.

P2   If an agent judges that it would be better to do x than to do y, then he wants
to do x more than he wants to do y.

P3   There are incontinent actions.

An incontinent (that is, akratic) action is defined:

D   In doing x an agent acts incontinently if and only if:
    (a)   the agent does x intentionally;
    (b)   the agent believes there is an alternative action y open to him; *and*
    (c)   the agent judges that, all things considered, it would be better to do y
than to do x.

This definition does not fit 'precipitate' akratic action very well, but it
fits apparently clear-eyed akrasia.

To get the problem off the ground we must suppose that the agent in
P1 believes he can do either x or y but not both; otherwise we may expect
him to do whichever is more convenient. Suppose I think that it would
be pleasant to kiss Amanda, but that my long-term happiness lies in
marrying Sophia. I want to marry Sophia more than to kiss Amanda,
but my best plan (as a temperate man) is first to kiss Amanda and then
to marry Sophia. This complication does not arise, of course, if x and y

are Øing and not Øing, and it might have been better to formulate P1 and P2 in terms of such alternatives.

Davidson's solution to the problem turns on a distinction between judging a course prima facie right (or prima facie better than an alternative) and judging it right (better than an alternative) absolutely or sansphrase (1980, p. 40). To put his view in the terms we have been using, he thinks a practical reason for Øing is something which renders Øing prima facie right, prima facie better than not Øing. It is fairly obvious that if a course is to be judged prima facie right the judgement must be relative to some circumstance which is a reason for it (or, as philosophers sometimes say, 'in favour' of it); it will be prima facie right given this reason. But Davidson also wants to hold the converse, that if a course is judged right relatively to a reason or set of reasons, it can be judged right only prima facie. Given this contentious converse, Davidson can maintain that his triad of principles is not, after all, inconsistent. The judgements of what is best in P2 are judgements of what is best sans phrase. The most, then, that can follow from P1 and P2 is that if A Øs intentionally A thinks that Øing is better than not Øing sans phrase. On the other hand A acts akratically only if he does something thinking that he could refrain and that it would be better *all things considered* if he refrained. His judgement that it would be better to refrain all things considered is precisely a judgement relative to everything he thinks relevant to the decision. Hence it is only prima facie. There is (says Davidson) no inconsistency between claiming that A thinks it better, relatively to all apparently relevant facts, not to Ø than to Ø, and claiming A thinks it is better absolutely to Ø than not to Ø.

In such a case there is, of course, something wrong with A's state of mind. What is wrong with it, however, is not that it is logically impossible. It is not logically impossible even that both of A's thoughts should be true. It might be better to Ø and at the same time all the relevant facts known to A might on balance favour not Øing. The trouble is that for A to believe that it is better to Ø when all the facts known to him favour not Øing is unreasonable or irrational.

A great merit of Davidson's discussion is that it is the first to focus attention on the notion of the prima facie in practical thinking. This notion is of central importance both to the moral philosopher and to the philosopher of action. Moral philosophers are inclined to think that if we cannot establish to everyone's satisfaction that particular actions are right or wrong, moral judgement must be irredeemably subjective; and conversely that if ethical subjectivism is false it must be possible to establish what is the best course in every concrete situation. In fact it is seldom hard to establish (at least to the satisfaction of members of one's own society) that a given circumstance is a reason pro or con a line of action and hence renders the course prima facie right or wrong; what is disputable is whether it is right or wrong sans phrase. Moral philosophers also (witness Hare) tend to think that general moral principles purport to determine what is absolutely right and wrong, and not just right or wrong prima facie. The result in the philosophy of action is that not only weakness of will but the whole phenomenon of moral conflict appears puzzling. In ordinary life it constantly happens that we have reasons pro and con the same course of action. To shed light on our predicament the philosopher must study the logical form of prima facie judgements and the logical relations between, say, the judgement that a promise to dine with a friend tells in favour of going and the judgement that an attack of migraine tells against. I shall consider work in this area by Davidson and others before trying to decide if he shows that clear-eyed akrasia is possible.

The term 'prima facie' was given a technical use in ethics by W. D. Ross in *The Right and the Good* (1930). Ross holds that what I earlier called 'social' relationships and also certain other factors give rise to prima facie duties which are:

> more or less incumbent on me according to the circumstances of the case. When I am in a situation, as perhaps I always am, in which more than one of these prima facie duties is incumbent on me, what I have to do is study the situation as fully as I can until I form the considered opinion (it is never more) that in the circumstances one of them is more incumbent than any other; then I am bound to think that to do this *prima facie* duty is my duty *sans phrase* in the situation. (p. 19)

Ross notes that the phrase 'prima facie' could be misleading. The claim that I have a prima facie duty to $\emptyset$ sounds like a tentative claim, a claim which I may have to abandon, that I have a full-blooded duty to $\emptyset$. In fact Ross wants it to be understood as a firm claim that I have a sort of half-blooded duty to $\emptyset$. It is not like the hesitant 'He may be a clever man but he looks a bit of a fool'; rather it is like the warning 'He looks a bit of a fool but he is in fact an extremely clever man'. As Ross puts it (1930, p. 20) 'What I am speaking of [when I speak of a prima facie duty] is an objective fact involved in the nature of the situation.'

Ross yields to no one as an Aristotelian scholar, and although he does not father his theory on Aristotle, it has an obvious resemblance to

Aristotle's. Aristotle has no word which corresponds to Ross's word 'duty', but he follows Plato (see especially *Statesman* 294 a–b) in holding that no general rule can tell us what we ought to do in every particular case. Modern aestheticians sometimes write as if it were a peculiarity of the fine arts that success cannot be achieved by blind adherence to rules; the Kantian idea lingers on that what is morally best is acting out of respect for moral principles. Aristotle says:

> There is nothing stable in the field of conduct or in what is advantageous, any more than in the field of medicine. And such being the position with universal principles, still less do principles concerning particular cases admit of exactness. Particular cases fall under no art or set of rules. The persons acting at any time must look to what fits the occasion, as in medicine and seamanship. (*EN* II.1104ª3–10).

Aristotle would hold, then, that a general principle of conduct can establish at best a prima facie rightness and wrongness; and the same must go, of course, for any particular circumstance that is a practical reason.

On how the 'persons acting at the time' are to weigh up the various reasons pro and con, Ross is content to quote Aristotle's tantalizingly brief statement elsewhere that 'perception must decide' (1930, p. 42) – perception here being not a sensory ability but the intellectual ability distinctive of men of prudence or practical wisdom. Whether we can improve on this we shall see later; for the moment we should try to understand prima facie rightness and wrongness by themselves.

Bernard Williams (1965/1973, p. 180) states what he calls the 'agglomeration principle' for ought-propositions as follows:

> 'I ought to do *a*' and 'I ought to do *b*' together imply 'I ought to do *a* and *b*'.

He observes that we get into difficulties if we accept both this principle and the principle that 'ought' implies 'can', since where a pair of practical principles conflict an agent will have grounds for judging both that he ought to ∅ and that he ought to refrain from ∅ing. Clearly it is not the case that he can do both. Williams recommends loosening the agglomeration principle, but he does not say exactly how or when. Neither does he distinguish between prima facie and absolute oughts. It seems to me that we are very strongly inclined to hold absolute oughts to be absolutely agglomerative. Prima facie oughts we take to be defeasibly agglomerative, agglomerative unless there is some reason (for instance that they cannot both be carried out) for thinking they are not. Those who think 'Before going to bed I should clean my teeth' and 'Before going to bed I should say my prayers' have no hesitation in inferring 'Before going to bed I should clean my teeth and say my prayers'. Williams might wish to maintain that even absolute oughts are only defeasibly agglomerative. If, however, I ought absolutely to $\emptyset$, there is a strong case for saying that I ought to $\emptyset$ all things considered. Now suppose it appears that all things considered I ought to $\emptyset$, and it also appears that all things considered I ought to ψ; suppose then it turns out that I cannot do both. What this shows is not, as Williams puts it, the weakness of the agglomeration principle; rather it shows that not everything has been considered, and at least one of the courses is not, all things considered, a course I should pursue.

Davidson compares judgements of prima facie rightness with judgements of probability. To stay with his examples, the general practical principles (1) if an act is one of fornication it is unlawful and (2) if an act is pleasant it is to be done, are analogous to (3) if the barometer falls, that it will rain is probable and (4) if there is red sky at night, that it will not rain is probable. From (3) or (4) and the fulfilment of the antecedent we cannot infer the detached consequent 'It will probably rain' or 'It will probably not rain', since it might happen that both antecedents are fulfilled: the evening sky might redden to a falling barometer. Similarly from (1) or (2) and the fulfilment of the antecedent we cannot infer that the act should be shunned or carried out.

Davidson suggests that we get these faulty inferences if we treat 'is probable' or 'is to be done' as signifying a property of events. Elsewhere Davidson is friendly to properties of events, but not here. 'If the barometer falls, that it will rain is probable' should not be taken to be of the form:

$p \rightarrow$ an R-type event is f.

Instead these linguistic items 'probable', 'good', 'evil', etc. are to be construed as combining with and modifying the sentential connectives. 'If the barometer falls, it will probably rain' is of the form:

That p makes-it-probable-that q

or

$pr\,(Rx,\ Fx)$

i.e. there being a falling barometer at spatio-temporal region x 'probabilizes' (Davidson's word) there being rain at x. Similarly "'Lying is (prima facie) wrong" . . . should be recognised to mean something like 'That an act is a lie prima facie makes it wrong"; in symbols "$pf(Wx, Lx)$".' Since $pr(Rx, Fx)$ means 'That x is F makes-it-probable-that x is R', $pf(Wx, Lx)$ ought to mean 'That x is L makes-it-prima-facie-that x is W'. The notion of rendering-prima-facie is one to which we shall return, but we may note here that Davidson does not seem to envisage it as applying to all values of p. Nothing makes it prima facie that Mars is red. He interprets general practical principles as involving a comparison: not between two positive courses of action ($\emptyset$ing and ψing) but between pursuing and not pursuing a course ($\emptyset$ing and not $\emptyset$ing). To say that lying is (prima facie) wrong is to say that the circumstance that x is lying and y is refraining from lying makes-it-prima-facie-that y is better than x.

Treating practical judgements in this way Davidson avoids the difficulties of agglomeration. From the premises:

1 $\emptyset$ing's being pleasant makes it prima facie better to $\emptyset$
2 $\emptyset$ing's being fornication makes it prima facie better not to $\emptyset$

we cannot infer that anything makes it even prima facie good both to $\emptyset$ and not to $\emptyset$. As regards the judgement that $\emptyset$ing is better all things considered, Davidson holds that this is the judgement: 'That p makes it better to $\emptyset$ than not to $\emptyset$' where p is the conjunction of all propositions which the agent judges to be both true and relevant (1980, p. 38). I shall discuss difficulties about this later, but first, what should we make of the rest of Davidson's account?

To a large extent Davidson is anticipated by Roderick Chisholm in 'The Ethics of Requirement' (1964; a revised version of the paper (1974) appears as 'The Logic of Requirement' in *Practical Reason*, ed. S. Körner). Chisholm uses a primitive notion of requirement according to which moral rules can take the form 'p, if it obtained, would require q', 'pRq' (e.g. 'someone's having promised to $\emptyset$ would require his $\emptyset$ing'). 'p does require q' is then taken to mean 'pRq and p obtains'. If p requires my $\emptyset$ing, I have a prima facie duty to $\emptyset$, and if p requires my $\emptyset$ing and nothing overrides it I have an absolute duty, a Rossian duty proper, to $\emptyset$ (1974, p. 13, cf. 1964, p. 149). Chisholm compares requiring to confirming: p confirms q if p would confirm q and p. Corresponding to the notion of absolute duty, or rather of what ought, sans phrase, to obtain, is the 'absolute probability' of a proposition, 'the probability which the proposition has in relation to the totality of those propositions which the person knows to be true' (1964, p. 149).

Peacocke (1985, pp. 55–62) challenges Davidson's parallel. He claims that pf in $pf(A$ is better than B, $E)$ is a mere relativization device, the content of the practical judgement being carried by the relativized clause 'A is better than B'; $pf(A$ is better than B, $E)$ says no more than that, relatively to E, A is better than B. In $pr(p, q)$, in contrast, pr is not a mere relativization device but carries a content of its own: $pr(p, q)$ says not just that relatively to q, p, but that relatively to q, p is probable. If Davidson wants a genuine parallel between practical judgements and judgements of probability, he should use the ternary operators btr (—is better than—relatively to—) and $morepr$ (—is more probable than—relatively to—). But then what corresponds to the all-out practical judgement 'It is better to $\emptyset$' will be a judgement of probability like 'It will probably rain' or 'It will more probably rain than not', not, as Davidson wishes, a straightforward judgement like 'It will rain'.

This conclusion would not disturb Chisholm since, as we have just seen, Chisholm accepts that the analogue of a judgement of absolute duty is a judgement of absolute probability. Davidson seems to imply the same in his original paper – he discusses the unrelativized judgement 'It will almost certainly rain' – and Charles (1982/3, p. 193) assumes it is what he means. His reply to Peacocke, however, shows that Peacocke has read his intention correctly. He insists that when all available evidence supports the hypothesis that p we should conclude not just that it is probable but that it is true that p (Davidson, 1985, p. 208).

Davidson may be right here, but Peacocke is equally right that his original parallel was faulty. If there is to be a true parallel between theoretical and practical thinking, and probability is to be eliminated from the content of the theoretical conclusion, goodness must be eliminated from the content of the practical conclusion. Peacocke suggests a way of doing this. Instead of:

$pf(\emptyset$ing is better than not $\emptyset$ing, $p)$

we can say

that p is a circumstance in favour of $\emptyset$ing

or, in his notation,

fav (I $\emptyset$, p).

This notion of favouring is a variant on Chisholm's notion of requiring.

fav (I $\emptyset$, p)

is then analogous to

$pr(q, p)$.

When p is the totality of relevant factors, the theoretical thinker moves to q ('It will rain') and the practical thinker to I $\emptyset$ ('I'll take an umbrella').

Since one of the most attractive features of Davidson's original account was that it promised to take moral concepts out of the content of practical thinking and put them into its form, we might expect him to welcome this proposal. In fact he dismisses it as 'a bad pun' (1985, p. 209). His objection seems to be that there is no analogy between the way in which a circumstance can tell in favour of a proposition and the way in which it can tell in favour of a course of action. I do not, however, see any other method of developing the parallel he wants. He might prefer

$pf(\emptyset$ing is better than not $\emptyset$ing)

to be understood as

that p renders-it-prima-facie-true-that $\emptyset$ing is better than not $\emptyset$ing.

But what is the content of this prima-facie-true proposition? That is a question which Davidson seems particularly ill-placed to answer since he holds that on occasion it is sufficient for the truth of 'A thinks it is best to $\emptyset$' that A $\emptyset$s intentionally.

Susan Hurley (1985/6) offers a different alternative to Davidson's account. Where that p is a practical reason for $\emptyset$ing, Davidson says that $\emptyset$ing is good relatively to p. So, in effect, say Chisholm and Peacocke. These relativized judgements are not subject to agglomeration because they are relativized to different circumstances. Hurley suggests that instead we might distinguish different kinds of reason. For the relativizer, though infinitely many different circumstances can constitute reasons, they may all be reasons of the same general kind, rendering a course good or bad in the same way. That Antiochus is passionate but considerate and that you promised to sleep with him are different reasons for sleeping with him but may make sleeping with him good in the same way; that he is your father and that he has AIDS are different reasons against, but may make sleeping with him bad in the same way. Hurley suggests that different kinds of reason make courses good or bad in different ways. Antiochus' diseases make sleeping with him unhealthy or, more generally, imprudent; his relationship to you make it contrary to a negative duty, since in Shakespearean society the relationship being a child of carries with it the duty to refrain from sexual intercourse with. Hurley calls this strategy with practical judgement 'indexation'. Her idea is that different kinds of rightness and wrongness might be indexed. That a prisoner is innocent renders it right/just to release him; that a mob is assembled to lynch him renders releasing him wrong/unkind. Where the relativizer says that agglomeration is dispensable for conclusions relativized to different reasons, Hurley says it is dispensable for conclusions with different indices, such as 'To keep him locked up would be unjust', 'Not to keep him locked up would be unkind'.

There are several differences between indexing and relativizing. First, an indexed conclusion seems to be more than prima facie. If a prisoner's being innocent makes it unjust to detain him, and this prisoner is innocent, it is not prima facie but genuinely unjust to detain him, and that remains true even if to release him is to ensure his death at the hands of the mob. And if detaining him is unjust, it is, as Hurley puts it, pro tanto wrong. Indexation allows us to detach conclusions in a way relativization does not. From this Hurley infers that the indexing treatment of practical judgement accounts for akrasia better than relativizing. Since indexed conclusions are detachable, we can understand the sheriff's releasing the innocent prisoner even when his all-things-considered judgement is that it would be best to keep him in jail. If the sheriff merely thinks that the prisoner's innocence renders it prima facie good to release him, while his innocence and the behaviour of the mob between them make it prima-facie good to keep him safely behind bars, it is a mystery how the less inclusive judgement comes to operate, especially, as Hurley emphasizes, because nothing comparable happens in thought about probabilities. If I think that red sky at night means no rain, but red sky at night plus a falling glass mean abundant rain, I cannot, for the reason that there is a red sky and in spite of the fact that there is a falling glass, conclude 'It will not rain'.

On these matters I find Hurley persuasive. She has some further remarks about agglomeration which seem to me more doubtful. 'The agglomeration principle,' she says (1985/6, p. 26), 'would hold for each kind of reason . . . If justice requires that p and justice requires that q, justice requires that p and q'. This could run into difficulties. Filial piety requires that I obey my father and filial piety requires that I obey my mother; what if, as so commonly happens, they give me conflicting orders? What if compassion requires me to relieve the distress of A, and compassion requires me to relieve the distress of B, but I have means to relieve only one? Hurley also suggests that since agglomeration does not hold 'across different kinds of reasons' (p. 26) there can be genuine conflict – as it might be between justice and mercy. Certainly there can be the detached conclusions 'Øing would be just', 'Not Øing would be merciful', and it would be incorrect to say that Øing is only prima facie just or not Øing prima facie merciful. But as Chisholm (1974, p. 15) says, it is 'intolerable' to think that it might be the case that I ought both to Ø and not to Ø all things considered, or that I have an absolute duty both to act and to refrain. In Ross's usage where prima facie rightness is 'an objective fact' one of the courses is only prima facie right. Hurley uses 'prima facie' in the way in which Ross says he is *not* using it, and hence exaggerates the difference between the prima facie and the pro tanto. The absolutely just or unkind is the pro tanto good or bad, but the pro tanto good or bad is just what Ross would describe as prima facie the course to be embraced or shunned.

Hurley's theory of indexation should be regarded less as a rival to the Chisholm–Davidson theory than as a development of it. If we recognize that the notion of goodness is not unitary, that there are different ways in which a course can be good, it is natural to say that different practical reasons render good in different ways. The sorts of reason distinguished in chapter 6 are more different than Hurley's reasons pertaining to different virtues, and insofar as they function in logically different ways they call out for different indices. Consider, for example, the circumstance that the flask contains wine. That is a reason (advantageous) to Stephano for drinking; a reason (necessary) to Laius, the driver, for not drinking; a reason (friendly) to Sidney for giving it to a thirsty man nearby; and a (technical) reason to Pedro for giving it to Osmin once he has adopted the goal of causing Osmin to become drunk.

II

Davidson's solution to the problem 'How is weakness of will possible' is that the judgement that it is best not to Ø, all things considered, is still only prima facie, and that there is no logical or psychological impossibility in holding it along with the judgement that it is best to $\emptyset$ sans phrase. Few philosophers have accepted this solution.

One difficulty is pointed out by Michael Bratman (1979, p. 160) and Ismay Barwell and Kathleen Lennon (1982/3, pp. 28–9). According to Davidson the akrates should think it best sans phrase to do what he does; but if asked, he would sincerely disavow any such judgement.

Another difficulty is this. Davidson seems to take an all-things-considered judgement to be of the following form:

$pf(a$ is better than $b, e)$

'where e is all the relevant considerations known to us' (1980, p. 38) As I said earlier, I construe e as the conjunction of all propositions believed to be both true and relevant by the agent ('us'). An all-things-considered judgement cannot be no more than this. Suppose that on a train I see a lady who is a complete stranger to me. It may well be that the only fact I know about her relevant to proposing marriage to her is that she is pretty. This fact is in favour of proposing. Nevertheless I do not think it best to propose all things considered, since the totality of the information at my disposal is far too little to warrant such a step. If I am to think it best, all things considered, to $\emptyset$ I must think not merely that all the facts known to me on balance favour $\emptyset$ing but that they collectively warrant $\emptyset$ing or even demand it. What does this further condition involve? I must think either that the facts make it best to judge, without further enquiry, that it is best sans phrase to $\emptyset$, or simply that they make it best to $\emptyset$ without further enquiry. In either case it seems I must judge that it is best sans phrase to $\emptyset$. Hence the judgement, say, that it is better all things considered not to elope with Helen is not compatible with an 'all out' judgement that it is best to elope.

What a musicologist might describe as an ornamented version of this argument is put forward in Paul Grice and Judith Baker (1985). In his reply (1985) Davidson restates his understanding of what it is to make an all-things-considered judgement. I judge that a is better than b all things considered if I think (1) if r were the case it would make it prima facie true that a is better than b; (2) r is in fact the case; and (3) r is 'all the reasons that are relevant' (p. 205). Davidson does not give an example, but he might accept the following. Paris judges it better not to elope with Helen all things considered if he thinks (1) if it were the case that (i) Helen marvellously resembled the immortal gods (ii) she were married to a powerful and jealous king (iii) I were a prince on a diplomatic mission, then relatively to (i), (ii) and (iii) it would be better not to elope; (2) (i), (ii) and (iii) are true; (3) (i), (ii) and (iii) are the only relevant facts (or the only ones known to me now). Davidson then says that an agent can fail to pursue a course 'all the relevant reasons support' just as a theoretical thinker, in breach of the principles of Hempel and Carnap, can fail to accept a hypothesis all the relevant evidence supports. This reply fails to take account of the point made above. To be a clear-eyed akrates, Paris must think it better to elope even though (i), (ii) and (iii) *demand* the conclusion that it is better not. The theoretical analogy would be refusing to accept a hypothesis when you think not just that the evidence supports it but that the evidence makes it irrational not to accept it.

A number of philosophers, among the latest of whom is Mele (1987), have argued that there can be 'doxastic incontinence'. Mele offers the following characterization:

> In believing that P during t, S exhibits strict doxastic incontinence if and only if the belief is motivated and free* and during t, S consciously holds a judgment to the effect that there is good and sufficient reason for his not believing that P. (p. 112)

Mele is unwilling to say exactly what it is for a belief of S to be 'free*' but apparently it is unfree* to the extent that he cannot help having it. As for the judgement 'to the effect that there is good and sufficient reason', this may, but need not, be based simply on evidential considerations. Mele points out that I may judge that the evidence available would warrant a certain belief, but that other considerations make it better for me not to accept that belief. A lady, for example, may think that there is strong evidence that her husband is unfaithful, but that she will be better off if she does not believe that he is. Mele says that if she then can and does refrain from believing her husband unfaithful she may be 'epistemically irresponsible' but she is not doxastically incontinent; on the contrary, she is incontinent if, though able to refrain, she believes that her husband is unfaithful and this belief is motivated by 'attraction to (apparent) truth' (p. 119). (This being so, Mele is able to hold, as he wishes, that akratic belief is not identical with self-deception.) Paraphrasing Davidson, then, we may say that I believe akratically that p if and only if (a) my belief that p is motivated, (b) I am able (Davidson would prefer to say I believe I am able) not to believe that p, (c) I judge that all things considered it would be better not to believe that p (or even to believe that not-p).

Mele argues that this kind of akratic belief can really occur. Might

Davidson take advantage of this conclusion and say that Paris judges that all things considered it would be better for him to judge that it would be better not to elope, but then akratically goes on to judge it is better to elope? A critic of Mele's theory of akratic belief might probe the issue of how far a person really can be able both to believe something and not to believe it. Let us grant, however, that akratic belief is possible in the cases Mele considers; these are not cases of thinking some course of action good or bad. The wife is not, say, judging that all things considered it is better for her to judge that she ought to refrain from reading her husband's letters, and then going on akratically to judge that she ought to read them. If she judges that her husband is unfaithful there is no particular course it is reasonable for her to pursue then and there, and neither is there any particular course to be pursued or shunned if she judges he is not unfaithful. Mele does not discuss the possibility of judging it best to judge it best not to $\emptyset$ and then akratically judging it best to $\emptyset$. There may be good reason for this omission. So long as an issue is theoretical a case can be made out for distinguishing the judgement 'I ought to conclude that p' from the judgement 'p'. But it seems artificial to distinguish 'I ought to judge that I ought to $\emptyset$' from 'I ought to $\emptyset$'. The judgement about a practical judgement seems to collapse into the practical judgement itself.

I think that we can distinguish between judging that it would be best to judge that p and judging that p in the theoretical sphere because judging and not judging theoretically are not within our power. Practical judgement, on the other hand, is inseparable from action. That means that it is, in a way, in our power, and to judge that I ought to judge that I should refrain from drinking this wine is eo ipso to judge that I ought to refrain.

III

Davidson fails to show that his P3 is compatible with P1 and P2. Which, then, of these three propositions should we surrender? By far the most popular candidate for ejection from the balloon is P2, which is a simplified and generalized version of Santas's value-strength principle (p. 51 above). Audi (1979), Taylor (1980), Charles (1984, ch. 4) and Mele (1983, 1987) are only four among many who maintain that it is all too easy to think it better to do x than to do y, but have a stronger desire to do y; and who use the possibility of a gap between judging better and wanting more both to defend the possibility and to explain the occurrence of completely clear-eyed akrasia.

The usual way of attacking P2 is to construct imaginary counterexamples. Audi and Taylor gives us scrupulous adulterers; Mele refreshingly provides a case of malakia: a biology student who needs some blood for an experiment and thinks it would be best to prick his finger, but is strongly motivated not to and refrains. But such examples, however *vraisemblable*, have no probative value until it is clear what is meant by 'stronger', 'greater motivational force' or 'wanting more'. There seem to be at least three possibilities, though individual modern champions of akrasia seldom get beyond noting two.

First, we can take the strength of a desire as a kind of introspectible quality of it, a phenomenologically felt violence or intensity (cf. Wiggins 1978/9, p. 257). If 'stronger' means 'more intense', P2 is manifestly false. The tropical explorer's desire to scratch an insect-bite is more intense than his desire to refrain, even though he knows that scratching will lead to ulceration and therefore to more pain in the long run. Similarly with the angry man's desire to retaliate at a moment at which he knows it is best to defer revenge. Equally P1 is false if 'wants more' is interpreted in this way.

Secondly we can say that the stronger desire is the desire which actually prevails, the desire on which the agent acts. If the explorer refrains from scratching his bites, his desire to refrain will eo ipso be stronger, in this sense, than his desire to scratch. If we use 'stronger' in this way we rule out any measuring of the strength of desires independently of how the agent acts, and the notion of a desire's strength therefore ceases to have any explanatory power. P2 becomes the principle that agents *do* what seems most advantageous – in other words (see below p. 136) that they behave rationally. Against this elimination of desire as an explanatory factor it might be objected that sometimes we think a desire ought to have prevailed, and would have prevailed but for some kind of accident. Cassio's desire to stay sober was really stronger than his desire for drink and would have prevailed but for the intervention of Iago. But we can still make this point by means of a counterfactual simply about action. Cassio would not have become drunk if Iago had not put forward all his wiles.

Third, suppose I think I ought to get a new vacuum cleaner; and suppose that (persuaded by Our Man in Havana) I judge that a Phastclean is cheaper, sturdier and more efficient than a Nuclean. Then I think it would be better to buy a Phastclean, and I can properly be said to *want* to buy a Phastclean *more* than a Nuclean. In this sort of case the strength of an agent's desire is determined by his value-judgement (so that P2 is analytic), not by what he does; though there is a logical presumption (in the absence of any other reasons or motives) that the stronger desire will prevail if either does: I buy a Phastclean and not a Nuclean if I buy either.

Both Santas and a number of other scholars seem to think the Greeks confused these senses of 'stronger'. The Greeks supposed, allegedly, that if an agent thinks one course more advantageous than a second he desires more intensely to pursue it, and also that the more intense desire prevails. It is true that the different ways of being stronger are not distinguished in the *Meno* or *Protagoras*. But I think it is difficult to atttribute confusions about them to the later Plato or to Aristotle. In the *Philebus* Plato distinguishes pure from impure or 'mixed' pleasures, and says the latter are more violent or intense than the former (52 c, 47 a); the same holds, surely, for the desires for them; and in the *Republic* IX.577 he denies that people always act rationally or that the desire to do what is most advantageous always prevails. We have seen that Aristotle distinguishes epithumia, a mode of desire which is more or less intense or violent, from boulesis which like Hume's 'calm passions' need have no felt intensity; and that he says that sometimes one prevails and sometimes the other (1224^a24–30).

Neil Cooper (1968, p. 151) suggests a more subtle confusion. 'If I think that I morally ought to do *A*' (he might have added 'or that it is best all things considered to do *A*'), then: 'I think that I ought to-do-*A*-preference-to-anything-else and hence I must want, in the minimal sense of ''want'', to-do-*A*-in-preference-to-anything-else'; but 'it does not follow from this that I must want to do *A* more intensely than I want to do anything else'. The belief that clear-eyed akrasia is impossible might result from failing to see that this does not follow; it might result from failing to distinguish between having a desire (of unspecified strength) to-refrain-form-$\emptyset$ing-rather-than-to-$\emptyset$, and having a desire to refrain from $\emptyset$ing which is stronger than your desire to $\emptyset$.

This is an ingenious suggestion, but I doubt if the distinction Cooper wants us to draw can be sustained. If I really loathe you I may have a desire to-rescue-someone-else-in-preference-to-you from drowning; I want you to see me, in your last struggle to stay afloat, preferring your worst enemy to you. But that is not thinking that I 'morally ought' to save your enemy or even that saving him in preference to you is best all things considered. I am normally said to want to $\emptyset$ in preference to anything else only if I want, more than anything else, to $\emptyset$. Whatever interpretation we choose for wanting more, if Ham wants to save Steerforth from drowning more than anything else then, in the corresponding sense of 'stronger', Ham's desire to save Steerforth is stronger than any other desire Ham has.

Those who think clear-eyed akrasia can occur mostly hope to explain it by saying that the agent is more strongly motivated to do the act he thinks bad than he is to refrain. They need, therefore, to maintain a version of P1: an agent does what he is most motivated to do. Once we distinguish the three interpretations of wanting more distinguished above, this looks a formidable task. On the first interpretation, P1 is false; on the second it is trivially true; and on the third, it rules out clear-eyed akrasia from the start. Since in his 1983 paper and his 1987 book Mele has proved himself one of the most determined and articulate of modern champions of akrasia, I shall concentrate on his handling of the difficulty.

In his 1983 paper he draws on Davidson's physicalism. The desire which in fact prevails is identical with some physical state which causes the action, and does so by virtue of some physical property (as yet unidentified by science). We can say that its motivational strength is identical with (or supervenient on) this physical property (p. 362). We can; but that will not license us to maintain, as a non-trivial truth, that the strongest desire prevails. If Davidson's physicalism is correct, if particular or 'token' mental states are identical with token physical states, it is probably true that

1   For any two desires x and y, if x prevails over y there is some physical state f such that x is more f than y.

But this is trivial. The f, the motivational strength, may be different in every case where one desire prevails over another, and hence the claim that the stronger desire prevails is vacuous. The simple converse of (1) namely:

2   For any x and y, if there is an f such that x is more f than y, x prevails over y

is false and leads to incoherence, since x and y will probably each have some property to a greater degree than the other. The interesting claim is:

3   There is some f such that for any x and y, if x is more f than y x prevails over y.

But that is not implied or even suggested by Davidson's physicalism. It is a theory of type-identity: the intensity of desire is represented as identical with the physical property f in all cases; and Davidson rejects type-identity (1980, Essay 11).

Mele's 1987 book reproduces most of his 1983 paper but omits the paragraph we have just been considering. Perhaps Mele has come to share my misgivings about it. Anyhow, he takes a different line. He points out various purely psychological factors which seem to contribute to the motivational force of a desire. Suppose I want to stop watching the television after lunch and resume my painting of a shed (Mele's example, p. 69). The strength of this desire, he says, depends on (a) the strengths of various supporting sub-desires, e.g. to make the shed weatherproof, to impress my family; (b) the strength of various contrary motives, e.g. my current enjoyment of the television, my aversion to the toil of painting; (c) cognitive factors such as the vividness with which I imagine the amazement of my family at seeing the shed finished, or their scorn at finding me still glued to the box. Further insight into these cognitive factors is provided when Mele proposes two ways of accounting for an agent's wanting more to pursue a course which he judges worse: (1) the benefits of this course are closer in time; and (2) it 'dominates' attention and is more 'salient' (pp. 84-7). Can considerations like these give enough content to the notion of motivational strength to allow Mele to put forward as a true empirical proposition. 'Of the courses he believes open to him, an agent will pursue the one to which he is most strongly motivated'?

The difficulty remains. In support of (1) and (2) Mele refers to experimental work by M. Miscel and E. Ebbeson, G. Ainslie and others. This work is based on what the experimental subjects actually do. Hence it can license conclusions only about when a desire is stronger by our second criterion, that is, about when it will prevail. There is no reason for thinking that desires prevail because they are 'motivationally stronger' rather than because the agent is led (perhaps irrationally) to think the desired course better. I shall, in fact, in chapter 8 appeal to similar experimental findings to show the possibility of explaining akrasia by a kind of intellectual failure.

If Mele does not see this difficulty it may be because beneath his urbane and sophisticated presentation there lurks a primitive philosophy of action. He says there might be 'desire-eradicating devices' which would enable us to get rid of unwanted desires by pressing a button (pp. 28, 56, cf. pp. 37-8). That suggests a Russellian conception of desires as non-cognitive feelings like headaches. If he also (forgetful of Hume, 1888, p. 418) thinks we always act on the most intense desire, then he will assume that any factor which changes the ability of a desire to prevail must affect its intensity (rather than the agent's valuation of alternatives). But whether or not this diagnosis hits the mark, it seems to me that the notion of motivational strength employed by Mele is a confusion of the first two notions of strength distinguished above.

Davidson's P2 is unsatisfactory as it stands (see also p. 51 above), but labouring its inadequacies does not show that or how akrasia is possible. What has emerged is that it is hard to find a notion of motivational strength which permits us to hold both that the strength of our desires determines what we do and that the strengths of two desires can be out of line with our evaluations of their objects. That leaves acting against the agent's best judgement at the moment of action as problematic as ever. But the friends of akrasia do not rely exclusively on demolishing P2.

Peacocke, as we saw, holds that an intention to $\emptyset$ is a disposition to $\emptyset$ (or to try to $\emptyset$) caused by a practical reason for $\emptyset$ing. He distinguishes two ways in which we may form such an intention: either we hold that some particular circumstance favours $\emptyset$ing, or we hold that the totality of circumstances on balance favours $\emptyset$ing. Paris, for example, might form the intention of abducting Helen because he thinks her charm will render sailing the Aegean with her pleasant, or he might form it because he thinks her charm, the strength of the walls of Troy, and the aversion of the Greeks to long sieges outweigh Menelaus' possessiveness and powerful connections, so that it is best all things considered to abduct. If his intention is caused by this latter belief it is formed rationally. If though he holds the latter belief, his intention is caused solely by the former, if the prudential considerations are causally inoperative (Peacocke, 1985, pp. 66–7) his behaviour may not be 100 per cent rational but at least it is not akratic. But if his intention is caused by the former belief and he also holds the belief (ineffective, alas, in intention-causing) that the totality of circumstances favours *not* abducting, then he sails off with Helen intentionally but akratically.

This account is hardly compatible with the conjunction of P1 and P2, but it does not of itself require us to reject P2. For all Peacocke says to the contrary, a weak-willed Paris might want to refrain more than to abduct, but (in defiance of P1) the belief that Helen's beauty is in favour of abduction might cause him to be disposed to try to lure her on board when the moment is ripe. The question, however, would then arise: 'Why does the belief that it would be better all things considered to refrain not cause an intention to refrain? If all-things- considered judgements can cause intentions, why does not this one?' The only plausible answer I can think of is that the belief 'Helen's beauty favours an abduction' is associated with a desire to abduct which has greater motivational strength than any desire associated with the all-things-considered judgement. But that answer brings us back to the standard explanation of akrasia; Peacocke's intentions are wheels with which nothing turns.

Pears (1984, ch. 8) distinguishes between what he calls 'weak' and 'strong' valuation. Weakly valuing an object or course is what is minimally required for wanting the object or wanting to pursue the course. If I want to $\emptyset$ I must think that there is something 'in favour' of $\emptyset$ing, and if I want x I must think there is something good about x. Strong valuation, which includes and may be exhausted by prudential and 'moral' valuation, is 'based on one's long-term interests or perhaps on other people's interests' (p. 196). Pears allows that the backward connection holds for weak valuation, but denies it holds for strong. I can $\emptyset$ intentionally without thinking that $\emptyset$ing is either morally or prudentially better than not $\emptyset$ing. That is what happens when I $\emptyset$ akratically. Drinking at the wedding, I neither withdraw nor forget my judgement that three glasses of champagne are too many for safety. But desire to drink can still move me to accept a third glass, and in accepting I act akratically: the desire issues in action without 'passing through the check-point of reason' at all. Insofar as my behaviour needs explanation, Pears wants to explain it in terms of a kind of salience, and by comparing it with misperceiving. An ornithologist sees a bird fly past at high speed, and misclassifies it as a falcon although it is not the shape of a falcon because it flies fast, and its speed is more salient than its shape. Where the ornithologist is trying to produce a state of mind, a belief, which corresponds to the external world, the flying bird, the bibulous motorist is trying to produce action in the world which corresponds to his own internal state of mind, his practical thinking. He does the wrong thing, takes the third glass, because the desire to drink is the salient part of that internal state.

This account does not involve an explicit rejection of P2. Rather it calls in question P1. Prudential considerations lead the wedding guest to desire not to drink. If he then drinks, presumably the desire to drink has some motivational strength. But if it bypasses the check-point of reason, it does not have to be any stronger than the desire to refrain. But is it really possible for the check-point to be bypassed?

Pears claims that I can Ø intentionally without strongly valuing Øing in three cases. First, where there is no scope for strong valuation, no serious prudential or moral reasons in favour either of acting or of refraining. For example 'someone walking along a beach sees what may be the keel of a surf-board or a dead fish and curiosity leads him to go and find out which it is' (1984, p. 205). Sometimes we act idly or on a whim, and there is then no strong valuation. Secondly we may have equally strong prudential or moral reasons for two incompatible courses. In such a Buridan's Ass situation we pick one course without strongly valuing it above the other. Thirdly there are cases of clear-eyed akrasia. Pears argues that since in the first kind of case, at least, a desire to Ø can lead to Øing without any judgement on moral or prudential grounds that Øing is good or even permissible, the same can happen when according to the agent's principles of prudence or morality Øing is bad. 'If there are any intentional non-compulsive actions that issue from mere desires, the backward connection [sc. to strong valuation] is not necessary' (p. 209).

This argument seems to me to be too quick. In the Buridan's Ass case Pears admits that the agent judges the course pursued to be at least morally or prudentially permissible. In the case of the seaside donder there is no possibility of a moral or prudential judgement. We need further argumentation to show that in cases where a moral or prudential assessment seems to be called for, an apparently foolish or selfish desire can pass into action without any sort of rational permit.

In the absence of such argumentation we may draw a different lesson from the parallel with misperceiving. The ornithologist mistakenly believes that 'That's a falcon' is a correct classification because the salience of the bird's speed makes him overlook its shape. Why not say that the bibulous motorist mistakenly believes that taking the third glass accurately reflects his practical judgement because the salience of his desire makes him overlook some part of his mind? A natural suggestion is that it prevents him from contemplating, as Aristotle would say, his knowledge that three glasses of champagne are too many.

IV

Davidson's P1 and P2 formulate, however infelicitously, connections between thinking good, wanting and acting which the argument of chapters 5 and 6 gives us (I believe) strong reasons to accept. Does any justification remain for not remedying the inconsistency between Davidson's three propositions by excising P3?

The main arguments for keeping P3 consist of thought-experiments such as I have already mentioned. One of the latest is offered by Mele (1987, pp. 28–9). A man feels a desire to watch strip-tease, but judges it would be better not to; although he knows he has his desire-eradicating device with him, he 'freely chooses' by a kind of Jamesian fiat not to press the button. It seems to me that saying one can conceive of something like this no more constitutes a philosophical proof of the separability of judgement and choice than it is a proof of the separability of mind and body to say: 'I have examined my idea of thinking thing, and find I can see that such a thing needs nothing else in order to exist except consciousness.'

Neither could any real example of akratic behaviour prove that P3 is true. Not only can no one other than the guilt-haunted adulterer know for certain that at the time he thought it would be better to refrain; he cannot know this for certain himself. Some introspectors may say that the harder they look into themselves the more confused they become; others who claim to see clearly report different things. Again we may take warning from Descartes: philosophical issues cannot be settled by proclaiming intuitions. To suppose they can is to construe them as more like questions of empirical fact than they really are. 'Can I do something intentionally, seeing clearly at the time that I should do better not to do it?' is a formulation in perhaps misleadingly concrete 'material mode' terms of a question about the concepts of thinking good and acting intentionally; it must be settled by analysing them.

The answer to which the present and the three preceding chapters point is 'No'. So much for our first main question. The second is how behaviour which looks like this, and which can properly be said to conflict with the agent's better judgement, should be explained. This is not a problem exclusively for the philosopher and in the next two chapters we shall use what light we can obtain on it from two disciplines adjacent to philosophy, psychology and economics.

8

Reason and the Economists

According to Davidson (1980, p. 41) what is wrong with the akrates is that he 'acts and judges irrationally'. Is that true, and if so, how far can akrasia be attributed to some failure of rationality? We talk of irrationality in connection with many things; in this chapter I shall be considering irrational action, belief, desire and deliberation.

When we describe behaviour as rational we may have either of two contrasts in mind. One is with the irrational, the other with the non- or sub-rational. Beasts are sometimes called 'irrational' but that is a slander. Horses and rabbits are no more irrational than trees. Plants, like planets, are non-rational. If we wish to deny that rabbits are rational we mean that, like plants, they lack certain psychological powers. Jonathan Bennett's book *Rationality* (1964) is about what distinguishes the rational from the non-rational. The word 'reason' is sometimes used for this important attribute and then signifies a certain intellectual capability. An organism has reason in this sense if it can do any of the following: generalize, draw inferences, understand causally, understand teleologically – and the list could be extended perhaps indefinitely.

Irrationality, as contrasted with non-rationality, is not opposed to having reason but requires it. An irrational agent is one that misuses or omits to use rational faculties that he, she or it possesses. When Elster says 'Rational behaviour on the standard definition means acting in accordance with a complete and transitive set of preferences' (1979, p. 147) he is offering a definition of rationality as opposed to irrationality.

Philosophers sometimes seem to make use of a further notion. If behaviour admits of explanation in terms of reasons – in the broad sense of 'reason' which embraces motives – it is said to be 'rationally explainable', and it may be thought that what is rationally explainable must be rational in a sense. In this sense of 'rational' irrational behaviour will always be rational, and so, I think, will be some sub-rational behaviour. For an organism can act for first-level reasons connected with bodily sensations, it can act to catch prey or escape a predator, without having the intellectual capacities usually thought to distinguish the rational from the sub-rational. I shall avoid this third use of 'rational' and our concern here, of course, is with rationality as contrasted with irrationality.

Elster's 'standard definition' (which we shall see and which he would probably agree to be a little unrealistic) is of rational behaviour as a whole, including deliberation. If we restrict our attention to action we find two types of irrationality (corresponding to Aristotle's 'precipitateness' and 'weakness'). It is irrational to act without considering circumstances, likely consequences, etc., that one ought to consider. Paris was irrational in this way if he went off with Helen simply because she marvellously resembled the gods, and never reflected that her husband was possessive, vengeful, and in a position to launch an irresistible armada to get her back. Eloping with a queen is a serious business and calls for more deliberation than stealing a kiss from one of her maids. It is also irrational to act against one's best judgement. Akratic action (as 'akratic' is understood today) is by definition irrational in this second way.

Frank Jackson (1984) appears to question this point. Having noted that Davidson observes the akrates need not act contrary to his judgement of what is *morally* best, Jackson undertakes 'to justify taking the extra step of entirely separating out the problem of weakness of will from that of acting contrary to what is judged best' (p. 1). He then asks us to imagine a 'convinced catholic' who 'is certain that it would be wrong for her to have an abortion, but she determines nevertheless to have one. When the time comes, however, her feelings of guilt overcome her resolve to have the abortion. Cannot such a case be one of weakness of will?' If this example is to redeem the promise to go one better than Davidson, the lady ought to think it not just morally better not to have the abortion but better all things considered. In fact she seems, like Sidgwick's Inquisitor, to be sacrificing her better judgement to her religious principles. Jackson's real ground, it appears from the rest of his paper, for saying that the problem of acting against one's

REASON AND THE ECONOMISTS

better judgement is separate from that of akrasia, is that the akrates never really does act against his better judgement. The weak-willed man, just as much as the strong-willed, does what he thinks best at the time, but his judgement is distorted by passion. We shall consider this theory in section III below; meanwhile I shall continue to say that akratic action has to be contrary to what (in some way) the agent thinks best.

Why is it rational to do what one thinks best? If I think it better not to $\emptyset$ than to $\emptyset$, what is irrational about $\emptyset$ing or, for that matter, preferring or deciding to $\emptyset$? That this question is not as silly as it sounds is attested by an elaborate attempt to answer it by David Charles (1982/3). In chapter 3 I took issue with Charles over the connection between thinking it good to $\emptyset$ and wanting to $\emptyset$. I claim that 'Aristotle and the truth' (as Plato would say) hold that thinking a course good is a *way* of wanting to pursue it. Hence if an agent thinks it better not to $\emptyset$ than to $\emptyset$, in the absence of reasons to the contrary he must prefer not $\emptyset$ing to $\emptyset$ing, and if he is free to $\emptyset$ and not to $\emptyset$ he must refrain from $\emptyset$ing. Doing what one thinks best is logically necessary, given freedom to act and absence of counter-reasons. We call it 'rational' and not 'necessary' in acknowledgement of this freedom and this absence. According to Charles, Aristotle and truth both draw a firm distinction between desiring and thinking good. There is therefore no logical pressure on agents to do or decide to do what they think best and the question 'Why should they?' becomes urgent.

Charles compares thinking it best not to $\emptyset$ but deciding to $\emptyset$ with thinking it most probable that not-p but at the same time thinking that p. The latter is irrational if or insofar as the evidence which supports 'It is most probable that not-p' is inconsistent with the truth of 'p'.

1   The sky is cloudless, the barometer is rising, the papers say an anticyclone is motionless overhead

supports:

2   It is most probable that there will not be a thunderstorm in the next half hour.

Insofar as (1) is inconsistent with:

3   There will be a thunderstorm in the next half-hour

it is irrational for anyone who accepts (2) to accept (3). Charles suggests that it is irrational for anyone who thinks:

    4   It is most desirable not to accept this proffered cigarette

also to think:

    5   I'll take it.

The source of the irrationality is not that evidence which supports (4) is inconsistent with (5), but that the satisfaction of the desires which support (4) is inconsistent with the execution of the intention expressed in (5). (These desires might be to conquer a craving and avoid a premature death from lung cancer.) The objection, then, to thinking it best not to take the cigarette and deciding to take it is not that we cannot both not take it and take it; it is not that the two courses are incompatible. Rather it is that the one course, taking the cigarette, is incompatible with satisfying the desires which recommend the other.

    Charles has here hit on a kind of practical inconsistency which is the practical analogue of inconsistency between beliefs about what is, was or will be the case. Two beliefs of that sort are inconsistent if they cannot both be true. Two desires, intentions or beliefs about what ought to be done are inconsistent not if the corresponding acts cannot both be done but if they cannot both be right – in which case the acts too may be called inconsistent. Not taking and taking the cigarette are inconsistent in this way as well as incompatible. Lighting one of one's own cigars would be compatible with not taking the proffered cigarette but inconsistent in that it would be wrong if refusing the cigarette would be right in the way indicated by Charles. Acts can, of course, be right in other ways besides by satisfying natural or rational desires. Judicial decisions aim at justice and two decisions are inconsistent if they cannot both be just. Treating like cases differently is inconsistent.

    We might rephrase Charles's explanation, then, of why it is irrational both to think it best not to take the cigarette and to decide to take it as follows: the factors which make it right not to take the cigarette are inconsistent with the rightness of taking it. I can use this to supplement my rather slender account of why doing what we think best is called 'rational' without thereby accepting Charles's general distinction between thinking good and desiring.

    As Charles himself points out, of course, further supplementation is going to be needed. For the man offered the cigarette could avoid inconsistency by giving up some of the desires which favour not accepting. Why do we think this would be less rational than giving up his intention (supported by a present craving) to accept? Because, says

Charles (1982/3, p. 209) the craving is 'less important' than those other desires and coheres less well with the man's 'theoretical and practical beliefs'. A theoretical belief, I suppose, would be that the pleasures of smoking are nothing to the pleasure a non-smoker can get from fine claret, and a practical belief would be that, having many children to rear, he ought to take care to avoid an early death. But here we need a procedure for ordering desires and balancing goods and evils; whether there are such procedures is the topic of section IV below.

II

In going off with Helen Paris could have acted rationally in that he could have thought it best to go off with her; but it might have been irrational of him to think this. Any course of action is likely to be good in some ways and bad in others. Moreover its goodness or badness will depend at least partly on its consequences: even if it is intrinsically an object of aversion it may have desirable consequences or vice versa. Insofar as the goodness of a course depends on its consequences it depends on two factors: the magnitude of the good or evil that may attend it, and the probability of the attendance. In this section I shall be concerned chiefly with beliefs about probability. Their importance is obvious from the case of Paris: surely he must have underestimated the probability of the disaster which in fact ensued. But first we should consider what in general is meant by 'rationality' in connection with belief.

We talk of reasons for thinking or believing; might we say, then, that it is rational for A to think that p (we need not distinguish between acquiring and retaining the belief) if A has a reason for thinking that p, and irrational if A has no reason, or a better reason for thinking that not-p? What, then, is a reason for thinking that p? Presumably q is a reason A has for thinking that p only if q is something A knows or believes. (Hence we can deny, what is in any case fairly clearly false, that it is reasonable to think that p if p: a belief can easily be both irrational and true.) For q, beyond that, to be a reason for thinking that p it is not necessary that q should logically imply that p, but if it does not logically imply that p it should be some sort of evidence or somehow render it probable that p.

As we have seen, there is a gap between thinking that something makes it probable that p and thinking that p is probable sans phrase. I doubt if any unitary account can be given of when it is reasonable or warrantable to move from the first thought to the second. But in any case you do not have to have a reason for believing that p for your belief to be rational. It is often rational to believe something straight off, not on evidence or by inferring it, and without believing anything else from which you could infer it. Being used to recognizing objects as human beings by sight. I normally think straight off, not on the basis of any inference, 'There's a human being there' – my first awareness of what I see or hear is as a human being. This is reasonable so long as the conditions of observation are good and I have no special reason (e.g. being at Mme Tussaud's) for caution. For our present purposes, then, I suggest we say that beliefs are rational unless there is some reason for thinking they are not. There is nothing special about a belief which makes it rational, but there has to be something special about it to lay it open to the charge of being irrational.

There are many things which can make a belief irrational. Philosophers, however, draw a broad distinction between what (since R.P. Abelson, 1963) are known as 'hot' and 'cold' cases. The chief forms of hot irrationality in belief are wishful thinking and self-deception, and it is these which are most conspicuous in akratic behaviour. I shall discuss them in chapter 9. But here I wish to consider whether they are the only kinds of irrational belief involved in akrasia and whether, indeed, a firm distinction between hot and cold cases can be sustained.

The term 'irrational' is normative: an irrational belief is one the believer should not have formed or retained. It is 'hot' if formed or retained because of some feeling or desire. The unreflecting might imagine that all irrational belief is hot, but Richard Nisbett and Lee Ross (1980) produce impressive evidence that this is not the case. In particular they show that we are prone to two main kinds of error. First, we prefer what is more available. We think it more frequent, more likely to occur, or more likely to be responsible for what we want to explain than an alternative which is less available. For example it is easier to think of words beginning with the letter 'r' – they are more available to memory – than of words with 'r' as their third letter, so people wrongly imagine that the former are more common. Or a possible cause which hits the eye, which is salient to perception, is more readily held responsible for an explanandum than one which is not. Secondly we expect explananda and explanantia to be representative of one another. For instance, since the process generating red and black at roulette is random, the inexperienced gambler thinks a run of five blacks less probable than one of four blacks followed by a red. We make constant use in our thinking of theories, generalizations and what are called 'schemas'. Schemas (herein resembling Kantian schemata) are neither concepts nor images but something in between, and we have them of types of person (the crusty but benign old rural doctor) and types of event (a meal at the restaurant). We tend to apply to the case before us theories and schemas which are available or of which the case seems representative. Nisbett and Ross do not pretend that these tendencies are bad in themselves. To arrive at the decisions we need when we need them we often have to pursue such strategies and they often pay off. The point is that we sometimes use them to excess instead of replacing or checking them by 'formal, logical and statistical strategies' (1980, p. 15) which we could use if we chose.

It is irrationality of this kind which is to be contrasted with the hot cases of akrasia: the case, say, where sexual desire makes a man lower his estimate of the probability of sexually transmitted disease. At first the distinction between hot and cold cases may seem both clear and sharp. Pears, however, suggests that there is a continuous spectrum or at least 'a gradation rather than a clear cut difference' (1984, p. 10), and even if there is a difference in principle between cold and hot irrationality the two may still be mutually reinforcing.

Pears, in accordance with his interest in Freud, distinguishes hot cases from cold by the presence and influence of wishes. Among the Nisbett–Ross types of irrationality is slowness to abandon a theory or first hypothesis. Pears can bring cold and hot cases together because once a person 'has formulated his first hypothesis he will wish to retain it, and this wish is personal and may even be accompanied by emotion' (1984, p. 10).

If we say that judgements are hot insofar as they are due to wishes, we should be able to distinguish fairly sharply among hot judgements by the kind of wish or desire involved. An epithumia (p. 104 above) is different in kind from a desire to retain a hypothesis or theory. But the notion of wish or desire is a slightly narrow basis for a distinction. If we use the broader notion of some kind of motivation, and say that hot irrationality is motivated and cold is not, it becomes doubtful whether any irrationality is completely unmotivated. I said that 'irrational' is a term of reproach. Blameless ignorance and innocent error are not irrational; irrationality is to a greater or less degree culpable; and faults, we may think, need motives. In the case of Nisbett–Ross irrationality one motivational explanation leaps to the eye: intellectual sloth. The irrational thinker takes the easy way when he should have thought harder or done more research. As Lucretius says, *Ardua dum metuunt amittunt vera viai*.

If we keep the word 'motive' for occurrent feelings, sloth is not strictly speaking a motive; rather it is a disposition. But is it (unlike knowledge of algebra) a disposition with regard to emotion? Grouped with paradigmatic vices of character in the Middle Ages, and gaining a special pre-eminence among vices in the Protestant Work Ethic, sloth has lost the attention of philosophers in recent years. The reason, perhaps, is that it is to be defined in terms of negative states: aversion to activity, insensibility to the usual motives, lack of interest and desire. Nisbett and Ross notice that negative information, being less vivid, tends to receive less weight than positive (1980, p. 48); they may themselves be guilty of this form of irrationality in their insistence that 'self-serving motivational factors need not be introduced to explain most of the fundamental inferential or judgmental biases discussed in this book' (p. 13).

But should we not distinguish intellectual laziness from physical? A confident answer should perhaps wait on empirical investigation but in the meantime we may ask *why* people are averse to applying knowledge of statistical theory, calculating probabilities mathematically, taking wider samples, and so forth. Plato and Aristotle would say that it is because we have bodies, and intellectual tasks require a physical effort. If that is not too wide of the mark there is a continuum from being unwilling to revise a hypothesis through being unwilling to service an engine thoroughly to being unwilling to dig a lot of potatoes. 'Cold' or Nisbett–Ross irrationality will appear as itself a form of what Aristotle calls 'soft' behaviour, not doing what you think you should because it is laborious or unpleasant.

Furthermore positive motivation is not as alien to Nisbett–Ross irrationality as their policy statements might lead us to expect. They observe that we tend to attach more weight to information which concerns us or our friends (p. 46) or which is presented in an emotionally moving form (p. 47). If I exaggerate the danger of bathing where there are sharks because a friend was attacked by a shark or because I saw a graphic film about sharks, am I not being moved to my miscalculation by what Aristotle calls 'pity' – 'distress or disturbance at evil which befalls the undeserving, and which you can imagine befalling you or yours' (*Rhetoric* 1385^{b}13–16).

On the one hand even the coldest irrationality seems to require some motivation. On the other the invasion of reason by passion is facilitated, so to speak, by the existence of certain well-trodden roads. Sexual desire, for example, may produce misleading schemas of persons and events, or suggest examples, which are perilously small samples, of people who have indulged with impunity and suppress examples of indulgers who have come to grief. Rashly to infer a fair interior from a fair exterior is an abuse of the Nisbett–Ross representativeness strategy which sexual desire notoriously encourages. And just as wine 'binds up' the ratiocinative powers of Aristotle's geometer, so passion may be expected to bind up the statistical knowledge of the impassioned deliberator and make it harder for him to do the mathematical calculation of probabilities the case demands.

III

Jackson's account of weakness of will (1984) starts from the point that in evaluating a course we consider both the values we attach to possible consequences and the probability of their ensuing. To adapt one of his examples, the total value I place on surfing in the South Pacific depends on the values I place on (1) the sensations of surfing, something intrinsic; (2) coming to feel more fit and (3) being eaten by sharks, possible consequences; together with the probabilities I attach to (2) and (3). Suppose I place low positive values of 4 and 3 on (1) and (2), and a high negative value, say – 20, on (3); and suppose I put the probability of (3) fairly high, say 0.2. Then even if I place the probability of (2) quite high, 0.7, the total value I place on surfing in the South Pacific is likely to be fairly low: I shall not want to do it. Jackson now points out that when attending a conference in Suva I may come to revise my total valuation upwards, and this may happen in either of two ways. The other philosophers might persuade me that the probability of being eaten by sharks is in fact very low, say 0.0001. Or, lured for once on to the beach, I might find the sensations of surfing so delightful that while they last I raise my positive valuation of them to 20 or even 40. For joys such as these, I feel, it is worthwhile to run a one in five chance of being eaten. Jackson suggests that in the first case, since what is changed is the estimate of probabilities, and probabilities are the business of reason, reason remains in control; so in staying on after the conference to surf I am not weak-willed. In the second case, however, where what is changed is the value I attach to the sensations of surfing, and the change is brought about by the sensations, passion has taken over and if I fail to get safely out of the water at the first opportunity my will is weak.

Jackson improves on Davidson in emphasizing that weak-willed behaviour involves the triumph of feeling over intellect. That is an idea firmly embedded in traditional thinking about akrasia, and Davidson's definition says merely that the akrates acts against his better judgement without specifying why; it could be from a dreary preference of calculated results over hunches, something which is at most on the periphery of weakness of will. But in other ways Jackson's account is unsatisfactory. There is no simple correlation of reason with estimates of probability and feeling with evaluation. New information can change the value we put on things. Hearing that Shakespeare slept in this bed, I may value owning it and lying on it more. And passion alters our estimates of probability. The delights of sports like surfing and fox-hunting often lead people to underestimate their risks. A tendency to cause factual error as distinct from misvaluation is one of the criteria, of what Aristotle (1105^b25–8) calls 'experiencing an emotion badly'.

The word 'evaluate' can confuse because it is used for estimating the monetary or exchange value of things, in itself an intellectual task, though any intellectual task, of course, can become suffused with feeling. Jackson is concerned not with this but with estimating the overall goodness of a course. Since thinking good is a way of desiring, in effect he is explaining akrasia as irrationality in desire. How does this compare with irrationality in belief?

The notion of a reason for desiring has been defended at some length. I said, however, that it can be reasonable to believe something straight off, without having a reason for believing it. Equally a possible change may enter our minds as an object of desire or aversion from the start, and it can be reasonable to desire or be averse to it without having any reason. I do not need a reason for aversion to falling out of a window or for wanting to drink a glass of something I conceive as pleasant. If we say that beliefs are rational unless there is some reason for thinking they are not, we may say the same about desires. On inconsistency in desiring, see above p. 138.

Does the parallel between desire and belief extend to a distinction between hot and cold irrationality? Desire for something can be irrationally affected by the frame or setting in which we see it. Elster (1983, p. 25) suggests that this is analogous to cold irrationality in belief. He takes from the work of Amos Tversky and Daniel Kahneman (1981) the example of: 'A customer who is willing to add £X to the total cost of a new car to acquire a fancy car radio, but realises he would not be willing to pay £X for the radio after purchasing the car at its regular price.' The customer allegedly values the £X less in the context of a large disbursement. Similarly how much a customer will pay for a jewel may depend on what is literally its setting, and the ardour with which I desire Amanda's love may vary with the number of other men who admire her.

In these cases there is no desire for the irrational desire or evaluation. Elster contrasts them with cases where a person's desires and aversions are adjusted to the possibilities. Sometimes this is a deliberate and rational process: didactic poets keep telling us that happiness consists in reducing one's desires to what is satisfiable. But sometimes it is 'a causal process occurring non-consciously', and then it is hot irrationality. One form of this is sour grapes – Elster uses this phrase not for the fox's belief that the grapes are sour but for its irrationally lowered evaluation of them. Another is lifting one's evaluation of what one has. Once she has chosen between two very similar suitors a lady may think the one she has chosen far superior to the one rejected.

The re-evaluations in Elster's second group are indeed welcome. They reduce what is called 'cognitive dissonance'. Leon Festinger (1957) carried out studies to show that if two 'cognitive elements' in a person's mind do not 'fit' together, if, in a broad sense of 'follow', 'the obverse of one element would follow from the other' (pp. 13–14), this 'dissonance' by itself generates 'psychological discomfort' and motivates the person to reduce it. 'Changing the attractiveness of alternatives' is 'the most direct and probably the most usual manner of reducing post-decision dissonance' (pp. 44, 61–71). Nevertheless the distinction between hot and cold here seems even less firm than the distinction in connection with belief. Cases like Jackson's do not fit easily into either group. The surfer raises his estimate of surfing neither because of the setting nor to reduce dissonance but simply because of the sensations at the time. And it is cases like these which are counted as akratic. A university student finds himself a popular member of a fast set and extricating himself to study becomes increasingly hard; the pleasures of astro-physics or cognitive psychology fade while those of graceful debauchery appear more worthwhile. Here framing, dissonance-reduction and present feelings all seem to contribute.

Even if considerations of desirability and dissonance do enable us to sort irrational changes of desire into two groups, neither group is significantly hotter than the other. Elster seems to me to exaggerate the causal character of his hot cases. No causal mechanism has yet been uncovered which effects the change, and Nisbett and Ross might explain it in terms of availability. The best criterion for distinguishing irrational adaptation of preferences from rational character-reform is not the presence of a causal mechanism; it is the falsity or truth of the beliefs involved. Are the grapes really sour? Is the accepted suitor really kinder and more intelligent? On the other hand when we allow the setting or framing to influence our desires more than we should, this irrationality is just as much motivated in one way or another (say by laziness, rivalry or squandermania) as cold irrationality in belief.

Empirical evidence that beliefs and desires can be affected by feelings provides support for an Aristotelian treatment of akrasia. But a doubt may be felt. I said that Nisbett–Ross irrationality may be viewed as a kind of malakia. But malakia is itself a kind of weakness of will. Does the Aristotelian, then, avoid admitting that clear-eyed akrasia occurs at the level of action only by supposing it occurs at the level of thought or deliberation?

No, for at that level it is unlikely to be clear-eyed. The Nisbett–Ross akratic fails to go through certain intellectual procedures which, if asked in a cool hour, he would agree are appropriate. He does not have to think at the moment of action that they are appropriate and that he ought to be applying them. Whereas it may sound odd to say that a man in the act of adultery possesses but does not contemplate the knowledge that adultery is bad, it is less paradoxical to say that he knows but does not contemplate the knowledge that when a marriage is at risk it is appropriate to consider base rates and not rely on a single reassuring example.

IV

Moral deliberation (in the broad sense of 'moral') is the weighing up of all the factors known to an agent pro and con a course of action. My deliberation is described as rational not if it is rational for me to do this weighing up (though it is sometimes sensible to act straight off) but if I do it in a rational way. Much recent discussion of rationality has really been about rationality in deliberation. It is a problem whether the weighing up of pros and cons can ever be a rational business, and if so, what the most rational procedure is. Substantial disagreements arise here between economists and moral philosophers and even within each of the two disciplines.

An apparently uncontroversial requirement for rational deliberation is consistency. This in turn seems to require transitivity. If I prefer X to Y and Y to Z (where X, Y and Z may be objects, courses of action or what you will) I ought to prefer X to Z. Kenneth O. May, however, points out (1954) that there is no logical necessity (on any normal definition of preference) that I will, and shows that in practice individuals often have circular preference-patterns. He asked students to suppose that X, Y and Z are potential spouses, each equipped with the basic minimum of brains, beauty and bullion; nevertheless X is more intelligent than Y and Y than Z; Y is better looking than Z and Z than X; and Z is richer than X and X than Y. He had no difficulty in finding pupils who preferred X to Y, Y to Z *and* Z to X. Apparently rats which are so unlucky as to fall into the hands of psychologists display a similar incoherence. Now the philosopher can certainly ask for transitivity here. He can say that if X's greater intelligence and wealth ought to outweigh Y's greater beauty, and Y's greater intelligence and beauty ought to outweigh Z's greater wealth, then on no account should Z's greater wealth and beauty outweigh A's greater intelligence. But how should we decide what outweighs what?

Economists tend to assume that there is some single thing on which the goodness or, as they sometimes call it, the 'utility' of any course depends; they then hope to grade rival courses by means of this. The older economists based utility on pleasure; their successors mostly prefer preference.

The classic pleasure-based theory is that of Bentham's *Introduction to the Principles of Morals and Legislation* (1780). Bentham starts by saying that utility is 'that property in any object whereby it tends to produce benefit, advantage, pleasure, good or. happiness', but he immediately adds: 'all this in the present case comes to the same thing' (1970/1780, p. 12), the only good thing being sensations of pleasure. The goodness of a sensation of pleasure is a simple function of its intensity and duration. Assuming that intensity can be measured, Bentham suggests that the utility of a course of action can be worked out quite easily. 'Begin with any one person of those whose interests seem the most immediately to be affected . . . Sum up all the values of all the pleasures on the one side, and those of all the pains on the other . . . Take an account of the *number* of persons whose interest appears to be concerned . . .' And there you are.

It is needless to rehearse modern criticisms of Bentham's account: his own friends saw it was oversimple. The younger Mill held that pleasures are heterogeneous to an extent which seems to preclude making a sum of them, and Ricardo says: 'One set of necessaries and conveniences admits of no comparison with another set'. (See Amartya Sen 1980/1, pp. 194–7 for further documentation and discussion.)

Modern economists mostly base utility not on some definite benefit like pleasure or monetary profit but on preference. It is assumed first that, presented with two options, I can always tell which I prefer, and second that this remains true when one (or both) of the options is a lottery (of indefinite complexity). I can tell not only that I prefer a glass of brandy to a cup of coffee and a cup of coffee to a cigarette, but also that I would (or would not) prefer the certainty of a cup of coffee to a lottery with one-third chance of the brandy and two-thirds chance of the cigarette. Granted this and also that our preferences are mutually consistent in various ways (see Luce and Raiffa, 1957, pp. 22–3) it becomes possible to produce a coherent ordering not just of objects (brandy, coffee, a cigarette) in order of preference, but of preferences themselves (coffee over a cigarette, brandy over coffee) in order of strength. The course with the most utility is then the one which offers the most preference-satisfaction. If there are several which offer the same amount they form what is called an 'indifference curve' (for a seminal exposition of this concept see Pareto 1971, pp. 118ff).

Unlike some pleasure-based theories this account does not discriminate against altruism; there is no reason why I should not prefer a course which satisfies someone else's preference to one which satisfies my own bodily appetites. But there are other fairly obvious difficulties. First, as Sen and Williams say (1982, pp. 12–13):

> It is natural to think of choosing and valuing as related, but it is hard to avoid the suspicion that, in this representation, the direction of the linkage has been inverted. It is not by any means unreasonable to respond to the question 'What should I choose?' by answering 'Whatever is most valuable'. But to respond to the question 'What is most valuable?', or even 'What is most valuable to me?', by answering 'Whatever I would choose', would seem to remove the content from the notion of valuing.

The difficulty is exacerbated if the same agent seems to have different preference-patterns on different occasions and it is not possible in practice to specify a disjunction or indifference curve of top preferences (cf. Wiggins 1978/9, p. 273).

Secondly, we often do not know what our preferences are; we do not know whether we rate one course higher than another, lower or equal to it. Von Neumann and Morgenstern say: 'Every measurement – or rather every claim of measurability – must ultimately be based on some immediate sensation . . . In the case of utility the immediate sensation of preference – of one object or aggregate of objects as against another – provides this basis' (1953, p. 16). Most philosophers would say that there is no such sensation. How then do I know, as I often do, that I prefer X to Y? A natural answer is that I know *why* I prefer it or what makes it (in my eyes) superior.

Many philosophers today (see for instance Wiggins 1978/9, Sen 1980/1) hold that there is no single criterion of goodness such as the economists desire. Courses are good and bad in many different ways, and it does not follow, because $\emptyset$ing is better than not $\emptyset$ing all things considered, that it is better by every criterion, that a sacrifice of present pleasure or profit, for instance, will be compensated in kind by profit or pleasure in the future. I agree. There is, however, a famous argument by Kenneth Arrow (1951) which shows that it may be impossible to produce a rational and transitive ordering of preferences within a society without giving one member dictatorial pre-eminence over all the rest. May (1954) contains a parallel argument to show that it may be impossible for a single individual to reach a rational ordering of his preferences without giving dictatorial preference to one criterion. Readers with an appetite for technicality will find an elaborate counter-argument in S. L. Hurley, 1985. I agree that May fails to prove his point; Hurley, however, makes no positive suggestion about how, in her words, we can get 'from rankings of alternatives under specific reasons [she has in mind justice, kindness, profitability, etc.] to all-things-considered rankings' (p. 501).

The economic theories we have been considering represent the deliberator as a kind of Robinson Crusoe who, in trying to work out his best policy, needs to consider only the ordinary laws of nature. Following von Neumann and Morgenstern a number of modern economists concentrate on the case of the person surrounded by other intelligent individuals competing with him for benefits and anticipating his moves. Different and more complicated methods are needed to find the best course in this second case. Since it is this case which prevails in many games, such as Poker and Diplomacy, the theory of rationality here is called 'games theory'. In real games the problem of how to compare the goodness of different possible outcomes does not arise. The rules of

Bridge, for instance, fix the penalties for undertricks doubled and vulnerable, and the players (unless irrational indeed) agree on the stakes before they start. The notion of a rational solution seems clear even if there are 'games' (Elster, 1979, p. 11 suggests hyperinflation) to which it does not apply, and the project of seeking rational solutions mathematically looks hopeful.

Even, however, when the theory identifies a single solution as the right one, applying the theory is not free from difficulty. In a real game players do not always aim at the result which is best according to the rules of the game. A Bridge player, for example, may prefer a lower total score if it includes a successful slam. When we come to a serious practical situation the problem how to balance pros and cons reappears with pristine force, and games theory does nothing to help resolve it.

Moreover there is room for dispute about rationality even within it. The game known as The Prisoners' Dilemma provides a simple illustration. Two prisoners (I follow the version in Luce and Raiffa, 1957, p. 95) are each given the following information:

> If one confesses to a crime in which both are said to be implicated and the other does not, the first gets a trifling sentence of three months and the second gets ten years. If neither confesses each gets a year. If both confess, each gets eight years.

It will be seen that confessing is best for each prisoner, whether the other confesses or not. Hence according to games theory it is rational for each to confess. But plainly the best solution for both is that neither should confess. Sen (1974) uses the case to contrast rationality as understood in games theory with morality, to the disadvantage of the former. But others (see Watkins, 1974; Elster, 1979, pp. 142–4) question whether games theory really should require the rational prisoner to confess.

Much work has been done on rationality in deliberation by economists in this century, but from the standpoint of philosophy the results are disappointing. Certainly they shed little light on weakness of will. Perhaps the most we can say is this. When, as in games theory, the rational course can be discovered only by lengthy and intricate mathematical calculation, the Aristotelian may expect passion to 'tie up' the arithmetical capacity. My personal experience is that emotion at high or low cards often produces something like akrasia in discarding at Piquet and in both bidding and play at Bridge.

Do moral philosophers do better? Some can hardly be said to try. Ross follows in the tradition of Shaftesbury and Hume in making moral judgement essentially similar to aesthetic judgement. There will be aesthetic or artistic reasons pro and con any word or image the poet considers, any shape or colour the painter considers. The artist (it is easy to think) makes a decision on the basis of a sense of fittingness or rightness which belongs more to feeling than to intellect. This is the model for a judgement of what an agent ought to do all things considered which is suggested by Ross (1930, p. 42) and also by Chisholm when he makes the fundamental notion of one thing's requiring another apply in art as well as in practical conduct (1974, p. 3). Chisholm holds that I have an absolute obligation to $\emptyset$ if something is the case which requires my $\emptyset$ing and nothing overrides this requirement. He also holds that wherever there is moral conflict 'there is a reasonable and proper way out' (p. 13), an optimistic view which is not entailed by the principle (see above p. 123) that we cannot have conflicting absolute obligations. (It would be consistent with that principle to hold that in some situations there is no absolute obligation.) But he offers no rational method of discovering the reasonable exit. To take familiar examples, how do we decide what overrides the obligation to keep trying to save a marriage, or to bear a child you have voluntarily conceived, or to obey a military superior?

I distinguished between first- and second-level reasons, and among first-level reasons I distinguished reasons arising from our sensitivity to bodily sensations, reasons to do with usefulness, reasons arising from social relationships, and reasons for enjoying activities. We act for reasons of all these kinds, and the mature adult has a system for balancing reasons of different kinds against one another. He does not normally know what his system is, and he does not adhere to it invariably, but it is the system to which he is *disposed* to adhere. As I intimated earlier, differences between systems correspond to differences in character. Suppose, for example, that I can devote my time and cash either to a young musician who needs patronage or to a sister with an alcoholic husband, but not both; and suppose the musician's talent weighs with me more than my sister's difficulties. If you in the same position would think you had stronger reasons for helping the sister, we are different in character, and it looks as if we attach different relative weights to reasons connected with aesthetic enjoyment and to reasons rooted in family or social relationships.

A system is the system of those weightings the agent thinks rational;

our question is whether there are any criteria of rationality for the agent's system as a whole. The most popular, consistency, is purely formal, but two or three others which bear more on the content of systems have been proposed.

First, it seems irrational regularly to give reasons connected with present sensations priority over prudential considerations, that is, considerations of usefulness and future sensations. Nagel (1970, ch. 7) defends the rationality of prudence (see above p. 98) roughly as follows. If a present sensation or bodily desire is a reason for action, then so long as I acknowledge my personal identity with my future self I must accept an anticipated future sensation as a reason for present action too. If a present feeling of sea-sickness would justify a swig of rum, my anticipated nausea on our projected yachting-trip justifies me now in buying a bottle of rum to take with me.

The argument is attractive, but the case is slightly more complicated than Nagel makes out. As our yacht pitches and rolls its way across the sea I reflect that I shall have sensations of desire for rum for the next three days as well as today. Should I drink only a quarter of the bottle now, and save a quarter for each of the following days? It is an intricate question how far different times should be treated alike. In the present example I may perish tonight in the waves, in which case three-quarters of the rum will be wasted; or perhaps the sea will get calmer or we shall hail a friendly ship that replenishes our supply. It seems rational generally for an individual, if not for a society, to discount the future to some extent relatively to the present. For a discussion of refinements see Elster, 1979, pp. 65–77. But we can safely say that a rational system of balancing should allow some weight to prudential reasons; and of course a system which always gave overriding importance to reasons connected with present sensations would make the commonest kind of akrasia impossible.

Economists tend to view altruism as intrinsically irrational and try to reduce it to egocentric behaviour. That would suggest that a rational system would always have egocentric reasons override reasons in friendship or enmity. Nagel, in contrast, tries to show that it is rational to give second-level reasons as much weight as first-level reasons. If it is reasonable for me to remove my gouty toes when others seem about to step on them, it is also reasonable for me to take care not to bring down my feet on the gouty toes of others (1970, ch. 11). Nagel's argument here is elaborate and I shall not try to reproduce it, partly because it is not generally considered successful. Perhaps to try to prove that altruism is rational is over-ambitious: such a proof has the appearance of an El Dorado of the mind. But again we may require a rational system of balancing to allow second-level reasons sometimes to predominate.

If human beings had a nature, and we knew what that nature was, we might be able to evaluate systems with an eye to that. We might then know how important society is to human beings, or to a particular human being, and how important friendship and aesthetic experience are, and whether enmity is sometimes good or always bad. Some philosophers (Sorabji 1973/4, pp. 114–15; John Cooper, 1975, pp. 59–64; Wiggins 1975/6) attribute this view or one like it to Aristotle. On their reading he thinks we can arrive at a correct weighting of factors pro and con by applying a general conception of the good for man or of the good, fulfilling, well-rounded life. The system of the truly virtuous man (whoever he may be) will be rational in the sense that it fits this conception; whereas the systems of the vicious, though they may be consistent internally, do not.

One trouble with this view is that many people seem not to have any such conceptions. Many people have never even thought of trying to form a conception of the good life; they have no notion of what such a conception is meant to be a conception of. Philosophers at least have that notion; but it does not seem to take them very far. Certainly if the philosopers I have mentioned are in possession of conceptions which enable them to decide on the relative weight to allot to considerations of friendship, duty, aesthetic fulfilment and personal advantage, they keep their cards very close to their chests.

But there is a more profound difficulty. Our ideas of what we are as conscious, purposive agents are problematic and normative. Insofar as we have such ideas they take shape as we form our characters and develop our systems of weighting pros and cons – for, as I said just now these are systematizations of the judgements we think rational. Our conceptions of what we are vary with our systems. Such a conception, then, cannot serve as an independent means of evaluating systems. If we try to use one, we are simply using our own system. It is not improper to evaluate someone else's system by means of one's own, but one ought to know when that is what one is doing.

These considerations show that we cannot establish that a system is rational by showing that it fits our nature. They do not prove that this is not what it is for a system to be rational or good. Perhaps I do have a nature, and perhaps the best system for me is the system that fits it best. But if I wish to decide whether a particular system is good, rather than appealing, or at least in addition to appealing, to a panel of academics drawn from philosophy, politics and economics, I do well to look at people who use the system and see what they are like and how they fare. I think the system fits my nature if it seems good, not the other way round.

9

Feeling and the Psychologists

If clear-eyed akrasia is impossible, there are two ways of explaining away apparent cases of it. We can say that the agent was psychologically incapable of refraining, or that at the moment of action he believed that the akratic course was all right. In the first two sections of this chapter I shall discuss these possibilities in the light of recent work both by philosophers and by psychologists; in the third I shall consider whether it is a help or a hindrance, in understanding akrasia, to partition the psyche in the sort of way proposed by Plato and Freud.

I

James Prichard wrote in the middle of the nineteenth century: 'the will is occasionally under the influence of an impulse which suddenly drives the person affected to the perpetration of acts of the most revolting kind, to the commission of which he has no motive. The impulse is accompanied by consciousness; but it is in some instances irresistible' (quoted in Nigel Walker, 1968, p. 105). Some philosophers are reluctant to accept this. We can always restrain our desires, they seem to think, if (in the words of Mr Dombey's sister Louisa) we 'make an effort'. 'Strictly speaking' says Joel Feinberg (1970, p. 282), 'no impulse is irresistible.' But English judges (not as a class notorious for soft-heartedness) take a more flexible line. Fitzjames Stephen (Walker, 1968, p. 106) maintained that a man can have 'disease affecting his mind from controlling his own conduct'. According to current law 'mental responsibility' for a crime is diminished by 'abnormal' mental states. These include not only a failure to recognize that what one is doing is an act of a certain criminal type, say killing or raping, but also desires and impulses so strong that they are 'difficult or impossible to control'. Lord Parker as Lord Chief Justice defined the relevant kind of abnormal state as follows:

> a state of mind so different from that of ordinary human beings that the reasonable man would term it abnormal. It appears to us to be wide enough to cover the mind's activities in all its aspects, not only the perception of physical acts and matters, and the ability to form a rational judgement as to whether the act was right or wrong, but also the ability to exercise will-power to control physical acts in accordance with rational judgement. (Walker, p. 155)

Lord Parker held that a man who had murdered and mutilated a girl under the influence of sadistic sexual desire was entitled to plead diminished responsibility on the ground that his desire was abnormally hard to resist or made it abnormally hard for him to regulate his behaviour in accordance with rational judgement.

Susan Khin Zaw (1978) protests that we cannot have every criminal pleading the strength of his desires as an excuse for his crimes and asks how we distinguish irresistible desires from desires which are resistible but not in fact resisted. Her own suggestion is that the weak-willed man who fails to resist a resistible desire is typically able to justify his action by specious reasoning and could have been persuaded by argument not to do it; whereas a so-called irresistible desire is one which, regardless of its strength, is not amenable to reason. A man who acts on a desire of this kind 'knows he cannot justify his actions and would not attempt to' (p. 132). As an example she offers a desire to spend every penny one possesses on buying more and more corduroy suits. Feinberg (1970, p. 285) takes a similar view. But can a firm line be drawn between what is and what is not amenable to reason?

As Gary Watson observes (1977, p. 329), once we allow that desires may be *hard* to resist it seems captious to deny that they can be *too* hard to resist. Watson argues that at the moment at which he acts the akrates could not refrain, but still deserves censure because he could have acquired techniques which would have enabled him to resist. Joseph Margolis (1981) reaches a similar conclusion. Those who insist that the akrates could refrain have to suppose either that he possesses enkrateia but does not exercise it, or that there is some effort he could have made and did not make. In either case we may ask: 'Why not? Was he *capable* of making the effort, exercising self-control?' If the answer is 'He was capable of making the effort; he just did not make the effort to make it' we have a regress. If the agent is not capable of making the effort, why not say from the start that he was not capable of refraining?

While holding that the akrates cannot refrain, Watson still wishes to distinguish akratic from compulsive behaviour. His proposal is that the akrates would have been able to refrain if he had acquired the techniques of self-control standard in his society, whereas compulsive desires are desires those techniques are powerless to curb. If that is right there will certainly be no firm line between akratic and compulsive behaviour. For as Watson points out, standards vary between societies and even between groups within a society. Suppose an unmarried mother who has nothing but a weekly dole takes money which she needs in order to feed her children and spends it on cigarettes for herself. She is akratic if she is the daughter of a professor, perhaps compulsive if she is one of the undeserving poor. Besides, the mastery of a technique is a matter of degree, and there will be people who, by the standards of their peers, are on the borderline between pass and fail.

Philosophical resistance to the plea of psychological impossibility probably owes much to philosophers' fears of the word 'impossible'. Lawyers use the weaker phrase 'difficult or impossible'. Feinberg allows himself to describe some desires as 'unreasonably difficult to resist', and this terminology expresses better than 'impossible' the notion that concerns us. It is unclear what strict psychological impossibility would be. Philosophers mostly seem to conceive it as a kind of causal impossibility, but I shall suggest below that we use causal models too freely for the workings of the mind.

For the present we may say that the akrates is psychologically incapable of refraining if his inability is of the same general order as inability to resist an obsessional compulsion or a phobia. Isaac Marks defines a phobia as: 'a special form of fear which 1. is out of proportion to the demands of the situation, 2. cannot be explained or reasoned away, 3. is beyond voluntary control, and 4. leads to avoidance of the feared situation' (1969, p. 3). An agoraphobic is afraid of going out of his home or into public places. In what way is he unable to leave his home? Not totally, as a psychotic patient is totally unable to rid himself of his delusions. If the house is on fire or the Gestapo are coming for him, his phobia disappears. But Marks observes:

A patient cannot be expected to muster her energies so that she treats every minor shopping expedition as she would a fire in the house. Not only agoraphobics but everybody can perform unexpected feats in an acute crisis; it would be unrealistic to demand such feats constantly of everybody as a matter of routine, and in an agoraphobic who has much anxiety any minor sally outside the house requires great effort, trivial though it would be for a normal person. (p. 141)

Watson (1977) says that a phobia or obsession 'may raise the cost of alternative actions prohibitively, and thus "coerce" rather than compel'. He is drawing on the distinction between, say, getting someone to leave the room by using your superior strength to push him out ('compulsion') and making him go by threatening him with a gun ('coercion'). The latter is an adequate model, since there are some orders we cannot *reasonably* be expected not to obey when they are backed by very fearsome threats. Is it possible, then, that the akrates is sometimes 'coerced' by passion? Can we find a continuum of cases from phobia and neurotic compulsion to weakness of will?

A phobia is an aversion to something the agent thinks good. Malakia, as distinct from akrasia in the strict sense, is aversion to doing what you think you should because it is unpleasant, and this could surely shade into phobia in proportion as the unpleasantness seems less and less real. Akrasia can include not acting, but only when the agent is inactive in order not to lose or forego pleasure. He lingers in bed, bath or deckchair instead of going to work, writing the letter or what not. This is pretty remote from the inaction of the house-bound agoraphobic. But phobic fear can also lead to action. A patient reports: 'At the height of a panic I just wanted to run – anywhere. I usually made towards reliable friends . . . I felt, however, that I must resist this running away, so I did not allow myself to reach safety unless I was in extremity' (Marks, 1969, p. 132). This is not so far from the language in which an akrates might describe his struggles with desire.

In the most typical cases of obsession (see A.J. Lewis, 1936; P.M. Salkovskis, 1985) the sufferer has an unpleasant intrusive thought which he often recognizes to be irrational but which he is not able to dismiss. Typical thoughts are that he will be contaminated or that he will hurt or kill someone. Thoughts of the latter kind may appear as urges, but they are not irresistible; obsessionals hardly ever act upon them. The intrusive thoughts, however, are accompanied by further unreasonable thoughts to the effect that the sufferer will be responsible for harm and will be blamed. The behaviour which is compulsive – endless washing, hiding away potential weapons, etc. – is designed to neutralize the risk of harm and blame.

In itself this behaviour is no more like akrasia than the agoraphobic's inaction. It does, however, provide another bridge over the apparent gulf between normal and compulsive behaviour. S. Rachman and R. Hodgson (1980, p. 2) emphasize that obsessional neurosis is rather an emotional than a medical condition. It appears that normal people have intrusive obsessional thoughts from time to time which they may even, occasionally, act to neutralize; and there is no firm line between these and the clinical cases (Salkovskis 1985, pp. 572, 580–1 and references). Freud suggested that all obsessional thoughts are substitutes for repressed sexual thoughts (III, pp. 45ff, with illustrative case histories, pp. 74–82). Even if it is doubtful whether this is universally true, there are some cases where the psychoanalytical diagnosis and treatment have been successful, and where, therefore, compulsive behaviour can be seen as rationally motivated by unconscious desires and beliefs. There are also cases where, though the agent has some conscious motivation and the behaviour may not be describable as obsessional in a strict sense, it is still accepted as at least partly compulsive.

Some stealing is of this kind. Lionel Haward (1981, p. 107) describes the case of a man who by the age of twenty-seven had accumulated thirty-two convictions for taking cars without consent. A belated psychological assessment revealed him 'to have deep-seated problems of sexual inferiority which could have explained the persistent need to drive large high speed cars despite the longterm consequences'. The Court of Appeal released this Mr Toad into Haward's hands for aversion therapy to taking without consent and psychotheraphy for the sexual problem. Similarly in 1974 the Court of Appeal removed a prison sentence from a woman convicted of persistent shoplifting when it found:

> She had a compulsion to steal attractive objects which she stored in her house, and derived sexual satisfaction thereby. She had responded to treatment but started shoplifting again when the doctor who was treating her, and with whom she had become closely identified, left the district. Psychiatrists were of the view that if she served her prison term she would return to compulsive shoplifting. (Quoted in M. and A. Craft, 1984, p. 53)

Melanie Klein (1927/1985, pp. 181–3) writes of a twelve-year-old boy whose delinquencies were 'breaking open the school cupboard and a tendency to steal in general, but mostly breaking up things and sexual attacks on little girls'. Her explanation was that as a result of witnessing sexual intercourse between his parents and being forced by an older sister to sexual acts at an early age, he was unable to release his aggressive tendencies via fantasy and sublimation. She claims that when the repression was weakened by analysis sublimation occurred, but as soon as the analysis was broken off the trouble started again, and 'I do not doubt in the least that he has started on the path of a criminal career' (see also 1927/1985, p. 258).

Aristotle takes eating too much of the wrong food as a central variety of akrasia. Some of his remarks in *EN* VII.3 have a disquieting aptitude to cases of bulimia. Not every reader may be acquainted with this affliction; the following particulars are taken from Suzanne Abraham and Derek Llewellyn-Jones, *Eating Disorders* (1984). Bulimia attacks one woman in fifty between the ages of fifteen and thirty-five. The victim does not overeat constantly but has 'binges' sometimes two or three times a week, often more rarely, in which she eats anything up to thirty times a normal quantity of food and goes especially for sweet things. She uses vomiting and laxatives to deal with this excessive intake. She eats secretly and with shame and tries to resist the impulse. Victims have gone to the extent of wiring their jaws together and cutting the tips of their fingers in order to make themselves unable to induce vomiting. A sufferer reports:

> I became increasingly aware of my increasing ability to relieve life's pressures through the intake of food. Although the induction of vomiting continued to be traumatic, the relief beforehand and the euphoria afterwards were, to me, of no comparison to it. The vomiting became more frequent as the food intake rose, and I accompanied my physically strenuous job with all the exercise I could muster. Some nights I could not sleep due to the immense guilt of either not having done enough exercise or having allowed too much food to digest. (1984, p. 88).

Modern writers make sexual infidelity the prime example of akrasia. Melanie Klein ascribes it, in contrast, to fear of dependence: 'I have found that the typical Don Juan in the depths of his mind is haunted by the dread of the death of loved people, and that this fear would break through and express itself in feelings of depression and in great mental suffering if he had not developed this particular defence – his infidelity – against them' (1985, p. 323). The Don Juan is driven not (just) by sexual desire but by desire to prove himself independent.

Sleeping with people with whom it would be better not to sleep is often part of what might be described as a mildly neurotic syndrome. The psychiatrist or social worker is constantly having to 'assess' the destitute unmarried mother who either cohabits with a violent criminal or voluntarily conceives a baby the begetter of whom is certain never to be a functioning parent. In the middle class it is often a sign that psychotherapy is going well that the patient gets rid of an unsatisfactory lover. Neville Symington, trying to prove that spontaneity on the part of the analyst can have a liberating effect on the patient, gives the following evidence (1983, p. 283):

> For two sessions [after he had performed an 'act of freedom' by putting up the patient's fee] she cried rather pitifully but then became resolved that she would meet the challenge. Soon she found a job that paid her one third more than her previous salary . . . Shortly after this she finally gave the push to a parasitic boyfriend . . . She had been able to do this because she had been able to give the push to a parasitic analyst. [Symington means, because the analyst had been able to give the push to her.]

Psychoanalytic theorists are like everyone else in their idea of what inner freedom consists in: it consists in being able to deliberate rationally, to arrive at a best judgement without cognitive disturbance by irrational influences, and to be able to act according to that judgement without disturbance from uncontrollable desires. Where they are peculiar is in their estimate of the extent of the area in which most of us enjoy that inner freedom: they think it is smaller than is generally supposed.

II

Where an agent could refrain from doing what he knows, or should know, to be bad, the alternative to acknowledging that he presents a case of clear-eyed akrasia is to say that at the moment of action he does not actually recognize the badness of his course. In chapter 8 we considered some kinds of more or less cold irrationality which could have this result; we must now pass to the warmer latitudes which are the home of wishful thinking and self-deception.

Wishful thinking is thinking that something is the case, although the information available does not warrant that belief, because you (consciously or unconsciously) want it to be true. Wishful thinking need not involve self-deception or even serious irrationality. If my new acquaintance is prepossessing I am inclined to believe that he or she is intelligent and trustworthy because I should like him or her to be so. Wishful thinking without self-deception can play a part in akratic-looking behaviour. A makes love to B thinking unjustifiably that B will treat the affair as just a bit of harmless fun because this, if true, would render A's behaviour permissible. But wishful thinking shades into self-deception when a belief is retained in the face of mounting evidence that it is false.

The standard case of self-deception is provided by the man who wants to pursue some course (which may be one of inaction) $\emptyset$ing; he accepts that if something p is the case, it is better not to $\emptyset$; he knows, believes or suspects that p; but because he wants to $\emptyset$ he makes himself believe that not-p, or at least stops himself from believing that p. In recent years there has been much debate about whether this is possible. The debate goes back to the chapter on 'bad faith' (*la mauvaise foi*) in Sartre's *Being and Nothingness* (1943; my references are to the English translation of 1958 though the translations actually used are my own). Sartre tries to conceive self-deception on the model of a man who deceives another man by lying to him, and says: 'I must know qua deceiver the truth which is hidden from me qua deceived. Indeed, I must know the truth very well to conceal it the more carefully; and this, not at two different moments of time . . . but in the unitary structure of the same project' (p. 49). Sartre (like M. R. Haight in her 1980 study) seems to assume that the belief the self-deceiver is trying to hide will always be true, but nothing turns on that. As described the case is puzzling. How can the same person at the same time believe both that p and that not-p?

Herbert Fingarette (1969) claims that this question springs from a misconception of the nature of consciousness. We are apt to think that being conscious of what he calls an 'engagement with the world' – an expression he uses to cover beliefs, desires, impulses, projects, etc. – is like seeing something which is before our eyes or receiving a bodily sensation. It then seems that the self-deceiver must both know and not know that he has the motive or belief he is trying to hide. In fact, being conscious of a belief or desire should be viewed as a kind of activity, an exercise of skill, similar to describing something in words. Fingarette calls it 'spelling out'. We do not, he says, spell out all our engagements; we need a reason for spelling one out. The first part (1969, ch. 3) of his account is that the self-deceiver is a person who has a reason for *not* spelling out some belief or desire; and not only refrains from spelling it out but, since being silent about it will otherwise attract attention when adjacent 'engagement's are spelt out, invents a cover story (p. 50).

This shift from discussing self-deception in terms of awareness to discussing it in terms of action does not in itself dispose of the Sartrian question. For how (Haight asks pretty much this question, 1980, pp. 92–3) can I intentionally refrain from spelling it out that I believe it would be futile or immoral to $\emptyset$ unless I am aware that I believe this? Since the content of belief or desire enters essentially into what I intentionally refrain from doing and invent a cover story to avoid, I must be aware of it.

Fingarette does not deal with this difficulty directly. He distinguishes, however, between a person and an individual. An individual is the organism begotten and born. A person is a 'synthesis which emerges in time' (1969, p. 82), a 'creation' (p. 83) which is gradually built up. More precisely, a person is a 'community' of engagements. Engagements get incorporated into a person by being acknowledged or 'avowed', and the process of spelling out is the process of avowal. When a belief or desire cannot be harmonized with other constituents of the person, it is reasonable to disavow it, and self-deception is this disavowal. If we take this second part of his account (ch. 4) literally, it may provide a way of avoiding the difficulty about believing both that p and that not-p. For we can say that belief strictly speaking belongs to a person; when an engagement is disavowed it is not part of the person, and the person, then, does not believe he has it.

The objection to this theory is that we cannot take the crucial distinction between the individual and the person literally. If we try to, the result is incoherence. The 'individual' builds the person, selecting and rejecting materials (p. 82): what can this individual be but the person? As though to conceal from himself the difficulty, Fingarette sometimes uses passive constructions: 'Certain forms of engagement . . . are taken up into the ever-forming, ever-growing personal self' (p. 86). But *what* takes them up?

Among recent attempts to defuse the problem are those of Robert Audi (1982) and Alfred R. Mele (1987). Audi suggests that where I should commonly be said to be deceiving myself in thinking that p (1) I unconsciously know that not-p, (2) I am ready to declare that p and do so sincerely, (3) I have some desire which explains at least in part why my belief that not-p is unconscious, why my declaration that p is sincere, and why I am unimpressed by evidence against p. It will be seen that on this analysis I do not actually believe that p, and hence I do not hold incompatible beliefs. This solution seems too simple. It turns self-deception into unconscious hypocrisy. And if one is going simply to deny that the self-deceiver holds incompatible beliefs, why deny he holds the one he thinks he holds rather than the one he is unconscious of holding? Some philosophers are sceptical about the possibility of unconscious mental states generally, so the unconscious belief would be the easier to get rid of.

Mele in effect takes that line. He hopes to dissolve the problem by denying that, in standard cases, self-deception is intentional. Even the deceiving of someone else, he says, *can* be unintentional: I deceive you if I cause you even inadvertently to acquire a false belief. In the same way I deceive myself if I cause myself to acquire a false belief, and this will be unintentional unless I have deliberately embarked on the sort of course which Pascal recommends to would-be theists (and which will be discussed below pp. 166–8). If in deceiving myself into thinking that p I do not mean to deceive myself or know I am deceiving myself, there is no need to suppose that I consciously or unconsciously believe that not-p.

Mele's argument could be set out like this:

1 A $\emptyset$s B if A intentionally or unintentionally causes B to be $\emptyset$ed.
2 B is deceived in believing that p if B believes that p and that p is false.
3 So A deceives himself if he even unintentionally causes himself to acquire or retain a false belief.

The argument is unsound. (1) holds only for some values of $\emptyset$ing. With verbs like 'redden' (see above p. 69) the intransitive and passive uses are indeed logically prior to the active. If I blush and my cheeks redden my cheeks become red; if I take some rouge and redden them I cause them to become red. But where a verb carries an implication of intention, like 'assassinate' or 'forgive', the passive use must be explained in terms of the active. The President is not just killed but assassinated if someone killed him intentionally for political reasons. Premise (2) rests on a usage of 'deceive' that is peripheral and slightly archaic.

In point of fact the positive account of how we deceive ourselves which Mele goes on to give does not depend on the idea that deceiving oneself is like causing the ratio of carbon dioxide to oxygen in a room to rise when one is asleep. Rather it implies the opposite. Mele claims that when I deceive myself into thinking that p I 'manipulate' evidence in various ways and the manipulation is 'motivated' by a wish. He hopes to temper the implications of this by insisting that my wish is not that I should believe that p but that p should be true. I agree that that is my primary wish. But suppose I am a Secret Service man in a Le Carré story. My wish that my superior may not turn out to be a Russian spy is not by itself a motive for averting my eyes from pointers to his guilt since such 'manipulation' will not cause him to be a loyal British patriot. The manipulation must be understood as being *in order that I may not come to believe* he is a traitor. In addition to the wish that he may be innocent I must be credited with at least an unconscious aversion to believing him to be guilty. The self-deceiver may not have the conscious intention of coming or continuing to believe something false, but self-deception is still (as Elster, 1979, p. 174 puts it) 'an intentional project'.

Neither will it do to say that there is 'nothing deeply paradoxical about holding beliefs which are incompatible' (Fingarette, 1969, pp. 14–15). We need to distinguish the following:

1 A believes that p and it is not the case that A believes that p.
2 A believes that it is the case that both p and not-p.
3 It is the case both that A believes that p and that A believes that not-p.
4 A believes both that q and that r, where from q it follows logically that p and from r it follows logically that not-p.
5 A believes both that q and that r where q strongly suggests that p and r strongly suggests that not-p.
6 A believes that p although the relevant information available to him supports p and not-p equally.

(The last four correspond to the four possibilities distinguished in this connection in Pears, 1984, p. 29).

(1) is logically impossible. There are difficulties in supposing that (2) is possible. To mention only one, believing that p seems to involve having the supposed circumstance that p function as a reason. How could the conjunction of p and not-p function as a reason for anything? As for (3) a person could act sometimes for the reason that p and sometimes for the reason that not-p (sometimes treating an employee as honest and sometimes as dishonest) without having any reason to change his mind or being conscious of changing it. We are concerned, however, with an agent's state of mind in $\emptyset$ing when the circumstance that p would be a reason for not $\emptyset$ing. If he believes that p, he will $\emptyset$ in spite of the fact that p and show signs of uneasiness, remorse or the like. If he believes that not-p, that not-p will not, strictly speaking, function as a reason with him; rather he will simply not be guilty or uneasy. In the case, then, which interests us, (3) is impossible too.

Haight (1980, ch. 2) offers a different but, to my mind, sound argument to the same effect. I conclude that self-deception conceived as Sartre conceives it is impossible. This conclusion is resisted by a number of writers including Sartre himself and Raphael Demos (1960). Demos undertakes to explain how 'lying to oneself' is possible by exploiting the concept of noticing: the self-deceiver knows but does not notice the inconvenient fact that p somewhat as, distracted by something interesting, one might cease to notice a headache. I agree with Haight that Demos's account fails because of an inevitable but disastrous slide from saying that the self-deceiver does not notice the inconvenient fact to saying he 'deliberately ignores' it (p. 593). The slide is necessary because self-deception is at least partly intentional; it is fatal because in order deliberately to ignore something I have to notice it. (Demos might, of course, be equivocating with the word 'notice': it used to be used for remarking upon or commending a person or action.)

Sartre represents self-deception as a decision 'not to ask too much' in order to be satisfied. He compares it to putting oneself to sleep, and suggests we are able to do it because all belief is conscious and once we are aware of a belief it becomes precarious (1958, pp. 68–9). Here too I agree with Haight's criticisms. Going to sleep is not something we do by deciding to do it, and Sartre exaggerates the extent to which thought generally is conscious or self-intimating.

Self-deception cannot be conceived on the model of lying to someone else, and the self-deceiver cannot (at least consciously) hold contradictory beliefs at the same time. It does not follow that self-deception is not available as an explanation of akratic behaviour. Three strategies of self-deception which escape Haight's criticisms are described by Pears (1984, pp. 59–63).

First, if I suspect but do not have overwhelming evidence that p I can take care to avoid being confronted with such evidence. I might do this quite consciously and it might even be rational, for instance if I suspect that my wife is unfaithful but at the same time think this suspicion jealous and unreasonable. Secondly, I can 'bias the processing of information' already at my disposal. Pears sees this as typically unconscious, though I might consciously refrain from pursuing certain dangerous lines of thought or deliberately stupefy myself with drink or drugs. Thirdly, I may be able to acquire a belief I wish to have by acting as if it were true.

The most famous description of this is in Pascal. If, he says, you wish to acquire belief in God, take the path taken by others who have been cured of incredulity 'Start the way they did: it is by doing everything as if they believed, taking holy water, having Masses said and so forth. That will make you believe' (*Pensée* 233). Pascal's technique sounds cynical, but it is clear enough that neglect of religious duties and adoption of a non-believer's life style can result in loss of religious belief. It also appears that we can acquire a desired belief by getting a hypnotist to induce it under hypnosis.

Elster (1979, pp. 47–54, 176–7) says that a difficulty for these kinds of belief-formation is raised by Bernard Williams. Williams (1970/1973) considers the bizarre possibility that, in the way in which I can hold my breath at will and in which it is imaginable that someone should be able to blush at will, I might be able to believe something at will. At a time when I am sure my sister is not in Paris or have no idea where she is, I can come to believe she is in Paris as a kind of basic action. Against this Williams argues that I could not 'in full consciousness regard this as a belief of mine, i.e. something I take to be true, and also know that I acquired it at will. With regard to no belief could I know – or, if this is to be done in full consciousness, even suspect – that I had acquired it at will' (p. 148). Elster thinks Williams's argument applies also to beliefs acquired by Pascal's technique or by hypnotism, and that it proves that for any such strategy to work the believer would have to forget that it had been employed.

What are Williams's grounds for the statements quoted? Why cannot I believe that *p* and at the same time know I acquired the belief by acting as if it were true or by hypnosis? All Williams himself says is that this is 'connected with the characteristic of beliefs that they aim at truth'. Since he finds it unnecessary to say more, he may be imagining the case of a man who (if possible) now believes that God exists and also knows or remembers that God does not exist or that there is no good evidence either way. That certainly seems impossible: it is case (3) or even case (1) of p. 163 above. But why should I not now believe that God exists and also know that I once did not believe this? I will not be stopped by a desire to hold only beliefs that are true.

Elster interprets Williams's argument as being that we do not want our beliefs to 'stem from the wrong causal process'; we want them to be based on rational grounds or direct sense-experience. That is true in general; but on Williams's own showing it is more important that our beliefs should be true than that they should be arrived at in any particular way, and so long as I am now sure it is true that God exists – especially if I now think that there are rational grounds for this belief – I may not mind too much that I acquired my belief through Pascalian practices (dictated, perhaps, by my parents).

Although Elster is censorious of acting in order to acquire a belief for which the agent has, at the time of acting, no rational grounds, he allows that we may both rationally and successfully act to strengthen in ourselves beliefs for which we do have rational grounds. Elster is thinking of general practical beliefs; by acting on these we make them our second nature, that is, we accomplish the laudable task of character-modification.

Aristotle suggested that passion can dull our perception of practically important features of a situation like wine; we can now see that there are plenty of ways in which passion can, more insidiously, distort it.

III

Sartre's chapter on bad faith is famous partly because it is a battle of giants: Sartre assails Freud's theory of repression. According to Freud there is a censor which keeps unwelcome knowledge and shameful tendencies in the Unconscious. Sartre argues that the censor must be aware of the tendency to be repressed 'precisely in order not to be consciousness of it'; it must choose and be aware of itself; and hence Freud has got rid of bad faith at the level of the human being only by establishing 'between the unconscious and consciousness a consciousness which is autonomous and in bad faith' (1958, p. 53). Sartre seems to be trying to show that psychoanalytic theory involves a regress. As Haight observes (1980, p. 55), the attempt fails. The censor is not trying to prevent itself from becoming conscious of the distasteful item; it is trying to prevent the human being from becoming conscious of it. Sartre might reply that the idea that there is an autonomous conscious entity inside each of us trying to deceive us is one which belongs to Descartes's *First Meditation*. But (especially now that homunculi are all the rage) psychoanalytic theory is not to be dismissed so fast.

I offered a brief sketch of Freud's partitioning of the psyche in chapter 2 and an even briefer summary will suffice here. In the first place he distinguishes mental states, beliefs, desires, etc., into Unconscious, Conscious and Preconscious. This, however, is rather a bipartite than a tripartite division. For our Preconscious states are states of which we can become conscious easily; states pass freely backwards and forwards between the Preconscious and the Conscious; whereas our Unconscious states are states of which we cannot, at the time, become conscious. Secondly Freud distinguishes the Superego, the Ego and the Id, and this tripartition, as we saw, has affinities with Plato's tripartition into Calculative, Spirited and Desirous Parts.

Freud's theories both throw light on akrasia, but in different ways. The theory of the Unconscious decisively confirms that there is no fundamental difference between akratic and (at least some) compulsive behaviour. The compulsive as much as the akratic agent acts for reasons. It also provides a clear content for the notion of psychological impossibility. If $Rp\emptyset A$, but A does not know that he believes that p, it will be difficult or impossible for him to refrain from $\emptyset$ing, and the difficulty or impossibility will be truly psychological. It is to do with cognitive states and reasons, not with physical states or causal factors. As long as A believes that p the belief must (as a matter of logical necessity) be reflected in his behaviour; and as long as he is not aware that he believes that p he cannot subject either the belief or his response to rational criticism: he cannot consider whether that p is a satisfactory reason for $\emptyset$ing, or whether it is even true.

The theory of the Superego, Ego and Id makes use of the notion of the Unconscious, but in itself it illuminates akratic behaviour in a completely different way. Whereas the theory of the Unconscious, at least as I have just interpreted it, does not require a real partitioning of the human subject, and could be used in an Aristotelian treatment of akrasia, the theory of the Superego, Ego and Id explains akrasia by internal conflict in the Platonic fashion, and the three parts have to be really distinct. Philosophers often criticize or defend both of Freud's theories together, but because of these differences I shall treat them separately.

An objection which has been brought against the theory of the Unconscious is that Freud's concept of an unconscious mental state is incoherent. A mental state is unconscious in Frend's technical sense so long as the person who has it is not merely unaware of it but unable to be aware of it. Some philosophers (for instance E. Nagel, 1959; A. Pap, 1959) say it is essential to at least some of Freud's unconscious states, such as wishes and hatred, that a person should be able to be aware of them. Hence an unconscious wish is either a contradiction in terms or a wish in a novel sense of 'wish'. This view way be inspired by an unconscious memory of Kant's statement that 'the "I think" must be able to accompany all my mental representations'. In point of fact Freud's unconscious states *can* become conscious thanks to analysis; even in ordinary speech we often attribute to people unconscious wishes which they sincerely disavow; and the fact that the concepts of belief and desire are connected with behaviour ensures that 'thinks' and 'wants' do not change their sense when preceded by 'unconsciously'. (For these and similar points, see A. MacIntyre, 1958, pp. 43–5; K. V. Wilkes, 1975, pp. 129–32).

A second objection is that Freud's concept of an unconscious desire involves a confusion of reasons and causes. According to Pap, unconscious desires are dispositional states. As such, they cannot be 'causal antecedents of overt behaviour, and it is a mistake to suppose that an item or pattern of overt behaviour has been explained when one says it expresses such and such an unconscious desire' (1959, pp. 286–7; similarly E. Nagel, 1959, pp. 44–7). A. MacIntyre seems to me to deal satisfactorily with this charge in *The Unconscious* (1958; much the same line is taken by Ilham Dilman, 1984, pp. 152–3). Freud wished to give a physicalist account and believed that such an account might underlie his theory. In practice, however, he operates almost exclusively with the notions of a reason and a purpose. Far from explaining intentional action mechanistically, he offers rational explanations of behaviour his predecessors had thought mechanical or random. MacIntyre is reluctant to speak of Freud as *explaining* behaviour because he keeps the word 'explain' for use in connection with causes; he prefers to speak of Freud as offering mere descriptions or redescriptions. But what MacIntyre calls 'description' is what I call 'teleological explanation'.

MacIntyre indicates a second confusion in Freud which really is between explaining and describing. Freud thinks that the repressing of a mental item, the confining of it to a realm or condition designated 'the Unconscious', is a causal mechanism. Childhood experiences cause adult behaviour through repression somewhat as heavy elements arise out of hydrogen through gravitational contraction and nuclear reactions. The Unconscious should be viewed as an entity of the same kind as an electron. In fact the notion of the unconscious which Freud uses in his writings is the notion of that which is very hard to acknowledge (MacIntyre, 1958, p. 61). The difficulty is explained teleologically by the sadistic, terrifying or otherwise unpleasant character of the repressed item; it is not explained causally by any mechanism.

This is important because it enables us to use the concept of the unconscious without making a real division of the psyche. Repression can be regarded as the same kind of project as self-deception. The strategies of motivated belief-formation are carried out at the best of times in a kind of twilight; to say that there is repression is to say that our nature is such that sometimes they are veiled in almost inpenetrable darkness.

But ought we to be frightened of slicing up the soul? Davidson has argued recently that some partitioning 'will be found in any theory that sets itself to explain irrationality' (1982, p. 303). This claim is not based simply on the success of Plato's and Freud's theories in illuminating otherwise puzzling behaviour; it rests on Davidson's conception of irrationality. According to Davidson it is part of being hotly irrational (he talks of irrationality indiscriminately, but he is thinking only of hot cases) that a desire accounts for behaviour in an abnormal, causal way. Paris's sexual desire for Helen is a 'reason' (as Davidson uses the term) for going off with her; that is (in my usage) the fact that she is charming is a reason and so, perhaps, is the fact that Paris is in a state of unsatisfied lust which prevents him from enjoying food, sleep and exercise. But Paris thinks it best all things considered not to elope. At this point his desire for Helen (like the Duke in *Measure for Measure*) makes a second appearance on the scene, no longer as an honest Davidsonian reason but as a causal factor compelling Paris to say 'Let's be off', blurring his perception of Helen's relationship to his host, and distorting his calculation of the probabilities of disaster for Troy and his ninety-nine siblings. In this second role the desire still has to be viewed as an intentional mental state and not, say, as a firing neuron; but it is a desire functioning causally: it functions causally as my desire functions causally relatively to you when, wanting you to do something, I get you to do it. Davidson claims that we can cast a desire for this double role only if we divide the person into two overlapping systems. There is the system which forms the best judgement, and to which the desire belongs as a 'reason'; and there is a second system in which the desire functions as a cause.

Davidson notes that his division is different from Freud's. The main differences are these. Freud's Conscious and Unconscious are differentiated by consciousness, not by their interactions – I have just said they need not be conceived as interacting causally at all. Davidson's systems are differentiated by their causal interacting. As for the Superego, Ego and Id, Freud divides the psyche into just those three parts and gives them widely differing modes of operation. Davidson's systems all operate in the same way, with a high degree of rationality, and he is coy about saying how many they are (1982, p. 300 and n.).

Plato, Freud and Davidson are a formidable trio. But the partitioning of the psyche is a divisive issue in more ways than one. 'The elimination of the Freudian unconscious as a theoretical entity,' says Elster (1983, p. 152), is 'a highly desirable goal.' Still more desirable, no doubt, is to eliminate the Supergo, Ego and Id. Such, at least, is the opinion of Irving Thalberg (see below), and we have already seen what Cross and Woozley (1964) think of Plato's tripartition.

The commonest philosophical objection to the Plato–Freud divisions is that the parts are personified and turned into little psyches or homunculi. This is pressed eloquently against Freud by Thalberg (1982). He notes that K.V. Wilkes tries to meet the objection. In her 1975 paper she argues that words like 'repress', 'censor', 'analyse' can be used either literally or at least in 'irreducible metaphors' of entities other than full scale human beings. Thalberg scores some good points ad hominem against Wilkes; he fails, however, to come properly to grips with her basic idea.

This idea goes back at least to 1959 when Fred Attneave (having in mind the psychology of perception, not akrasia or compulsiveness) argued that 'the charge that an opponent is "assuming a little man inside the head" has been accepted as an argument-stopper for too long' (1961, p. 781). Attneave puts forward proposals for the use of homunculi in psychology which have since been developed by philosophers and find their most lucid exposition in D.C. Dennett (1978). According to Dennett, we start with the notion of a 'whole person or cognitive organism' defined by its functions – speaking a language, say, making tools or playing strategic 'games' – and we want to understand how it discharges these functions. The recommended procedure is to break it

> into an organization of subsystems, each of which could itself be viewed as an intentional system (with its own beliefs and desires) and hence as formally a homunculus. In fact, homunculus talk is ubiquitous in AI [artificial intelligence], and almost always illuminating. AI homunculi talk to each other, wrest control from each other, volunteer, sub-contract, supervise and even kill. There seems no better way of describing what is going on. Homunculi are *bogeymen* only if they duplicate *entire* the talent they are rung in to explain. If one can get a team or committee of *relatively* ignorant, narrow-minded, blind homunculi to produce the intelligent behavior of the whole, this is progress. (p. 123)

Each homunculus's function is further divided till we get to functions so simple that they could be performed by machines; and lo, we find they are, the machines being neurons. Dennett also says that introspection reveals humunculi, for example something which throws up ideas and something which selects and judges, and he suggests that these correspond to the subconscious and the conscious (pp. 86–8).

Julia Annas accepts this as an adequate justification for Plato's division: 'Desire, for example, is what gets the person to gratify particular wants. It includes the ability to figure out how to do this . . . So it is cleverer than mere animal craving. But it is much less clever than the whole person' (1981, p. 145). Attneave and Dennett had in mind the normal functioning of a coordinated personality; the partitionings with which we are concerned are intended to explain malfunctioning and internal conflict. These are not goals, and 'How do we behave irrationally?' is to that extent a different question from 'How do we solve chess problems?' It is not clear, however, why a functionalist answer should not be given to both. Dennett and Wilkes have declared physicalist aims, but dividing the psyche into their homunculi does not of itself settle any questions about determinism and moral responsibility. The functionalist method can, after all, be applied with demonstrable success to collectivities such as multinational companies and states. It is a little worrying that neither Annas nor Wilkes says what the next step might be after the inititial tripartition. How do we divide up the Spirited Part or the Superego? But our anxiety will be containable if a satisfactory answer can be given to a different problem.

How are we to conceive the parts of the psyche as interacting? That they interact is the whole point of the tripartitions of Plato and Freud. But the notion of purely teleological interaction seems incoherent, and there are difficulties is making them interact causally.

Davidson's division is based precisely on the idea that a desire in one part of the psyche acts causally on another part. Unfortunately it is extremely hard to see how it can. Pears (1984) tries for twenty pages (pp. 83–102) without, as it seems to me, making much headway. Davidson's model, as we saw, is my acting in order that you may do what I want: 'Wishing to have you enter my garden, I grow a beautiful flower there [cf. Catullus 1x. 39ff]. You crave a look at my flower and enter my garden. My desire caused your craving and action' (1982 p. 300). Yes; but I acted causally on the garden with spade and watering-can. What kind of intra-cerebral gardening can we attribute to Paris's desire for Helen?

How do the Ego and Superego interact, or the Calculative and Desiring Parts? Plato in the *Republic* offers as a model economic or political groups with interests that can conflict, the sort of sub-systems a functionalist might distinguish if he were asking how states make war and peace or go bankrupt. As we saw in chapter 8, modern theorists sometimes try to explain collective choices and behaviour in a purely teleological way, purely in terms of the preferences, wants or evaluations of sub-groups and individuals. But in this they are abstracting; in real life people interact causally; they talk to one another, write letters and move about. Wilkes (1978, ch. 7) hails Aristotle as a forerunner of Dennett because he divides the soul into Nutritive, Perceptive and Intellective Parts. I think a more deserving subject for her encomia would be Aristotle's follower Alexander of Aphrodisias, but in any case there are imporant differences (as R. de Sousa, 1976, observes) between the Platonic and the Aristotelian divisions. The Aristotelian Parts are ordered vertically, the nutritive subordinated to the perceptive and the perceptive to the intellective. They do not conflict but nutrition produces organs of perception and locomotion by which the organism hunts, with or without intelligence, for food. The Platonic Parts, like the Freudian, are all pretty much on the same level, and it is essential to them that they can conflict or cooperate. The Aristotelian functions are referred to distinct parts of the body which really do interact causally. Plato in the *Timaeus* and Freud in his *Project for a Scientific Psychology* want to locate parts of the psyche in different physical habitats, but Freud had to give up the idea, and Plato seems less than fully serious about it (see *Timaeus* 72).

The functional analysis of societies ends with individuals who interact causally but whose causal action is teleologically explainable. If the analysis of the individual ends with parts like this we have homunculi who, however stupid they may be, are bogeymen. The physicalist wants his analysis to lead to entities like neurons which interact in a purely causal way. The lusts of the Id and the gloomy moral principles of the Superego are lost somewhere in the process. Presumably mechanistic explanations are found for behaviour we class as self-punitive or libidinous. This being so, the partitioning of the psyche will be valid only at a certain level of explanation. There may be no parts of the brain that you could separate with a scalpel corresponding to the functions of Freuds's or Plato's parts, and (as Spinoza liked to insist) even if there are, the division of a causal system into sub-systems has no objective basis independently of the interests and purposes of the divider.

(Freud's interests were perhaps mainly therapeutic, Plato's may have been more legislative.)

We do not have to choose between bogeymen and physicalist reductions. Both spring from wanting to use a causal model for relationships between mental states. We say that desires can conflict with principles or dull or distort cognition, and we try to conceive this on a model of causal interaction. It does not matter whether we assign the mental states owners that fight, plot or cooperate, or let the mental states float free like logs in a river and interact. If we want to liberate ourselves from this model we must see teleology as a genuine, thoroughgoing alternative. We confine ourselves to a single owner of mental states, the person. Instead of partitioning the person we divide desires and modes of thinking into different groups. (This has to be done in any case by those who divide the psyche.) We allow beliefs and desires to appear only as reasons and purposes; that is, we must always be ready to restate our explanations in the form: 'It was for the reasons that p and q, and in spite of the facts that r and s, and in order that B might become f and lest C should become g, that A $\emptyset$ed'. We avail ourselves of a moderate concept of repression. A mental state is repressed if we are very unwilling to become conscious of it or, as Fingarette says, spell it out to ourselves, and our reluctance is explained teleologically by features of the repressed item.

The working out of such a theory is an empirical undertaking and belongs to psychology or psychiatry, not to philosophy; but I can indicate what I have in mind. What happens when Paris's sexual desire affects his cognitive grasp of the situation? Does it, as Davidson might like to say, cause a cerebral event in a deviant fashion? Or does Paris's Desirous Part tyrannize over his Calculative? Rather he does not think of factors or do computations he should and could, and this is to be explained teleologically by Helen's smile, her body-odour or what not. What happens when Don Giovanni compulsively pursues Zerlina? Is a stern Superego forcing his Ego to repeat a childish ritual? Not exactly. He grabs Zerlina in order not to be dependent on Elvira and experience misery at her dying. Why does he think she is going to die? Because his mother withdrew her breasts from him in infancy. Not a very good reason for thinking Elvira is going to die now? No, it is not; and he would see that himself if he realized that this *was* his reason. So what he needs is not hellfire but psychotherapy.

The theory of the Unconscious, then, can be made acceptable to philosophers of widely differing views. Partitions carried out in the

Plato–Freud, as distinct from the Aristotle–Alexander fashion require us to think of our mental life in a fundamentally causal, as contrasted with a teleological, manner. To philosophers to whom this is satisfactory, a partition will have a provisional validity at a certain level of theory; a level not profound but perhaps appropriate for certain practical purposes.

10
Conclusion

At the beginning of this book I raised two principal questions about weakness of will. First, does it ever in fact happen that a person does of his own free will something he clearly perceives at the time it would be better not to do? Secondly, since people certainly do behave in ways in which we should normally say they know they would do better not to behave, how is this akratic behaviour to be explained?

We soon found that there are two well supported positions on each of these issues. In the first place, our civilization accommodates two conflicting views of human nature. The Judaeo-Christian tradition equips us with two distinct psychological capacities, a deliberative or reflective capacity, which enables us to consider what is good or bad, and an executive capacity, the will, which is responsible for how we actually behave. In ancient Greek philosophy, in contrast, no purely volitional capacity appears and there is no firm separation between thought, desire and action. On the first of these views clear-eyed akrasia presents no problem whatever; on the second it seems impossible.

When we come to the second main issue we find the two contrasting opinions both already active in Greek thought. Plato – I mean the mature Plato of the *Republic* and the *Laws* – favours a psychological approach both to the explanation and to the treatment of akrasia. He divides up the psyche in the manner of Freud; it seems to him common for men to act against their rational calculation of what is best; and he views this action as in some sense compulsive. He thinks that the law-giver or statesman should be a kind of psychotherapist (*Statesman* 295 b, 309, etc.). Aristotle, in contrast, favours a philosophical approach to the explanation of akrasia and a layman's way of dealing with it. He is the forerunner of the modern cognitive psychologist as distinct from the psychoanalyst, of the economist who tries to give a quasi-mathematical

account of rational choice, and of the tough-minded citizen who would
send the akrates not to the shrink but to the beak.

The second issue is one chiefly of emphasis. Both emotional disorder
and cognitive failure can result in akratic conduct. Sometimes an agent
seems almost perfectly rational but his behaviour compulsive; sometimes there is nothing compulsive about the behaviour but the agent
appears in one or another way irrational. It is not for the philosopher to
say which factor predominates in any particular case, let alone generally.
There are, however, certain more or less conceptual questions on which
the philosopher might hope to say something useful.

First, is there a difference of kind or only of degree between behaviour which is weak-willed and behaviour which is somehow neurotic:
between akratic eating, stealing or sexuality and compulsive, or
between phobic failure to do what one ought and the failure of the
malakos? Allied to this is the question whether there is a firm distinction between 'cold' and 'hot' irrationality. Some thinkers have assumed
that there are discontinuities here without much investigation. Perhaps
the main burden of the investigation must be empirical; but
philosophers can contribute. They can comment on the results of the
empirical investigation: I did that in arguing (chapters 8 and 9) that
there are, in fact, no discontinuities. More important, they can interpret
psychological theories. The theory of the unconscious is a case in point.
We saw that at first philosophers thought (not wholly without justification) that this involved conceptual confusion; but that it then
proved possible to eliminate the confusions and save the theory by
construing it as fundamentally teleological and not causal. So interpreted it provides a useful concept of psychological impossibility.

In holding that the akrates is sometimes unable to act otherwise, that
the area within which we are free agents may be smaller than the tough-
minded citizen supposes, I side with Plato and the clinical psychologists. But on a second issue I am less sympathetic towards them. That
is the issue of partitioning the psyche. We saw that the objections
brought by some philosophers against the Plato–Freud divisions can be
parried by interpreting the division as functional analysis. The parts
then become harmless Dennettian homunculi. The price of this piece of
salvaging, however, is that we have to take a fundamentally mechanistic
view of human beings.

Many philosophers today are either happy to do this or convinced
they have no alternative. However that may be, the question whether
human behaviour can be explained mechanistically seems to me crucial

for the question how far philosophy, as distinct from psychology, can be expected to shed light on akratic behaviour.

It is not immediately obvious how a philosopher's approach to human behaviour and a psychologist's should differ. Of course the philosopher is supposed to sit in his armchair and the psychologist is supposed to carry out empirical studies and do statistics; but what are these different methods meant to achieve? This standard answer is that the psychologist achieves a substantial explanation: he finds out why, in fact, people do certain things that they do; whereas the philosopher achieves only a conceptual analysis. But this answer ignores the fact that there are other academics working in the same field, notably political and economic theorists. Their thinking is often more normative than empirical; they operate with ideal conceptions of rationality, justice and so forth, and say how individuals and collectivities *ought* to reach decisions. What kind of validity has this work if human behaviour is to be understood by the methods of the psychologist?

Political and economic theorists have a teleological view of human behaviour as explainable in terms of reasons and purposes. I suggest that insofar as our behaviour really can be explained in this way, it is the business of philosophers. Not of philosophers alone: the poet and the novelist think of men as agents with reasons and purposes. But the poet, like the philosopher, is an armchair man. On the teleological view, mind 'is the cause of what it understands'. A philosopher distinguishing different kinds of reasons, goods and evils is offering at a very general level the appropriate kind of explanation for intentional action and inaction as such. The poet on the one hand and the political or economic theorist may be seen as developing separately two capacities present though rudimentary in the philosopher: creativity and technical expertise. They stand to him somewhat as cigars and snuff stand to the tobacco plant.

Now at a superficial level the mechanist can tolerate the teleologist. People can be supposed to act for reasons and purposes, enkratically or akratically, and a functionalist account can be given of that. But at a deeper level it is not so clear that teleological and causal explanation are compatible. That is a problem which falls outside the scope of this book. But I have indicated that, whether they are compatible or not, I wish to hold on to the teleological view, and to that extent, on the issue of how akratic behaviour should be understood, I favour the Aristotelian position more than the Platonic.

The other main issue, between the Greek and the Judaeo-Christian

views of the human agent, is not simply one of emphasis. Either we have
wills or we have not. Since the Judaeo-Christian gene is dominant in
modern Western culture, the corresponding philosophy of action seems
to us intuitively the more convincing. Knowledge, whether of what is
right in general or of what we ought to do on a particular occasion, is
relatively easy to attain. There may be a philosophical problem about
whether it should be conceived on the model of knowledge of objective
matters of fact or rather, in Hume's fashion, as a 'calm passion' which
can either ride or be swamped by the waves of violent emotion; but
there is little practical doubt about its content. The difficulty is to
behave as we know we should. Doing what we think right often requires
an effort, and so does refraining from what we think wrong. The word
'refrain' was originally the word for the action of a person driving horses
who hauls on the reins to stop them. This action calls for muscle as well
as skill, and we need moral muscle-power to prevent our passions from
running away with us.

By comparison with this account of human conduct, confirmed by
introspection and formulated in many pronouncements from the pulpit
and the bench, the account we find in Plato and Aristotle seems not
only unconvincing but almost unintelligible. For them in a significant
number of cases the main difficulty is not to do what you know you
should, but to know what it is you should do. They are willing to distinguish theoretical thinking from practical. They distinguish the
thought of a scientist or the craftsman's thought about a technical
problem from the ordinary thinking that guides our actions. But they
see no natural gaps between our cognitive awareness of our
surroundings and practical judgement, between practical judgement
and desire, or between desire and action. The modern man's first
reaction may be that the Greeks were just primitive. They failed to draw
obvious distinctions.

If the argument of chapters 4–7 is sound, the verdict of philosophy is
different. Philosophy can make nothing of the Judaeo-Christian
concept of the will. Neither can it understand cognition divorced from
any kind of appetite. It requires us to conceive a person as a true unity
whose beliefs and desires are separated neither from action nor from one
another.

So we still face today the problem that confronted our predecessors in
the time of Constantine: how can we combine what is intuitively
convincing about the Judaeo-Christian view with Greek philosophy?
One idea which we quite cherish is that to behave well requires an

effort. I have argued that the only sound conception we have of trying is simply the notion of purposive causal action. Various circumstances may make this exhausting, painful or boring, and a strenuous effort may be required to continue preventing a change we think bad (the boat's becoming filled with water) or finally to accomplish a change we think good (reaching the shore). This is the field of karteria and malakia.

In the field of akrasia and enkrateia, where the problem is not that we feel an aversion to a course we think good but that we feel an inclination to a course we think bad, the notion of trying is less easy to apply. We have, indeed, seen a limited space for it. To arrive at the right practical judgement it may be necessary to do some hard thinking. We may have to calculate probabilities carefully and at some length, gather addition information which is not readily available, and make some estimates, say about other people's thoughts and feelings, which can easily be biased by our own emotions. We can fail to do this hard thinking properly through a kind of weakness. It is also possible that a course we think bad (taking a drug) may promise relief from a painful sensation we can hardly bear. To say, however, that the akrates fails because he did not make sufficient effort in these ways is to assimilate akrasia to malakia. The assimilation is not always plausible. The akratic drinker, as contrasted with the advanced alcoholic, does not really suffer unpleasant sensations; neither does the akratic adulterer.

There is another kind of effort which might be appropriate for people like the akratic adulterer. Their undesirable desires involve thought of the forbidden object and often images of it. They can try to dismiss these thoughts and images, perhaps by calling up other, harmless or edifying ones. This may have been the technique for dealing with bad emotions which Descartes had in mind in *Passions* I.50; thought-control is discussed by spiritual writers of his day as well as by psychologists of ours. The bad thoughts of the akrates do not seem to be radically different in kind from the unwanted thoughts of the obsessed, and if the notion of effort in resisting applies there it can apply here.

On the whole, however, the model of holding back horses seems to me of doubtful value in understanding akrasia. It is not just that if we try to press the analogy between trying to keep out an unwanted idea and trying to keep out an enemy who is literally pushing at the door we run into Rylean difficulties: the model is fundamentally causal. It seems to me wrong to conceive the akrates as an object caught between opposing forces like an abandoned ship blown one way by the wind and carried another by the tide. He is more like Buridan's Ass, torn between attractive prospects. The strongest reason is the reason which makes the course of action it favours appear best. In a competition between reasons, effort is out of place.

I suspect that the Judaeo-Christian tradition puts so much emphasis on volitional effort because it has so much confidence in its moral beliefs. From the time of the Maccabees onwards Jews and Christians have been ready martyrs. If an agent can be supposed to have no doubts about what he ought to do, failure to do it can be attributed only to a weakness in some executive capacity. If the importance of effort is merely derivative from the importance of moral certainty, the prospect brightens. Greek philosophy can allow us to have the second while limiting the area within which we can deploy the first. For as we have seen, general moral principles are only (in the technical sense) prima facie, and (pp. 90–1 above) we can allow people to hold them with all the certainty they like and yet not act upon them.

It may well be that the ancient Greeks were indeed a little primitive in their moral code, if not in their philosophy of action. The modern Western world may be in possession of a code which is far more detailed, and the prescriptions of which are reliable for a high percentage of cases. Perhaps our system stands to that of Pericles almost as a modern motor-car to an ox-cart. All that needs to be insisted is that although the tolerance permissible in car-manufacture is much less than that permitted to a cartwright, the difference is still one only of degree. No rule determines with perfect accuracy what should be done in every possible case.

But that means that moral certainty cannot be complete about what the agent ought to do here and now. Many philosophers will say that sometimes it *is* complete, yet the agent still fails to behave accordingly. They stand by the doctrine that the agent's problem can be, and even that in the morally important cases it actually is, exclusively volitional. Is this, I wonder, a doctrine for which we should really wish to go to the stake? What is the point of separating cognition and volition in this way?

It is common ground that the akrates is aware of one circumstance which to him is a moral reason (in one of the narrow senses, see p. 108 above, of 'moral') for refraining from a course of action; and of another circumstance which is an egocentric reason, or perhaps (so Hurley) an equally moral one, for pursuing that course. Why does he have to think it morally better in the wide sense of 'morally', why does he have to think it better, on balance, to refrain? Why not say that he really questions whether refraining is best all things considered, really wonders if the reason for refraining should not be overridden in this case? Our tradition, reinforced by our policing and judicial procedures, may put pressure on him to say that he knew at the time that he should refrain. But perhaps we are pressing him to redeem wrong-doing by hypocrisy. Aristotle compared the irreproachable utterances of the akrates with those of an actor, and the Greek word for 'actor' is 'hypocrite'.

Whether misconduct can be an exclusively volitional affair is not a question that can be settled by introspection (see p. 134 above); we need reasons for answering it one way or the other. For my part I find it preferable to say that there can be no wrong-doing without some impairment of intellectual vision. Doing what is bad involves stupidity, false belief or both: that is what makes it intrinsically a thing to be shunned. I think I speak here not only for myself or for the classical Greek philosophers, but for the Homeric Greeks; if J.L. Kupperman (1981) is right, for the ancient Chinese; and perhaps for primitive people everywhere. It is quite a common opinion that a man who does what he knows he should refrain from doing is either a stupid or a clever fool.

The great justification of the volitional theory is that it preserves moral responsibility. Ignorance, even if temporary, is some excuse. If the criminal did not know his action was wrong, how can he be blamed? And if he cannot be blamed, how can the virtuous people who knew and did refrain be praised?

Moral responsibility is indeed a valuable thing, but as we have seen, postulating a faculty of will does not secure it. For we are immediately obliged to ask what determines the will, and to this the volitionist can give no satisfactory answer. The notion of volition which is crucial for moral responsibility is the notion according to which acting or not acting is volitional if it is voluntary or intentional; and it is voluntary or intentional if it is explainable by a reason.

If the Judaeo-Christian view commends itself to us because it represents us as conscious, purposive agents acting and refraining from action of our own free will, and because it represents at least some things in the world at large as happening because of what Socrates in the *Phaedo* (see above p. 25) calls 'mind': then the will is a superfluous liability. What we need is teleological as distinct from causal explanation. We must see man as a causal agent, certainly, but one that acts causally or stays inactive for reasons and purposes. I have been advocating an account in which not only are these modes of explanation valid, but the concepts of belief and desire and psychological concepts generally are explained in terms of them. This account preserves, I think, what is most valuable in each of the two pictures of man we have inherited: it preserves the unity of human activity and the responsibility of the human person.

Bibliography

First date given is that of edition cited in text; dates in parentheses are those of first publication if different. In the text the two dates are given thus: 1957/1963.

Abelson, R. P. 1963: Computer simulation of 'hot' cognition. In S. Tomkins and S. Messick (eds), *Computer Simulation of Personality*. New York, Wiley, 277–98.

Abraham, S. and Llewellyn-Jones, D. 1984: *Eating Disorders*. Oxford University Press.

Annas, J. 1981: *An Introduction to Plato's Republic*. Oxford, Clarendon.

Anscombe, G. E. M. 1956/7: Intention. *Aristotelian Society Proceedings*, 57, 321–32.

—— 1963 (1957) *Intention*. Oxford, Basil Blackwell.

—— 1965: Thought and action in Aristotle. In R. Bambrough (ed.), *New Essays on Plato and Aristotle*. London, Routledge and Kegan Paul.

Arrow, K. 1951: *Social Choice and Individual Values*. New York, Wiley.

Attneave, F. 1961 (1959): In defence of homunculi. In W. A. Rosenblith (ed.), *Sensory Communication*. Cambridge, Mass., M.I.T. Press.

Audi, R. 1979: Weakness of will and practical judgement. *Nous*, 13, 173–96.

—— 1982: Self-deception, action and will. *Erkenntnis*, 18, 133–58.

Austin, J. L. 1961 (1956): A plea for excuses. In *Philosophical Papers*. Oxford, Clarendon.

Ayer, A. J. 1936: *Language, Truth and Logic*. London, Gollancz.

Bambrough, R. 1960/1: Universals and family resemblances. *Aristotelian Society Proceedings*, 61, 207–22.

Barwell, I. and Lennon, K. 1982/3: The principle of sufficient reason. *Aristotelian Society Proceedings*, 83, 19–33.

Bennett, J. 1964: *Rationality*. London, Routledge and Kegan Paul.

—— 1976: *Linguistic Behaviour*. Cambridge University Press.

Benson, J. 1968: Oughts and wants. *Aristotelian Society*, Suppl. 42, 155–72.

Bentham, Jeremy 1962 (1827): *The Constitutional Code. Works*, ed. J. Bowring, vol. 9. New York, Russell and Russell.

—— 1970 (1780): *An Introduction to the Principles of Morals and Legislation*. London, Athlone.

Braithwaite, R.B. 1932/3: The nature of believing. *Aristotelian Society Proceedings*, 33, 129–46.

Bratman, M. 1979: Practical reasoning and weakness of will. *Nous*, 13, 153–71.

Broadie, A. and Pybus, E. 1982: Kant and weakness of will. *Kant-Studien*, 73, 406–12.

Burnet, J. 1900: *The Ethics of Aristotle*. London, Methuen.

Charles, D. 1982/3: Rationality and irrationality. *Aristotelian Society Proceedings*, 83, 191–212.

—— 1984: *Aristotle's Philosophy of Action*. London, Duckworth.

Charlton, W. 1980: Aristotle's definition of soul. *Phronesis*, 25, 170–86.

—— 1983: Aesthetic reasons. *British Journal of Aesthetics*, 23, 99–111.

—— 1983/4: Force, form and content in linguistic expression. *Aristotelian Society Proceedings*, 84, 123–43.

—— 1985: Aristotle and the harmonia theory. In A. Gotthelf (ed.), *Aristotle on Nature and Living Things*. Bristol, Classical Press.

Chisholm, R. 1964: The ethics of requirement. *American Philosophical Quarterly*, 1, 147–53.

—— 1974: Practical reason and the logic of requirement. In S. Körner (ed.) *Practical Reason*. New Haven, Yale University Press.

Cooper, J. 1975: *Reason and Human Good is Aristotle*. Cambridge, Mass., Harvard University Press.

—— 1982: Aristotle on natural teleology. In M. Schofield and M. Nussbaum (eds), *Language and Logos*. Cambridge University Press.

Cooper, N. 1968: Oughts and wants. *Aristotelian Society Proceedings*, Suppl. 42, 143–54.

Craft, M. and A. (eds) 1984: *Mentally Abnormal Offenders*. London, Bailliere Tindall.

Cross, R.C. and Woozley, A.D. 1964: *Plato's Republic*. London, Macmillan.

Danto, A. 1965: Basic Actions. *American Philosophical Quarterly*, 2, 141–8.

Davidson, D. 1980 (1963–78): *Essays on Actions and Events*. Oxford, Clarendon.

—— 1982: Paradoxes of irrationality. In R. Wollheim and J. Hopkins (eds), *Philosophical Essays on Freud*. Cambridge University Press, 289–305.

—— 1985: Replies to essays I–IX. In B. Vermazen and M. Hintikka (eds), *Essays on Davidson: Actions and Events*. Oxford, Clarendon.

Demos, R. 1960: Lying to oneself. *Journal of Philosophy*, 57, 588–95.

Dennett, D.C. 1978: *Brainstorms*. Montgomery, Vt., Bradford Books.

Descartes R. 1964–74: *Oeuvres*, ed. C. Adam and P. Tannery. Paris, Vrin.

Dihle, A. 1982: *The Theory of Will in Classical Antiquity*. Berkeley, University of California Press.

Dilman, I. 1984: *Freud and the Mind*. Oxford, Basil Blackwell.

Donegan, A. 1983: Review of B. O'Shaughnessy, *The Will*. *Journal of Philosophy*, 80, 298–303.

Elster, J. 1979: *Ulysses and the Sirens*. Cambridge University Press.

—— 1983: *Sour Grapes*. Cambridge University Press.

Eysenck, H.J. 1982: The paradox of 'freedom'. *Metamedicine*, 3, 367–74.

Feinberg, J. 1970: What is so special about mental illness? In *Doing and Deserving*. Princeton University Press.

Festinger, L. 1957: *A Theory of Cognitive Dissonance*. Stanford University Press.

Fingarette, H. 1969: *Self-Deception*. London, Routledge and Kegan Paul.

Frege, G. 1956 (1918): The thought. Tr. A. and M. Quinton, *Mind*, 65, 289–311.

Freud, S. 1966–74: *The Complete Psychological Works*. London, Hogarth (references to volume and page).

Gallop, D. 1964: The Socratic Paradox in the Protagoras. *Phronesis*, 9, 117–29.

Gardiner, P.L. 1954/5: On assenting to a moral principle. *Aristotelian Society Proceedings*, 55, 23–44.

Gauthier R.A. and Jolif J.A. 1958–9: *L'Ethique à Nicomaque*. Louvain University Press.

Gotthelf, A. 1976: Aristotle's conception of final causality. *Review of Metaphysics*, 30, 226–54.

Grice, H.P. 1961: The causal theory of perception. *Aristotelian Society Proceedings*, Suppl. 35, 121–52.

—— 1971: Intention and uncertainty. *Proceedings of the British Academy*, 263–79.

Grice, P. and Baker, J. 1985: Davidson on 'weakness of the will'. In B. Vermazen and M. Hintikka (eds), *Essays on Davidson: Action and Events*. Oxford, Clarendon.

Gulley, N. 1968: *The Philosophy of Socrates*. London, Macmillan.

Haight, M.R. 1980: *A Study of Self-Deception*. Brighton, Harvester.

Hardie, W.F.R. 1968: *Aristotle's Ethical Theory*. Oxford, Clarendon.

—— 1971: Willing and acting. *Philosophical Quarterly*, 21, 193–206.

Hare, R.M. 1952: *The Language of Morals*. Oxford, Clarendon.

—— 1963: *Freedom and Reason*. Oxford, Clarendon.

Harman, G. 1975/6: Practical reasoning. *Review of Metaphysics*, 29, 431–63.

Haward, L. 1981: *Forensic psychology*. London, Batsford Academic.

Hornsby, J. 1980: *Actions*. London, Routledge and Kegan Paul.

Howard, G.S. and Conway, C.G. 1986: Can there be an empirical science of volitional action? *American Psychologist*, 41, 1241–51.

Hume, David 1888 (1739): *A Treatise of Human Nature*, ed. L.A. Selby-Bigge. Oxford, Clarendon.

—— 1902 (1751): *An Enquiry concerning the Principles of Morals*, ed. L.A. Selby-Bigge. Oxford, Clarendon.

Hurley, S. 1985: Supervenience and the possibility of coherence. *Mind*, 94, 501–25.

—— 1985/6: Conflict, akrasia and cognitivism. *Aristotelian Society Proceedings*, 86, 23–49.

Irwin, T. 1974: Review of Leo Strauss, *Xenophon's Socrates*. *Philosophical Review*, 83, 409–13.

—— 1977: *Plato's Moral Theory*. Oxford, Clarendon.

Jackson, F. 1984: Weakness of will. *Mind*, 93, 1–18.

James, William 1907: *Principles of Psychology*. London, Macmillan.

Kenny, A. 1963: *Action, Emotion and Will*. London, Routledge and Kegan Paul.

—— 1966: The practical syllogism and incontinence. *Phronesis*, 11, 163–84.

—— 1975: *Will, Freedom and Power*. Oxford, Basil Blackwell.

—— 1978: *The Aristotelian Ethics*. Oxford, Clarendon.

Kipp, D. 1985: Self-deception, inauthenticity and weakness of will. In M. W. Martin (ed.), *Self-Deception and Self-Understanding*. University of Kansas Press.

Klein, M. 1985 (1921–45): *Love, Guilt and Reparation*. London, Hogarth.

Kupperman, J.L. 1981: Confucian ethics and weakness of will. *Journal of Chinese Philosophy*, 8, 1–8.

Lemmon, E.J. 1962: Moral dilemmas. *Philosophical Review*, 71, 139–58.

Lewis, A.J. 1936: Problems of obsessional illness. *Proceedings of the Royal Society of Medicine*, 29, 325–36.

Luce, R.D. and Raiffa, H. 1957: *Games and Decisions*. New York, Wiley.

Lukes, S. 1965: Moral weakness. *Philosophical Quarterly*, 15, 104–14.

Macaulay, Thomas 1889 (1828): History. In *Miscellaneous Writings and Speeches*. London, Longmans Green.

MacIntyre A. 1958: *The Unconscious*. London, Routledge and Kegan Paul.

Mackie, J.L. 1974: *The Cement of the Universe*. Oxford, Clarendon.

Margolis, J. 1981: Rationality and weakness of will. *Journal of Chinese Philosophy*, 8, 9–27.

Marks, I. 1969: *Fears and Phobias*. London, Heinemann.

May, K.O. 1954: Intransitivity, utility and the aggregation of preference patterns. *Econometrica*, 22, 1–13.

Mele, A. 1983: Akrasia, reasons and causes. *Philosophical Studies*, 44, 245–68.

—— 1987: *Irrationality*. New York, Oxford University Press.

Mellor, D.H. 1977/8: Unconscious belief. *Aristotelian Society Proceedings*, 78, 87–101.

Midgley, M. 1972: Is 'moral' a dirty word? *Philosophy*, 47, 206–28.

Mortimore G. (ed.) 1971: *Weakness of Will*. London, Macmillan.

Nagel, E. 1959: Methodological issues in psychoanalytic theory. In S. Hook (ed.), *Psychoanalysis, Scientific Method and Philosophy*. New York University Press.

Nagel, T. 1970: *The Possibility of Altruism*. Oxford, Clarendon.

Neumann, J. von and Morgenstern, O. 1953 (1943): *Theory of Games and Economic Behaviour*. Princeton University Press.

Nisbett, R. and Ross, L. 1980: *Human Inference: Strategies and Shortcomings of Social Judgment*. Englewood Cliffs, N.J., Prentice-Hall.

Nowell-Smith, P. 1954: *Ethics*. Harmondsworth, Penguin.

Nussbaum, M. 1978: *De Motu Animalium*. Princeton University Press.

O'Brien, M. 1967: *The Socratic Paradoxes and the Greek Mind*. Chapel Hill, University of North Carolina Press.

Ogden, G.K. and Richards, I.A. 1923: *The Meaning of Meaning*. London, Routledge and Kegan Paul.

O'Shaughnessy B. 1980: *The Will*. Cambridge University Press.

Pap, A. 1959: On the empirical interpretation of psychoanalytical concepts. In S. Hook (ed.), *Psychoanalysis, Scientific Method and Philosophy*. New York University Press.

Pareto, V. 1971 (1909): *Manual of Political Economy*, Tr. A. Schwier. London, Macmillan.

Peacocke, C. 1979: *Holistic Explanation*. Oxford, Clarendon.

—— 1985: Intention and akrasia. In B. Vermazen and M. Hintikka (eds), *Essays on Davidson: Actions and Events*. Oxford, Clarendon.

Pears, D. 1978: Aristotle's analysis of courage. *Midwest Studies in Philosophy*, 3.

—— 1984: *Motivated Irrationality*. Oxford, Clarendon.

Putnam, H. 1978 (1975): The meaning of 'meaning'. In *Philosophical Papers*, vol. 2. Cambridge University Press.

Rachman, S. and Hodgson, R. 1980: *Obessions and Compulsions*. Englewood Cliffs, N.J., Prentice-Hall.

Ramsey, F.P. 1978 (1926): Truth and probability. In *Foundations*. London, Routledge and Kegan Paul.

Robinson, R. 1977 (1954): Aristotle on akrasia. In J. Barnes, M. Schofield and R. Sorabji (eds), *Articles on Aristotle*, vol. 2. London, Duckworth.

Ross, D. 1923: *Aristotle*. London, Methuen.

—— 1930: *The Right and the Good*. Oxford, Clarendon.

—— 1949: Aristotle, Prior and Posterior Analytics. Oxford, Clarendon.

Russell, Bertrand 1921: *The Analysis of Mind*. London, Allen and Unwin.

Ryle, G. 1949: *The Concept of Mind*. London, Hutchinson.

Salkovskis, P.M. 1985: Obsessional-compulsive problems. *Behaviour Research and Therapy*, 23, 571–83.

Santas, G. 1964: The Socratic Paradoxes. *Philosophical Review*, 73, 147–64.

—— 1966: Plato's *Protagoras*. *Philosophical Review*, 75, 3–33.

—— 1969: Aristotle on practical inference. *Phronesis*, 14, 162–89.

1979: *Socrates*. London, Routledge and Kegan Paul.

Sartre, J.P. 1958 (1943): *Being and Nothingness*, Tr. H. Barnes. London, Methuen.

Scruton, R. 1974: *Art and Imagination*. London, Methuen.

Searle, J.R. 1962: Meaning and speech-acts. In C.D. Rollins (ed.), *Metaphysics and Experience*. Pittsburg University Press.

Sen, A. 1974: Choice, orderings and morality. In S. Körner (ed.), *Practical Reasoning*. New Haven, Yale University Press.

—— 1980/1: Plural Utility. *Aristotelian Society Proceedings*, 81, 193–215.

Sen, A. and Williams, B.A.O. (eds) 1982: *Utilitarianism and Beyond*. Cambridge University Press.

Shaftesbury, third Earl of 1977 (1699): *An Inquiry concerning Virtue and Merit*, ed. D. Walford. Machester University Press.

Sidgwick, H. 1893: Unreasonable action. *Mind*, 2, 174–87.

Smith, P. and L. 1987: *Continence and Incontinence*. London, Croom Helm.

Sorabji, R. 1973/4: Aristotle on the role of intellect in virtue. *Aristotelian Society Proceedings*, 74, 107–29.

Sousa, R. de 1976: Rational homunculi. In A. Rorty (ed.), *The Identities of Persons*. Berkeley, University of California Press.

Spinoza, B.:*Opera*, ed. C. Gebhart. Heidelberg, C. Winters.

Stevenson, C.L. 1945: *Ethics and Language*. New Haven, Yale Univesity Press.

Strang, C. 1982: Tripartite soul, ancient and modern: Plato and Sheldon. *Apeiron*, 16, 1–10.

Symington, N. 1983: The analyst's act of freedom as an agent of therapeutic change. *International Review of Psychoanalysis*, 10, 283–91.

Taylor, C.C.W. 1976: *Plato: Protagoras*. Oxford, Clarendon.

—— 1980: Plato, Hare and Davidson on akrasia. *Mind*, 89, 499–518.

Thalberg, I. 1982: Freud's anatomies of the self. In R. Wollheim and J. Hopkins (eds), *Philosophical Essays on Freud*. Cambridge University Press.

Tversky, A. and Kahneman, D. 1981: The framing of decisions and the rationality of choice. *Science*, 211, 543–58.

Urmson, J.O. 1968: *The Emotive Theory of Ethics*. London, Hutchinson.

Walker, N. 1968: *Crime and Insanity*, vol 1. Edinburg University Press.

Walsh, J.J. 1963: *Aristotle's Conception of Moral Weakness*. New York, Columbia University Press.

Watkins, J.W.N. 1974: Self-interest and morality. In S. Körner (ed.), *Practical Reasoning*. New Haven, Yale University Press.

Watson, G. 1977: Skepticism about weakness of will. *Philosophical Review*, 86, 316–339.

Wiggins, D. 1975/6: Deliberation and practical reason. *Aristotelian Society Proceedings*, 76, 24–51.

—— 1978/9: Weakness of will, commensurability and the objects of deliberation and desire. *Aristotelian Society Proceedings*, 79, 251–77.

Wilkes, K.V. 1975: Anthropomorphism and analogy in psychology. *Philosophical Quarterly*, 25, 126–37.

—— 1978: *Physicalism*. London, Routledge and Kegan Paul.

Williams, B.A.O. 1973 (1965-70): *Problems of the Self*. Cambridge University Press.

Wilson, J. Cook 1879: *On the Structure of the Seventh Book of The Nicomachean Ethics, Chapters I-X*. Oxford, Clarendon.

Wollaston W. 1897 (1722): *The Religion of Nature Delineated*, excerpted in L.A. Selby-Bigge (ed.), *British Moralists*, vol. 2. Oxford, Clarendon.

Zaw, S.K. 1978: Irresistible impulse and criminal responsibility. In G. Vesey (ed.), *Human Values*. Brighton, Harvester.

Ziff, P. 1960: *Semantic Analysis*, Ithaca, N Y, Cornell University Press.

Index

Wiggins, D., 37, 41, 46, 75, 127, 148–9, 153
Wilkes, K.V., 34, 170, 172–4
Williams, B.A.O., 117–18, 148, 167
Wilson, J. Cook, 41
wishful thinking, 161–2
Wittgenstein, L., 10

Wollaston, W., 99–100
Woozley, A.D., 28, 172

Xenophon, 14–18

Zaw, S.K., 156

i – ₱?

894008

894

TEIKYO WESTMAR UNIV. LIBRARY

BJ 1468.5 .C43 1988
Charlton, William, 1935-
Weakness of will (90-312)

DEMCO